ROUTLEDGE LIBRARY EDITIONS: COMPARATIVE EDUCATION

Volume 20

PROGRESSIVE RENAISSANCE

PROGRESSIVE RENAISSANCE

America and the Reconstruction
of Italian Education,
1943—1962

STEVEN F. WHITE

LONDON AND NEW YORK

First published in 1991 by Garland Publishing, Inc.

This edition first published in 2018
by Routledge
2 Park Square, Milton Park, Abingdon, Oxon OX14 4RN

and by Routledge
711 Third Avenue, New York, NY 10017

Routledge is an imprint of the Taylor & Francis Group, an informa business

British Library Cataloguing in Publication Data
A catalogue record for this book is available from the British Library

ISBN: 978-1-138-54113-9 (Set)
ISBN: 978-1-351-00358-2 (Set) (ebk)
ISBN: 978-1-138-54419-2 (Volume 20) (hbk)
ISBN: 978-0-429-50760-1 (Volume 20) (ebk)

Publisher's Note
The publisher has gone to great lengths to ensure the quality of this reprint but points out that some imperfections in the original copies may be apparent.

Disclaimer
The publisher has made every effort to trace copyright holders and would welcome correspondence from those they have been unable to trace.

Progressive Renaissance

America and the Reconstruction
of Italian Education, 1943–1962

Steven F. White

Garland Publishing, Inc.
New York & London 1991

Library of Congress Cataloging-in-Publication Data

White, Steven F., 1955–
Progressive Renaissance: America and the reconstruction of Italian education, 1943–1962/
Steven F. White.
p. cm.——[Modern European history. Italy]
Includes bibliographical references.
ISBN 0-8153-0672-5 [alk. paper]
1. Education——Italy——American influences——20th century. 2. Italy——History——Allied
occupation, 1943–1947. 3. Italy——History——1945– . I. Title. II. Series.
LA791.8.W55   1991
370'.945——dc20   91-31238

Designed by Marisel Tavárez

Printed on acid-free, 250-year-life paper.
Manufactured in the United States of America

To Guglielmo Balbi and Jim Martin,
Master Teachers

CONTENTS

ACKNOWLEDGMENTS

Many persons have helped me as I have prepared this book.   I
owe a special word of thanks to my dissertation advisor, Professor
Hans Schmitt, and to his wife Florence, for their insight and
encouragement. Dr. Tracy Koon made many helpful suggestions in the
early stages of this project. Dr. James Miller of the U.S. State
Department provided expert advice concerning federal archival
holdings. Professor Robert Evans of the University of Virginia's
Department of Government and Foreign Affairs, and Professors Joseph
Kett, Duane Osheim, Woodford McClellan and Enno Kraehe offered
helpful suggestions at various stages of the research and writing.
Professor Alexander De Grand at North Carolina State University and
Professor David Roberts at the University of Georgia have each read
the present revision of the dissertation. I am grateful to each
for their counsel. Responsibility for any errors of fact or interpretation naturally remains my own.

A Fullbright Fellowship made it possible for me to spend nine
months conducting dissertation research in Italy. I am greatly
indebted to Dr. Cipriana Scelba, Director of the Italian Fulbright
program, and to Dr. Luigi Filadoro, her assistant, for their
professional and personal support. Many Italian scholars shared
generously of their time and experience with me. In particular,
I would like to acknowledge the assistance of Dr. Giovacchino
Petracchi at the Ministry of Public Instruction, Dr. Giovanni
Gozzer, Professors Lucia Boncori, Giacomo Cives and Aldo
Visalberghi at the University of Rome and Professors Tina Tomasi
and Lamberto Borghi at the University of Florence. I am also
grateful to all the Italian educators who shared with me their
personal experiences of educational reconstruction. Although I am
not uncritical of the role played by Christian Democrats in this
work, the Hon. Maria Badaloni was especially gracious and
considerate in our conversations.

The professional staffs of the Archivio Centrale dello Stato,
the Biblioteca Nazionale in Rome, the Ministry of Public
Instruction Library, the Chamber of Deputies Library, the
Biblioteca Magistrale Laziale , the Associazione Italiana Maestri
Cattolici and the Istituto Gramsci were most accomodating. Here
in the United States I am indebted to the archivists and librarians
of the National Archives and Records Administration, the Teachers
College Library and Herbert Lehman Center of Columbia University
and the Alderman Library Manuscripts Department at the University
of Virginia. Ms. Robin Dove and Drs. Samuel and Constance Fletcher

viii

offered invaluable logistical support in preparing the final manuscript.

Most of all, I wish to thank my wife Alica for her assistance and encouragement at every stage of this work.

Gettysburg, Pennsylvania
Summer, 1991

INTRODUCTION

Education for a New Italy

The last half-century has revolutionized Italy, bringing unprecedented levels of prosperity, education and cultural awareness to a society long synonymous with provincialism and self-absorption. Rejecting the autarchic chimera of the Fascist era, Italian writers, educators, artists, statesmen and entrepreneurs have opened the nation's physical and metaphysical borders to a lively exchange of goods and ideas. The terms of this exchange have been dictated by the great ideological heirs of the Resistance: Italy's Marxist, Catholic and "secular-progressive" subcultures. The Italian Communist Party has exchanged the frigid orthodoxies of Stalinism for the protean musings of Gramsci's prison notebooks (published posthumously in 1947), the literary iconoclasm of Vittorini and Moravia and the Eurocommunist politics of Berlinguer. The windows of Pius XII's cramped, apprehensive Church have been thrown open by John XXIII, Paul VI and the ecumenical spirit of the Vatican II Council. The secular progressives (now represented by the Socialists and smaller lay parties) have championed a liberal, consumeristic, Western-oriented Italy. In the last decade Bettino Craxi and other Italian Socialist leaders have played leading roles in shepherding the EEC toward a fully integrated market. More broadly, Italian students and intellectuals from across the political spectrum have participated enthusiastically in various initiatives for fuller cultural integration within the European community, including the newly established European university in Florence.[1]

The renewal of Italian schooling since the fall of Mussolini has been forged through prolonged struggle and dialogue between both indigenous and foreign actors. Between 1943 and 1945, educational reconstruction was dominated by Anglo-American officials who initiated a systematic "purge" of Fascist influence from the Italian teaching corps and curricula. In addition, Deweyian educators within Allied ranks promoted progressive education as the optimal template for a new, democratic Italy. In particular, these educators urged a locally-rooted, pupil-centered brand of education for all young Italians through the eighth grade. Within its sphere of activity, the Allied Control Commission's Education Subcommission was among the most energetic Anglo-American agencies operating in liberated territory. Sometimes assisting, sometimes obstructing Allied efforts were a wide variety of Italian educators and statesmen, some functioning within Italy's central educational ministry, others in the ranks of the anti-Fascist Resistance. The latter gave rise to their own impressive, if shortlived, educational initiatives in 1944 and 1945.

After the war the sacrifices and dreams of the liberation

struggle gave way to more prosaic work of physical rebuilding. The Allied education subcommission closed its doors in April, 1946, leaving further responsibility for reconstruction in Italian ministerial hands. Three months later the Christian Democratic party obtained control of the educational ministry--a stronghold it has monopolized, with brief interruptions, ever since. In power the Christian Democrats worked intently to instill Catholic values through both parochial and public schools. Secular-progressives and Marxists countered with their own, more positivistic and non-confessional conceptions of democratic education. Yet in the scholastic as in the wider political sphere, Italy's anti-clerical forces were no match for partisan Catholicism through the late 1940s and 1950s.

American progressive ideology encountered stiff, widespread resistance through the immediate post-war decade. Inevitably, its reception was colored by the contradictory associations which America herself aroused. American (and British) military might had freed Italy--at the cost of destroying much of it. The same nation which generously shared her cornucopia through the Marshall Plan did so only after brazenly interfering in the 1948 elections--all in the name of anti-communism. The intensely conformist milieu of the late 1940s and early 1950 seemed ill-suited to a pedagogy of liberal individualism. Communist intellectuals attacked the progressive focus on individual self-realization as at once naive and abstract, as it seemed to slight the socio-economic determinants of education. For their part, Catholic commentators feared that the new, pupil-centered pedagogy might eclipse the family's pivotal role in the socialization of the child. In 1955, after years of tenacious pedagogical and political preparation, the Christian Democrats introduced a new primary school curriculum to replace the "American" syllabus of 1945. A "harmonious Christian humanism" supplanted the hybrid pragmatist and idealist philosophical underpinnings of the earlier document.[2] Deweyian progressivism, with its radically optimistic assessment of human nature, would obtain a fair hearing only as the Cold War polarization of Italian politics began to abate. For Italy, that process began in the fall of 1954, with the resolution of its long-standing border dispute with Tito's Yugoslavia. The accompanying withdrawal of U.S. and British forces from the Free Territory of Trieste closed the last chapter of Allied military governance in Italy.

The years between 1955 and 1962 brought the Italian economic miracle and new evidence that the global cold war might be abating. In a transformed international and domestic environment, a genuinely pluralistic culture began to emerge in Italy. A renewed openness to compromise and a reconsideration of political alignments culminated in the "Opening to the Left" of 1962, which brought the Socialist Party back into a governing coalition along side the Christian Democrats for the first time since the dawn of the Cold War. Accompanying these broad political and socio-economic changes was an expanded pedagogical dialogue among Italy's three major ideological subcultures. Florence's secular-progressive publishing house "La Nuova Italia" helped to launch the debate, bringing out the major works of John Dewey in translation beginning in the late 1940s. In 1954 the Salesian University in Rome began publishing *Orientamenti pedagogici*, Italy's first scientific journal of educational psychology. The new publication testified to a less dogmatic, empirical spirit emerging within Italy's Catholic subculture. Similarly, the appearance of the communist journal *Riforma della Scuola* in 1955 heralded a new attitude of critical and yet constructive engagement on the part of Italian Marxists.

Institutionally, the quickening of national concern for educational problems bore its most dramatic fruit in 1962, when Italy adopted Europe's first truly comprehensive middle school, designed for all students, regardless of socio-economic background or vocational destination. This landmark legislation, inspired in part by American precedent, represented a compromise between each of Italy's major political parties. Reconciliation on this issue was pivotal in bringing Christian Democrats and Socialists together again in the Opening to the Left. This social and ideological watershed clearly steered Italy in the direction of a cosmopolitan, pluralistic mass society. Two major reforms of 1969 confirmed contemporary Italy's progressive, egalitarian spirit: the creation of a nationwide network of state-funded pre-schools, and the opening of Italian university faculties to graduates from all types of secondary schools. The election of various councils--including students, teachers, parents and neighborhood residents--since the early 1970s has begun to realize the principle of participatory democracy in Italian schools. All of these innovations testify to widespread support for pedagogical progressivism in contemporary Italy--despite its tarnished reputation in its native land.[3]

The Coming of the Americans

The Second World War marked the opening of a new chapter in the history of American progressivism. By the outbreak of the war, progressives had concluded a forty year crusade to wrest control of American education from selfish "bosses" and entrust it to non-partisan school boards and professional administrators, counselors and pedagogues. Nationwide, primary and secondary schools had become "workshops of democracy," training children from various class and ethnic backgrounds in the dynamics of social accomodation and political compromise. Some progressives also stressed "life adjustment skills," from personal and social hygiene to good sportsmanship. These skills seemed fundamental to all forms of American associational and civil life. They formed a kind of "pre-political matrix" which guaranteed the stability and effectiveness of our democracy. John Dewey offered intellectual justification for such views in his book *Freedom and Culture*, published in 1939. All successful governments, he observed, depended on a supportive fabric of cultural attitudes. As Dewey put it, "political institutions are an effect, not a cause."[4]

The rise of inimical "totalitarian" systems of education in Italy, Germany, Japan and the Soviet Union between the wars reinforced American progressives' pride in their democratic accomplishment. With the onset of the Second World War, progressive intellectuals within and outside the Roosevelt administration began to proselytize for the eventual cultural reconstruction of each of the Axis peoples. The lion's share of this activity focused on Nazi Germany. However the successful invasion of Sicily and the overthrow of Mussolini in July of 1943 shifted the attention of reformist policy-makers and educators to Italy. The ensuing experiment with educational rehabilitation--with "progressivism at gunpoint," if you will--presaged later, larger reeducation campaigns in American-occupied Germany and Japan.[5]

Responsibility for educational reconstruction in Italy fell to an Educational Subcommission operating under the umbrella of the Allied Control Commission, or ACC. Like other branches of the ACC, the Educational Subcommission had to coordinate policy with its functional equivalent in the co-belligerent Italian regime: the Ministry of Public Instruction. As more and more of Italy was wrested from the Germans--especially after Rome was freed in June, 1944--the Ministry of Public Instruction assumed greater control. After reaching a peak strength of 18 Allied officers in 1944, the Education Subcommission staff was steadily scaled back until the office formally closed in April, 1946.[6]

Eighty percent of the subcommission's staff were Americans, but its first director, George Robert Gayre, was an Englishman. This Oxford physical anthropologist had achieved recognition in the interwar period as a spirited critic of Nazi racial theory. After eight tempestuous months spent trying to eliminate Fascism (which Gayre regarded as a slightly shallower and less efficient version of Nazism), he was reassigned to London to help plan England's reeducation program for Germany. Gayre's succesors at the helm of the subcommission all came from the United States. Thomas Vernor Smith, education director from February to September, 1944, was a political philosopher at the University of Chicago and an ex-Democratic Congressman at large from the state of Illinois. A strict philosophical and cultural relativist, Smith brought a cautious and patient approach to his responsibilities. Smith was followed briefly by Henry Rowell, a Johns Hopkins classicist affiliated prior to the war with the American Academy in Rome. After a tenure of barely a month, the conservative Rowell was reassigned to the Pacific theater at the beginning of October, 1944. The subcommission's final, and most influential director was

Carleton Washburne, a disciple of John Dewey who had earned a nation-wide reputation as an innovative Superintendent of Schools in Winnetka, Illinois. Washburne labored zealously to expose Italy to wider currents of European and American pedagogy, first as education director for the ACC and then as director of the United States Information Service's northern Italian office between mid-1946 and mid-1948.[7]

The Anglo-Americans envisioned a two-stage process of reconstruction. First, ideologically committed Fascist teachers and administrators had to be purged, and explicitly Fascist doctrines expunged from textbooks and lesson plans. Second, instructional practices and materials needed to be redefined so as to foster democratic rather than authoritarian values. Here the revision of national primary and secondary school curricula would be especially significant.[8]

But how was the transition from the first, essentially "negative" stage of "defascistization" to a constructive process of "democratization" to be managed? Who would manage it? Clearly Allied representatives had an important role to play in screening school personnel and cleansing textbooks of Fascist militarism and hero worship. But should foreigners direct the longer-range work of democratic reconstruction? Could foreigners hope to accomplish this without imposing their own ideology or without favoring one or another of Italy's intensely competitive non-Fascist political forces?

Allied educators and their superiors disagreed on these fundamental questions. G. R. Gayre and later Carleton Washburne tackled both the "negative" and the "positive" aspects of reconstruction with great confidence. Yet neither man's national background or philosophy equipped him for the controversies he would encounter--particularly in the exquisitely sensitive area of balancing the educational interests of the Catholic Church and the Italian state. Gayre came under intense fire for unduly favoring the Church, and Washburne--subsequently--for discriminating against it. Such embroglios underlay Secretary of State Cordell Hull's March, 1944 proclamation that the Allies sought only to "eliminate the teaching of Fascism," while "leaving the formulation of a now positive program to the Italians themselves." T. V. Smith's blunt judgment in July, 1944 was that the American experience had little to offer "these tired peoples of a dazed land."[9]

Italian Bureaucrats and Reformers

Smith's remark reflects the subcommission leadership's ongoing frustrations with the central Italian bureaucracy. The state civil service rivaled the Vatican hierarchy in its resolute defense of traditional perogatives. Where post-war Florence enjoyed a reputation for pedagogical and cultural cosmopolitanism, Rome--at least bureaucratic Rome--remained singularly closed to change. This was particularly true of the Ministry of Public Instruction, the state's largest and geographically most inclusive employer. "La Minerva," the elephantine ministerial seat in Rome's Trastevere district, still exudes the ambiance, at once pretentious and dilapidated, of the turn-of-the-century Liberal Monarchy. This continuity finds expression less in the person of the minister or major educational legislation (which have changed markedly through the Fascist and post-Fascist eras) than in the paternalistic attitudes and archaic circulars which still define her daily practice. The reforms of the Fascist era are best understood as elaborations on an older bureaucratic base. In 1925 the Fascists underscored the importance of the ministry for their totalitarian project by renaming it the Ministry of National Education. During the *ventennio* a succession of ministers, from Gentile to Bottai, tried with mixed results to reshape La Minerva into a supple instrument of Fascist political socialization. Briefly interrupted by Mussolini's overthrow and the ensuing "Forty-Five Days," these efforts were resumed in attenuated fashion in the northern Italian Social Republic until its final defeat.[10]

The most traumatic episode of the war for the central bureaucracy was the precipitate flight of King Victor Emmanuel III and portions of his cabinet south to Brindisi following the signature of the armistice with the Allies in early September, 1943. Disoriented and discredited by that event and by the brutal German occupation which followed, the Roman bureaucracy assiduously courted the Anglo-American leadership following the liberation of the Eternal City in June, 1944. This diplomacy paid dividends in the spring of 1945. Confronted by the twin spectres of incipient communist and separatist insurgency, the Allies backed the government of Rome as opposed to the partisans' Committees of National Liberation as the war drew to a close.

The referendum of June, 1946 ended the reign of the House of Savoy; delegates to a Constituent Assembly were elected at the same time. The Italian republic which was then conceived was schizophrenic in nature, combining an innovative constitution (especially in its expansive guarantees of human rights and its provisions for regional government) with an essentially unreformed civil service. As regards education, the new constitution was decidedly traditional, conserving for the Church the privileged position it had obtained in the Lateran Accords of 1929. Instruction in the catechism remained an integral part of all public school currricula, both primary and secondary.[11]

The volatile years between the collapse of the dictatorship and the inauguration of the republic brought a colorful array of educational statesmen to the post of minister of public instruction. Yet none of them possessed the requisite political muscle to divert policy far from established bureaucratic channels. Giovanni Cuomo, educational minister in the first Badoglio

government (September, 1943 to April, 1944) was a monarchist
conservative opposed to any kind of sweeping political or
pedagogical renewal.   Cuomo was followed by three liberals: Adolfo
Omodeo (April-June, 1944), Guido de Ruggiero (June to December,
1944) and Vincenzo Arangio Ruiz (December, 1944 to December, 1945).
Despite common intellectual and political ties with Benedetto Croce
(who had himself served as Minister of Public Instruction in 1921),
these men diverged temperamentally and ideologically in office. The
Action Party leader and historian Adolfo Omodeo heralded his
determination to break with Italy's recent past by reviving the
pre-Fascist name of Ministry of Public Instruction. But Omodeo's
relentless pursuit of educators whom he suspected of Fascist
sympathies eroded his public support, and he was replaced by a
fellow historian and Actionist, the more diplomatic De Ruggiero.
Yet De Ruggiero's ministry foundered on related grounds: unwilling
to remove the top echelons of La Minerva from their posts upon
reoccupation of the ministerial headquarters in July, 1944, De
Ruggiero found his own liberal reform program stymied by his
ministerial subordinates. His successor, Liberal Party secretary
Arangio Ruiz, allowed previously initiated reforms such as the new
elementary curriculum to reach completion, but otherwise lapsed
into habitual defense of the status quo.   Arangio Ruiz was
unsympathetic to a creative array of educational initiatives
undertaken by the northern Italian Resistance upon liberating
territory from the neo-Fascist Republic of Salo.   Throughout the
north, the arrival of the Allies resulted in the suppression of
such grass-roots efforts, whether Actionist, Socialist or Communist
in inspiration.[12]
        The dawn of the post-war era augured more favorably for
Italy's Catholic subculture. Following the uneventful tenure of
Labor Democrat Enrico Mole, Guido Gonella became Italy's first
clerical Minister of Public Instruction in June of 1946. Over the
ensuing five years, Gonella patiently converted La Minerva into a
nearly impregnable Christian Democratic fiefdom.   A staunch
integralist, he was hostile to key components of political and
pedagogical progressivism.   Accustomed to acting within a
centralized, hierarchical organization, Gonella saw no special
virtue in decentralization or in the "grass roots" formulation of
educational policy.   Resentful of the "spiritual agnosticism" of
traditional Italian state institutions, he also harbored suspicions
of the Americans' new, child-centered pedagogy, with its emphasis
on the development of a secular brand of social and civic
consciousness.   In particular, the "American" elementary curriculum
of 1945 came in for mounting criticism through the late 1940s and
the early 1950s, culminating with its repacement in 1955.[13]
        While Gonella represented a backward-looking, defensive brand
of political Catholicism, his associate Giovanni Gozzer was quite
different.   A native, like Alcide De Gasperi, of Trentino, Gozzer
brought a sober, utilitarian, technocratic approach to his work.

Shortly after World War II he and a team of Italian educators from across the peninsula spent a year studying educational innovations in Switzerland.   Gozzer also administered Gonella's 1947 *Inchiesta sulla Scuola*, a mammoth, nationwide survey of public opinion on the status and future of Italian public education.   Gozzer helped to mastermind the new elementary curriculum of 1955, and rally Catholic support for the middle school reform of 1962.   Like De Gasperi, Gozzer believed that Catholic values should compete freely with other ideological orientations, rather than simply being imposed by state power.[14]

An equally dedicated protagonist of reform was the communist didactic director Dina Bertoni Jovine.   An active member of the Roman Resistance, she was instrumental in reviving the Italian elementary schoolteachers' union.   Together with other Roman activists, she helped fashion a grassroots, democratic governance structure and a new primary curriculum for local schools.   To her dismay, these initiatives were rebuffed by the educational ministry during the winter of 1944-45.   Still, Bertoni Jovine was included on the ministerial commission which drafted the new *istituto magistrale* (normal school) curriculum of 1946.   A decade later she helped to found *Riforma della scuola*, a communist periodical which featured lively debates on the pedagogy of Dewey, Anton Makarenko of the USSR, and others.   During the 1950s Bertoni Jovine also published several pioneering histories of modern Italian education.[15]

The preeminent secular-progressive innovator of the immediate post-war period was Ernesto Codignola of Florence.   This former nationalist and protege of the Idealist pedagogue Giuseppe Lombardo-Radice played a pivotal role, along with Washburne, in the development of the elementary *programmi* of 1945.   Following the war Codignola established a progressive lab school in Florence, the Scuola-Citta Pestalozzi, and the similarly titled journal *Scuola e Citta*.   The new journal combined analyses of educational innovations at home and abroad with broadsides aimed at governmental clericalism.   "La Nuova Italia," the publishing house Codignola directed, launched a major campaign to publish the works of Dewey and Washburne, as well as kindred Italian spirits.[16]

This trio of reformers is suggestive of the diverse ideological and geographical roots of contemporary Italy's educational renaissance.   Each knew Carleton Washburne, and each found in American progressivism a stimulating, if imperfect, conception of democratic education.   All of these Italian educators admired the altruism and practical energy of American reformism, but criticized its philosophical grounding.   In Italy, progressive methodologies of education bore fruit only as they were appropriated, and enriched, by the country's several ideological subcultures.

Historiography

The reception and spread of American-style progressivism in post-Fascist Italy has attracted the attention of a variety of Italian, British and American commentators. To date, their interpretations have fallen into two broad categories. One approach, exemplified by British historian David Ellwood and Giovanni Gozzer, has portrayed the Educational Subcommission as well-intentioned but naive--indeed utopian--given the traumatic legacy of the war. A second approach treats the Allied educational program as a function of the larger, increasingly conservative political agenda of top Allied political and military officials between 1943 and 1945. Leftist scholars such as Dina Bertoni Jovine, Tina Tomasi and Francesco Susi all focus on the Allies' commitment to the rickety Italian state apparatus rather than partisan or other grassroots elements. Consequently, Anglo-American initiatives appear limited, cautious and even repressive at points. Taken together, these interpretations are suggestive of the complex nature of the American presence.[17]

With the passage of time, the declassification of official records and the accumulation of scholarship on both sides of the Atlantic, it is now possible to place educational reconstruction in fuller historical perspective. The documentary base of this work includes the archival record of the Allied Control Commission's Education Subcommission, official Italian ministerial documents and the memoirs of American, British and Italian educators. Newspaper articles, schoolteachers' periodicals, reconstruction textbooks, lesson plans and interviews with retired schoolteachers, conducted by the author in 1981-82, provide evidence of reform on the classroom level. Drawing on these sources, I have retraced the history of Italy's progressive renaissance through the formative years of 1943 to 1962.

The book opens with a background chapter on the Liberal Monarchy and the Fascist *ventennio*, synthesizing the extensive Italian and English-language scholarship on education in these two periods. Animating that history is an ongoing struggle between reformist forces demanding greater popular enlightenment and entrenched, institutionalized authoritarianism. As Lamberto Borghi has shown, despite their mutual ideological antagonism, 19th and early 20th century Italian Liberalism, Catholicism and Fascism shared a profoundly authoritarian approach to education. For Mussolini's regime, historians Giuseppe Di Palma, Tracy Koon and Michel Ostenc have gone on to distinguish between novel, relatively transient "totalitarian" and more enduring "authoritarian" dimensions of educational policy. The cumulative impact of this scholarship is to emphasize the continuities in the history of Italian schooling prior to 1943. I share this line of interpretation, the more to dramatize the break with tradition which, in their differing ways, the Anglo-Americans and the partisans each envisioned.[18] Chapter three introduces the Allied educational mission in Italy, during the first eight months of the Italian campaign. The Anglo-Americans exercised their greatest freedom of action in Italy during this period, prior to the establishment of a full-fledged client Italian government in Salerno. Mounting Italian bureaucratic and clerical opposition to Allied initiatives dominates chapter four, which encompasses the 1944 calendar year. Chapter five turns to the didactic reforms which Carleton Washburne successfully promoted after assuming the helm of the subcommission in the fall of 1944. The liberation of northern Italy and the concomitant upsurge of partisan activism in the spring and summer of 1945, and the Allies' ambivalent reactions to these developments, are chronicled in chapter six. Finally, chapter seven documents the Catholics' post-war consolidation of control over educational reconstruction.

The ongoing struggle over schooling sheds light on a number of wider political and social questions in this period. The whole issue of the purge has recently attracted studies by Lamberto Mercuri and Roy Domenico. These studies concentrate on the fate of top level Fascist party and governmental figures; my work examines Allied and Italian-imposed vetting among rank and file educators--the largest single category of public servants in Italy. The relatively heavy toll of the purge among schoolteachers and professors, compared with the lighter punishments meted out to many senior civil servants, suggests that Carlo Sforza's famous dictum "strike high, but let the small fry go" wound up being applied in reverse. Allied-Resistance relations remain another area of sometimes heated historiographical debate. Remo Fornaca and Umberto Margiota have carefully documented a host of innovative schools established by the partisans across central and northern Italy as World War II drew to a close. Fornaca's studies on Piedmont have begun to flesh out the Anglo-Americans' mercurial relationship with these indigenous innovators. My own work extends that analysis across the peninsula, confirming a pattern of Allied caution toward the forces of the Resistance and correct, if not always cordial relations with the Ministry of Public Instruction.[19]

The Church's pivotal role in shaping the course of post-Fascist Italian schooling will not be fully comprehensible until the Vatican opens the appropriate archival documents to the public. In the meanwhile, wider studies of the postwar Italian Catholic sub-culture have shed new light on the pedagogical and ideological struggles of the period. Representative of such scholarship is A. Giovagnoli's collective portrait of the Catholics' leadership during the period of the *secondo dopoguerra*. Italian Catholics took the Church's educational vocation very seriously during these years; a diversity of Catholic voices make themselves heard in the pages that follow.[20]

The Church's effectiveness in conditioning Italian educational reconstruction becomes very clear when one juxtaposes the Allies' legacy in Italy with that in Germany and Japan. The epilogue of this work sets the Italian case in such a cross-cultural framework, building upon several earlier comparative studies. In 1985 Keith Wilson and Nicholas Pronay co-edited a pathbreaking study of "political re-education," broadly conceived, in each of the ex-Axis nations. In addition, Marlene Mayo and Ed Beauchamp have begun to identify elements of continuity between American reconstruction policy in German and Japanese schools. My epilogue documents continuities and discontinuities in American educational policy and personnel in all three of the defeated Axis nations.[21]

As Victoria De Grazia has noted, America's post-war cultural and social influence throughout Western European society remains less well-studied than her military, political and economic impact. Pier Paolo D'Attore has echoed De Grazia's judgment, specifically with reference to Italo-American cultural relations. Certain media of cultural exchange (notably cinema and literature) have received considerable attention. Yet much additional spade work needs to be done before we will be ready for synthetic treatments of American cultural influence comparable to James Miller's recent work on the U.S.-Italian diplomatic and political relations between 1943 and 1950, or John Harper's study of Italian economic reconstruction. Within its own sphere, the present work seeks to complement Miller's and Harper's studies. The story of progressivism in Italy is an unpredictable and sometimes entertaining one. Like the characters in Roberto Rossellini's 1946 film classic *Paisa*, American, British and Italian educators repeatedly misinterpreted one another as they groped toward a common idiom of societal and pedagogical renewal. Yet despite a host of obstacles--the disruption of war, the hubris of the "liberators" and the *miseria* and mistrust of the Italians themselves--the saga eventually reaches a satisfactory conclusion.[22]

ENDNOTES

[1]Donald Sassoon, *Contemporary Italy: Politics, Economy and Society since 1945* (London: Longman, 1986), pp. 122-161, 221-255; Jeffrey Schapp, "Cultural Integration and Disintegration in the Europe of 1992," *Italian Journal*, IV, 5 (1990), 3-6.

[2]Giovanni Gozzer, "Originalità dei nuovi programmi," *Scuola di base* II, 3-4 (July-Dec. 1955), 10-11.

[3]Dario Ragazzini testifies to Italians' continuing fascination with Dewey in "Tra americanismo e pedagogia (la fortuna di Dewey)," *Riforma della scuola* 22, 8-9 (1976), 15-23 and in *Repertorio bibliografico di storia dell'educazione* (Florence: Sansoni, 1986),

pp. 34-36. See also Paul Ginsborg, *A History of Contemporary Italy: Society and Politics, 1943-1988* (London: Penguin, 1990), pp. 268-270; Giovanni Genovesi, "L'educazione prescolastica," in Tina Tomasi, ed., *L'istruzione di base in Italia (1859-1977)* (Florence: Vallecchi, 1978), p. 56; Martin Clark, *Modern Italy, 1871-1982* (London: Longman, 1984), p. 365; Fred Coombs and Richard Merritt, "The Public's Role in Educational Policy-Making; An International View," *Education and Urban Society* (February 1977), 186-187.

[4]On the evolution of American progressivism, see David Tyack, *The One Best System* (Cambridge, Mass.: Harvard University Press, 1974) and George S. Counts, *School and Society in Chicago* (New York: Harcourt, Brace, 1928); see also Edward Purcell, *Crisis of Democratic Theory. Scientific Naturalism and the Problem of Value* (Lexington, Ky.: University of Kentucky Press, 1973), p. 212.

[5]John Diggins, *Mussolini and Fascism: The View From America* (Princeton: Princeton University Press, 1972), pp. 365, 387-388; representative of American educators' wartime comparisons of our own and rival school systems is Thomas Vernor Smith and Glenn Nagely, *Democracy vs. Dictatorship: Teaching American Youth to Analyze and Understand Their Own and the Enemy's Way of Life* (Washington, D.C.: National Educational Association, 1942)

[6]Memo, Washburne to Public Relations branch, AFHQ, 10 Sept 1945, National Archives and Records Administration (NARA), Record Group 331, 10000/144/605.

[7]Allied Commission. Education Subcommission. (T. V. Smith), *Swan Song from the Ex-Director of the Education Subcommission, Allied Control Commission.* n. p., 1944; Carleton Washburne, "La riorganizzazione dell'istruzione in Italia," *Scuola e Citta* XXI (1970), 273-274.

[8]Carleton Washburne, "Education Under Allied Military Government in Italy," *Educational Record* XXVI, 4 (October, 1945), 261-268.

[9]Harry L. Coles and Albert K. Weinberg, eds., *Civil Affairs: Soldiers Become Governors*, (Washington, D. C.: Dept. of the Army, 1964), p. 404; (T. V. Smith) Monthly Report, Education Subcommission, July 1944, NARA, RG 331, 10000/144/165.

[10]Giorgio Canestri and Giuseppe Ricuperati, eds., *La scuola in Italia dalla legge Casati a oggi* (Turin: Loescher, 1976) pp. 189-266.

[11]Fiorenza Fiorentino, *La Roma di Charles Poletti (giugno 1944-aprile 1945)* (Rome: Bonacci, 1986), pp. 49-51; on the constitution see Remo Fornaca, *I problemi della scuola italiana dal 1943 alla Costituente* (Rome: Armando, 1972).

[12]While Omodeo's and De Ruggiero's historical and philosophical writings are widely known, their respective experiences as educational ministers are not. On their intellectual millieu see Eugenio Garin, *Intellettuali italiani del XX secolo* (Rome: Riuniti, 1974), esp. 47-68 and 105-136.

[13]Francesco Susi, *La scuola italiana dopo la seconda guerra*

mondiale (Rome: Societa Editrice Libraria, 1981), p. 46; Mario Alicata, *Intelletuali e azione politica* (Rome: Riuniti, 1976), p. 227; Giovanni Ferretti, "Guerra all'intelligenza" and "Il bilancio del Ministero Gonella'" in his *Scuola e democrazia* (Turin: Einaudi, 1956), pp. 17-19 and 34-45.

[14]Gozzer's Swiss trip, funded by private American sources, is described in his article "Missione a Ginevra," *Scuola e Professionalità* (May, 1970), 7-11. See also Dina Bertoni Jovine's *La scuola italiana dal 1870 ai giorni nostri* (Rome: Riuniti, 1958), pp. 407-409 and 462-464, as well as Canestri and Ricuperati, eds., *La scuola in Italia*, p. 414. Gozzer offers an unusual, Catholic challenge to mainstream clericalism in *I cattolici e la scuola* (Fiume: Vallecchi, 1964).

[15]Bertoni Jovine's rather critical appraisal of Washburne, and her increasingly positive assessment of pedagogical progressivism, emerge in *Scuola italiana dal 1870*, pp. 398-404 and 486-487. See also Tina Tomasi, *Scuola e pedagogia in Italia, 1948-1960*, (Rome: Riuniti, 1977), p. 170.

[16]On Codignola's pedagogical and political transformation from the 1920s through the 1940s, see Bertoni Jovine, *Scuola italiana dal 1870*, pp. 298-300, 473-475 and Tomasi, *Dalla dittatura alla repubblica*, pp. 159-162. Two major Italian "Deweyians" whose works were published by La Nuova Italia were Lamberto Borghi and Aldo Visalberghi.

[17]David Ellwood, *Italy 1943-1945* (New York: Holmes & Meier, 1985), pp. 146-147; Gozzer, "Originalità dei programmi," 10-11; Tomasi, *Dalla dittatura alla repubblica*, pp. 14-16; Susi, *La scuola italiana*, pp. 22-24.

[18]Lamberto Borghi, *Educazione ed autorità nell'Italia moderna* (Florence: La Nuova Italia, 1951); Tracy Koon, *Believe, Obey, Fight: Political Socialization of Youth in Fascist Italy* (Chapel Hill: University of North Carolina Press, 1985). The first critical study of Fascist educational politics and administrative practice was undertaken by the Educational Commission during the period of Allied occupation: Allied Commission, Education Subcommission, *La politica e la legislazione scolastica in Italia dal 1922 al 1943* (Rome: Garzanti, 1946); Marxist historians Canestri and Ricuperati have gone so far as to identify this volume, "so rich in implicit recommendations for future educational reforms," as the subcommission's most positive legacy. *La scuola in Italia*, p. 191.

[19]Roy Domenico, "Sanctions Against Fascism, The Politics of Purges in Italy, 1943-1948" Unpublished Ph.D. Dissertation, Rutgers University, 1987; Lamberto Mercuri, *L'epurazione in Italia 1943-1948* (Cuneo: L'Arciere, 1988); Remo Fornaca, "La politica scolastica degli Alleati in Italia e in Piemonte dopo la liberazione," *I problemi di pedagogia*, 2 (1975), 256-280; Umberto Margiotta, "La formazione della coscienza politica degli italiani durante la Resistenza" in Mario Gattulo and Aldo Visalberghi, eds.,

La scuola italiana dal 1945 al 1983 (Florence: La Nuova Italia, 1986), pp. 15-18.

[20]A. Giovagnoli, *Le premesse della ricostruzione. Tradizione e modernità nella classe dirigente cattolica del dopoguerra* (Milan: Nuovo istituto editoriale, 1982), pp. 228-233.

[21]Keith Wilson and Nicholas Pronay, eds., *The Political Reeducation of Germany and her Allies after World War II* (New York: Barnes & Noble, 1985). On German and Japanese reeducation efforts, see James F. Tent, *Mission on the Rhine: Reeducation and Denazification in American-Occupied Germany* (Chicago: University of Chicago Press, 1982) and Marlene J. Mayo, "Psychological Disarmament: American Wartime Planning for the Education and Reeducation of Defeated Japan, 1943-1945," in *The Occupation of Japan, Educational and Social Reform: the proceedings of a symposium sponsored by the McArthur Memorial Foundation*, October 16-18, 1980 (Norfolk: Gatling, 1982), especially pp. 33-35 and 57-61.

[22]Victoria De Grazia, "Mass Culture and Sovereignty: The American Challenge to European Cinemas, 1920-1960," *Journal of Modern History* 61:1 (March, 1989), 56; Pier Paolo D'Attore, "Guerra fredda e trasformazioni delle societa occidentali nella storiografia americana," *Italia contemporanea*, 140 (Sept. 1980),83-90; James Miller, *The United States and Italy, 1943-1950* (Chapel Hill: University of North Carolina, 1986); John Harper, *America and the Reconstruction of Italy, 1943-1948* (New York: Cambridge University Press, 1987); Peter Bondanella, *Italian Cinema from Neorealism to the Present* (New York: Ungar, 1983), pp. 42-50.

CHAPTER 2

AN AUTHORITARIAN EDUCATIONAL HERITAGE

The Genesis of Popular Schooling

Since the dawn of the Risorgimento, the fortunes of popular education in Italy turned on the slow and erratic growth of national sentiment. Universal primary schooling, which originated in northern Europe during the Reformation, was introduced to the Italian peninsula only in the late 18th century. In Lombardy, the Austrians under Joseph II promulgated a system of elementary schools, and teacher normal schools, as the major foundation of national well being. The short-lived Jacobin republics and their successor Napoleonic kingdoms extended these institutions through much of the peninsula.[1] These foreign imports satisfied the state-building needs of foreign conquerors; they reflected no indigenous craving for literacy.

In Italy, as elsewhere in Europe, the Catholic Church was the great antagonist of nationalist, public schooling. In a religiously homogeneous territory such as Italy, the traditional, life-long socialization provided by parish churches in every village and neighborhood had continued for centuries. Formal congregational or parish "schools" provided a universal formative bedrock and generally developed for socio-economic rather than ideological purposes. A few children of the "lesser classes" in the towns learned basic trade-related skills and the rudiments of the catechism, while Latin schools prepared the children of the propertied classes for the clergy or other literate professions.[2]

After the Napoleonic interlude, ideology could not help but assume a larger place in the educational policies of the Papacy and the peninsula's Restoration kingdoms and dutchies. Italy's rulers were profoundly frightened by a revolutionary refrain which advocated civic instruction, "careers open to talent" and the nation-state. They repudiated universal elementary schooling; the very principle of popular education was suspect, linked now to subversive republicanism. Clerical supervision guaranteed the religious orthodoxy of instruction in the few schools which survived. Gradually secular goals began to permeate Piedmont and the Austrian sphere of the North and Center, but failed to penetrate the Papal States and the Kingdom of Naples. Everywhere except in Piedmont, the four and a half decades of Restoration brought a decline in the overall number and quality of schools.[3]

If Restoration rulers deliberately neglected popular education, Risorgimento democrats saw it as a major tool in the achievement of their aims. Giuseppe Mazzini in particular centered his revolutionary tactics on the educational campaign of "Young Italy" to awaken Italians to their God-given destiny as a unified,

republican nation. The most important function of his Italian state
would continue to be "National Education," binding together the
energies and allegiances of the highly particularistic Italians
through the inculcation of a new "civic religion."[4]

The problem of popular political education posed by Mazzini
proved a difficult one for Cavour and his fellow Piedmontese
statesmen who masterminded Italian unification between 1859 and
1870. These Liberals doubted the wisdom of broad popular political
suffrage in the new kingdom. The suffrage law of 1861 enfranchised
only literate males holding substantial property--some 2% of
Italy's 26 million inhabitants.[5] In the short term, their hesitancy
was understandable. Outside of the Po Valley, the Piedmontese
seemed at least as alien to local populations as the monarchs and
dukes they had supplanted. Furthermore, in 1861 only prosperous,
formerly Austrian, Lombardy possessed a majority of literate
inhabitants. Illiteracy stood at 61.5% in the North, 78.3% in the
Center, 86.3% in the peninsular Mezzogiorno and 88.8% on the
islands of Sicily and Sardinia.[6] At unification, no more than 3%
of the peninsula's population used Italian rather than the local
dialect as a first language.[7]

How was this disparate population to be integrated into a
cohesive and loyal nation? Drawing on Napoleonic precedent, the
Piedmontese erected a highly centralized scholastic bureaucracy to
cement the cultural foundation of the new state. The Casati law
of 1859 had established the hierarchical structure of the Ministry
of Public Instruction for Piedmont and Lombardy; through the 1860's
that structure was relentlessly extended, with scant regard for
local tradition or legislation. The ministry was headed by the
minister himself and by the *Consiglio Superiore*, a consultative
council of professors and civil administrators appointed by the
king. Separate ministerial divisions administered primary,
secondary and higher education. Each division enforced uniform
administrative procedures and standardized curricula through
provincial superintendents.

Most of the Casati law and of the new state's educational
expenditures were devoted to secondary education. The classical
lyceums would train the nation's ruling elite, exposing their
students to common classical and Renaissance exemplars of civic
virtue. Like Napoleon before, them, some Liberals also championed
state secondary schools as the best means of combatting
anti-national, intransigent Catholicism. Anti-clericalism thus
supplemented distrust of the working and peasant classes as an
inducement for maintaining a restrictive, centralized scholastic
system.[8]

According to the Casati law, all communes were expected to
provide local boys and girls with two years of primary schooling.
At unification, one third of the nation's communes lacked even
these two-year schools. Even two years of schooling often proved

insufficient to insure against eventual return to illiteracy among graduates.[9] Yet the Casati law required only communities with over 4,000 inhabitants to offer an additional two years of schooling. It took decades to implement this rudimentary level of popular education. Until the late 1870s, there were no sanctions against communes which did not set up schools or against parents who kept their children at home.[10] Even after sanctions were established, they often remained a dead letter. Provincial educational authorities were reluctant to cross local landowners dependent on child labor or distrustful of the unsettling social potential of popular schooling.[11] Furthermore, these same landowners usually controlled the purse strings of the communes, which the Casati law made financially responsible for the construction and maintenance of primary schools.

The modest primary school system envisaged by the Casati law was devoted to inculcating social obedience and rudimentary literacy. The national curriculum for the first two years emphasized the study of the catechism as well as the Italian language: the nation's Liberal leaders granted religion a positive socializing value in elementary school which some of them denied it at the secondary level. Schoolteachers stressed to their pupils the duties which bound them to "God, to their parents, their brothers and sisters and their country."[12] Only in the third and fourth years, not taught in many rural communities, were elements of geography and episodes of national history included to bolster the civic component of the curriculum.[13]

Perhaps the greatest flaw of the Casati law lay in its neglect of elementary schoolteachers. The communes hired teachers at subsistence wages on a year to year basis, with no provisions for pensions or other benefits. Teachers were routinely harassed or fired for political or personal reasons. Even in a wealthy municipality like Milan, janitors and domestic servants both earned more in 1860 than the average male schoolteacher, and more than twice the pay of a female schoolteacher. Such pay differentials help explain why male schoolteachers outnumbered females for the first decade and a half after unification.[14] Often communes hired persons lacking even minimal teaching credentials. In the mid-1860s, the nation's normal schools were graduating only one quarter the number of teachers necessary to fulfill even the modest terms of the Casati reform. These training institutions were concentrated in the North and Center: many of the most impoverished southern provinces had none.[15]

A succession of parliamentary commissions denounced the government's educational policies, but no significant reform was attempted until the parliamentary Left swept the Liberals of the Right from power in the elections of 1876. The new government accepted the obligation of helping to finance schoolteachers' salaries, but increased them by no more than 10%. Compulsory lower level elementary schooling was extended to three years, increasing the full elementary program to five.[16]

During its eighteen years in power, the Left government pursued anti-clerical and chauvinistic policies even more openly than had its predecessor. Elementary religious instruction was made optional, left to the discretion of each commune. By 1900, the majority of children, particularly in urban areas, were no longer receiving public instruction in the catechism. Government laws and circulars implementing compulsory attendence referred frequently to the "scholastic obligation" of Italian youth.[17] When a new shortage of teachers developed as a result of these decrees, prominent Masonic officials within the Ministry of Public Instruction proposed that authorities employ junior officers from the army. No wonder many peasants continued to distrust the village schoolmaster nearly as much as the government recruitment officer. Although the Left boosted the national educational budget slightly, it increased the military budget much more. At the end of the 1880s, Italy was spending only 1.3 lire per inhabitant on schooling, while Belgium spent the equivalent of 5 lire per inhabitant, France and Great Britain 3.8 lire, and Prussia 2.7 lire.[18] Gauged by Western and Central European standards, the educational record of the Left represented only a moderate improvement over that of the Right in the 1860s and early 1870s.

In the last two decades of the century, a vigorous new advocate of public popular education emerged: the Italian Socialist Party. From their first appearance in the Chamber of Deputies in 1882, Socialists were the most outspoken and determined critics of the mounting imbalance between the nation's military and instructional budgets. But with the deepening of the economic crisis in the early 1890s, this concern took a back seat to agitation for immediate relief of the *miseria* of workers and peasants. Socialists echoed a persistent *leit-motif* of earlier Italian social critics, denigrating mere educational reform: what good is the "bread of science," they asked, when one lacks bread for the table?[19] After the mid-1890s, however, the economy entered a period of sustained expansion, and socialists once again took the lead in establishing adult evening schools and supplementary primary education through working class *scuole popolari*.[20] Like many Italian Liberals, and the radicals of the parliamentary Left, the socialists also championed public popular schooling as an antidote to clerical influence, which continued to be particularly strong in rural areas.

Since unification, Italy's Catholics had adopted an even narrower and more defensive approach to popular education than had the nation's major lay currents. Above all, this was true late in the papacy of Pius IX. In his *Syllabus of Errors*, Pius insisted on ecclesiastical control over family life and education. Any state-initiated instructional efforts required the Church's constant supervision and corrective influence; Pius explicitly condemned the separation of Church and State in the educational as in every other sphere. Furthermore, he eliminated the intellectual basis for any compromise with liberals or democrats by denouncing the doctrine of popular sovereignty and denying the independence of reason from ecclesiastical authority.[21] In 1872, the Jesuit periodical *Civilta Cattolica* reiterated this intransigent position: only the Church and the family could be entrusted with the delicate work of educating the young.[22]

Despite   their   ultimately   exclusive   and   authoritarian educational preferences, however, Catholics were forced to make use of traditional liberal arguments in favor of "liberty of instruction" and free competition between state and private institutions in order to protect parochial schools. Confronted by a hostile national educational bureaucracy, they were also among the earliest and most eloquent advocates of a more decentralized school system. The reforms of the late 1870s mobilized Catholics behind the defense of religious instruction in state primary schools. By the mid-1880s, this concern took on a more positive coloration: moderate Catholics began to warn their brethren against an overly narrow focus on the inculcation of the catechism. Instead, Catholics should support the general qualitative and quantitative strengthening of universal public primary education along side a vigorous and free parochial system. Even *Civilta Cattolica* admitted in 1886 that popular education had become an "ineluctable necessity of modern society," though it prescribed what it termed "moral education" rather than reading and writing as the appropriate focus for the nation's popular schools.[23] Catholics also contributed to a national quickening of interest in pedagogy during the 1880s.[24]

For most of his papacy, Leo XIII remained close to the conservative political and pedagogical views of the Jesuits. And yet his social doctrine demonstrated a certain democratic sensitivity to the aspirations of the poor and downtrodden. In the last years of his papacy, Leo XIII argued in his encyclical *Graves de communi* that all elements in society should participate in its guidance, and that government ought to benefit all--especially the lower classes. In this spirit the *Opera dei Congressi* launched the *Lega degli Insegnanti Cattolici* (League of Catholic Schoolteachers), which addressed the economic and social as well as the spiritual needs of teachers. Nor was the league the only Catholic organization concerned with popular education. Once Catholics were permitted to begin participating in local elections in the 1890s, parish priests in Lombardy taught local peasants to read and write so that they could qualify to vote for Catholic candidates.[25]

Leo's   successor,   Pius   X,   undid   most   of   the   advances represented by this progressive interlude. He lost no time in resurrecting an exclusive and authoritarian approach to popular education. The important scholastic reforms of the early 20th century would only be implemented in the face of militant Catholic opposition.

Popular Schooling in the Giolittian Era

When Italy entered the twentieth century one out of two of her citizens could neither read nor write. In 1900 Italian elementary school enrollments were less than half of those of France, although Italy's population had nearly equalled that of her Latin neighbor.[26] After Giovanni Giolitti assumed the prime ministership in 1903, however, the Italian state finally confronted the nation's popular educational needs in a serious and effective manner, introducing a series of measures comparable in scope to France's Ferry Reforms of the early 1880s. The Nasi law of 1903 granted female teachers pay equal to that of their male counterparts for certain categories of instruction, and improved the juridical status of all elementary teachers. *Maestri* now joined their secondary counterparts within the ranks of the state civil service. The Orlando law of 1904 extended compulsory education up to the age of 12, and created the first state schools for adult illiterates. Most significant of all was the Daneo-Credaro law of 1911. It transferred rural and small town schools from communal to state administration, and provided the first major state appropriations for the construction of new elementary schools. The law also required each commune to establish scholastic assistance offices, or *patronati scolastici*, which helped to outfit classrooms and provided books, clothes, and even meals to needy schoolchildren. Finally, steps were taken to improve the didactic effectiveness of teachers, through upgraded normal schools, practice teaching, and university in-service training courses.[27] By 1921, this complex of reforms enabled Italy to reduce illiteracy nationwide from 48.5% (in 1901) to 30%.[28]

These gains were supported by powerful new teachers' associations, and by all left-of-center parties. Inspired by the growing trade union movement, Italian primary and secondary schoolteachers established national professional organizations. In 1900 they organized the *Unione Magistrale Nazionale* or UMN (National Elementary Schoolteachers' Association) absorbing the Catholic *Lega degli Insegnanti* and several smaller groups.[29] In 1903, a unitary secondary teachers' association, the *Federazione Nazionale Insegnanti della Scuola Media* (FNISM), was formed. The two organizations collaborated only sporadically. Despite their common juridical status as members of the civil service, elementary and secondary teachers regarded their respective roles very differently. Primary *maestri* proudly carried on their educational mission among the whole people, while secondary *professori* conscientiously groomed the nation's socio-economic and political elite.[30]

The *Unione Magistrale* also declined to establish formal ties with any particular political party. UMN president Luigi Credaro argued that Italy's "family of schoolteachers" should become a "national party of the school" standing above partisan and class loyalties.[31] But Credaro's dream proved impossible in the highly polarized atmosphere of the pre-war decade. In the early years of the *Unione*, socialist militants opposed Credaro's position. Spiralling disaffection proved to be even more serious among Catholic schoolteachers. This group opposed the transfer of primary schooling from communal to national governmental administration, fearing an anti-religious offensive under the Bloc of the Left after the 1904 elections. The repudiation of the Concordat and the suppression of Catholic schools by a leftist government in France only heightened Catholic fears. Credaro's membership in the Masonic Order led to charges that the entire UMN association was becoming a "slave of the Freemasons."[32] In 1907 a sizeable minority within the association, including many of its women members, seceded and formed the rival Catholic *Associazione Magistrale "Nicolo Tommaseo."* The new Catholic organization quickly retreated from broader questions of popular and civic education to resume the traditional defense of religious instruction in state primary schools and the liberties of private educational institutions.[33]

More than anything, however, the schism reinforced many schoolteachers' inclinations to steer clear of political involvements and focus their collective energies on socio-economic questions. After decades of suffering at the hands of capricious local authorities, they placed great importance on their juridical rights as state dependents. Elementary teachers' new-found intermediary position between state and and people was expressed in the *Unione's* motto "neither slaves nor rebels."[34] In 1910 and 1911 schoolteachers gained direct representation at the apex of the national educational bureaucracy: two elementary teachers and a didactic director now sat on the newly-formed primary subcommission of the *Consiglio Superiore*. In addition, females were no longer restricted from serving on the council.[35]

The Italian educational system finally appeared to be evolving in a genuinely democratic direction. Few realized that elementary schools now consolidated into the national educational hierarchy could instead become channels for a highly illiberal and anti-democratic program of political socialization. The national administration of primary schooling had other drawbacks as well. In the long run, it inhibited schools from serving as democratic catalysts in their own communities.[36] The schoolteachers' new responsibilities to provincial and national authorities, like their increased professional mobility, tended to remove elementary teachers from local aspirations and concerns.

At the same time, the unprecedented expansion of primary schooling during the Giolitti era opened teaching to persons of even the most humble backgrounds. Sons and daughters of agricultural and unskilled industrial laborers now attained the status and security of a state post. They ascended to the "lowest rungs of the bourgeoisie," although their low pay meant that materially, schoolteachers were little better off than the families of their poorest pupils. Sometimes this rekindled a sense of proletarian solidarity; more often, it made these young teachers cling all the more to a fragile sense of cultured superiority.[37]

At the national level, too, Italians embraced popular education more readily as an avenue of socio-economic advancement than as a vehicle for social reform or more effective self-rule. Even as popular education finally took root across the peninsula, Italy's political leaders had great difficulty deciding whether or how to strengthen political democracy. In particular, they were troubled by the persistence of high illiteracy rates on the one hand and pressures to liberalize suffrage laws on the other. Some political moderates pointed to substantial popular illiteracy in urging modest suffrage reform. In 1908 Rome's daily *Il Messagero* warned that "giving the vote to illiterates was like giving explosives to a baby."[38] In 1912, however, the Chamber of Deputies endorsed universal manhood suffrage. Ironically, conservatives and Catholics assured the outcome, expecting to increase their control over an electorate so much of which was still poorly educated. During the parliamentary debate, an unusual coalition of conservatives and socialists also advocated the enfranchisement of women. But Liberals, Radicals, and Republicans rallied behind Giolitti and succeeded in blocking women's suffrage, for fear that it would add to the clerical vote.[39]

Having abruptly endorsed universal manhood suffrage in principle, the nation's political leadership arranged to circumvent it in practice. Giovanni Giolitti manipulated the elections of 1913 even more flagrantly than he had those of 1904 and 1909. For the first time, he incorporated Catholic support within a transformist governing coalition, negotiating a pact with the president of the Catholic Electoral Union, Ottorino Gentiloni, which permitted Catholics to vote for those Liberal candidates who pledged themselves to respect parochial schools and defend religious instruction in public schools. The Catholic masses now began voting "as a minor under papal guardianship."[40]

Italian involvement in World War I revealed equally manipulative attitudes on the part of the nation's elite toward the common man. Giolitti's successor Antonio Salandra committed Italy to the Allies against the wishes of the great majority of his countrymen. After a period of vacillation, Italy's *classe magistrale* set aside its humanitarian reservations and dutifully rallied behind the war effort. On April 1, 1915 UMN president Giuseppe Soglia pledged that Italy's *maestri* would become "sentinels of civil mobilization." On the front lines, attitudes differed widely. Many bourgeois officers hoped to renew the spirit of the Risorgimento through a noble crusade against Italy's traditional foe. Like the young teacher-turned soldier Adolfo Omodeo, they were dismayed at the indifference and selfishness of the army's semi-literate peasant and worker conscripts. Yet those sentiments only deepened as General Cadorna continued to sacrifice Italy's poorly-armed infantry against Austrian machine guns and barbed wire. In the end, the bloodbath of 1915-1918 polarized an already deeply divided nation.[41]

From Caporetto to the Gentile Reform

Although Benito Mussolini had once been a schoolteacher, his movement at first paid little attention to the problems of the school. What Mussolini and his comrades valued was a collective war-time experience whose action and violence were the antithesis of the sedate life of the classroom. The *Partito Nazionale Fascista* did not address an educational issue until its 1921 congress, when it demanded that the nation's primary schools "provide Italy's future soldiers with a rigorously national physical and moral training."[41] In addition, the congress held that the state needed to monitor teachers carefully, "especially in those communes dominated by anti-nationalist parties."[42] All concurred that the socialists and Italy's infant communist movement were "anti-national;" some Fascists applied the epithet to the Catholics as well. Whether lay or Catholic, Italy's schoolteachers and its school system were viewed as unreliable vehicles for the Fascist Revolution. The Fascists expected the patriotic indoctrination of young Italians to take place chiefly in their own para-military youth groups, and only secondarily in conventional schools.[43]

This distrust of the nation's schoolteachers was not confined to Fascism. In 1919 the Idealist educator Ernesto Codignola accused the majority of teachers within FNISM of treasonous pacifism, charging that under them "the secondary schools had prepared Caporetto." Following the war Codignola and Giovanni Gentile spearheaded the formation of a new teachers' association, the *Fascio di Educazione Nazionale*. Codignola and Gentile shared Mussolini's disdain for socialism and "Masonic, pacifistic and humanitarian democracy."[44] However, the new association originated and functioned completely independently of the *fasci di combattimento*.

In the wake of the Daneo-Credaro law, public concern with elementary education had waned. Fierce debates swirled around secondary schooling, however, between 1918 and 1923. A revolution of rising socio-economic expectations in motion before the war, and greatly reinforced by that conflict, threatened to overwhelm the nation's rickety, archaic secondary school structure: in 1920 secondary enrollments were five times those of the turn of the century.[45] Meanwhile, opponents and proponents of religious instruction within the Socialist and new Catholic Popular Parties attacked one another in ever more heated terms. In 1921 a new, Liberal minister of public instruction, Benedetto Croce, backed by Italy's leading pedagogical Idealists, proposed a single, rigorous matriculation examination (the *esame di stato*) for both public and private schools. Croce was confident that stiffer standards and livelier competition would rescue the state schools from the overcrowding which was compromising their "seriousness." Croce's proposal was an important stepping stone toward the reconciliation of Catholics and moderate non-clerical forces on a traditionally highly divisive issue. The ensuing debate over the *esame di stato* contributed to the broader political isolation of its chief critics, the socialists, while it cemented a cultural and political alliance behind the man who would finally institute the examinations in 1923--Giovanni Gentile.

When Mussolini formed his first cabinet in October, 1922, he had no clear-cut political, and hence educational, program beyond a generic nationalism. He was eager to legitimate his new authority as widely as possible; by appointing a distinguished philosopher as minister of public instruction, he appealed to the nation's intellectuals. In this sense his selection of Gentile may be compared to his courtship following the march on Rome of big business, the army, the church and the civil service.

Mussolini allowed Gentile virtually a free hand to reconstruct the entire Italian educational system. For the first time since the era of Casati, a minister of public instruction was granted *pieni poteri* ("full powers") to legislate solutions to the problems he faced, without parliamentary or other consultation. When Gentile's comprehensive reform was enacted in 1923, Mussolini quickly hailed it as "the most fascist of reforms." It is hard to say what Mussolini really meant by this statement; perhaps he was impressed by the authoritarian method, or style, with which the reform was introduced.[46] The statement cannot be applied to the systematic Idealist presuppositions and conservative content of the reform.

Gentile had developed his philosophy of education in the pages of *La Critica*, which he co-edited with Benedetto Croce from 1903 to 1922, and in a series of independent works, the first of which appeared in 1901. His entire pedagogy revolved around his Idealistic conception of the relationship between pupil and teacher. True education only took place when, in a moment of perfect communication, schoolmaster and student together became vehicles of the Spirit in action. As ultimate reality, the Spirit enjoyed absolute freedom: each of its realizations by individual masters and pupils was unique and non-repeatable. This emphasis on individual differences and relationships could be interpreted in a liberal and even democratic sense, as Gentile's colleague Giuseppe Lombardo-Radice would demonstrate. Ultimately, however,

Gentile's philosophy of the Spirit lent itself more directly to authoritarianism. Like Hegel, Gentile believed that the Spirit's highest historical realization lay in the State, which rationalized all partial and individual interests within itself.[47]

Still, the new elementary school curriculum, drafted by Lombardo-Radice, was surprisingly tolerant and progressive in spirit. At its heart, music and art, popular literature, tales and myths, and a modicum of grammar nurtured the "intensely imaginative world of the child." If necessary, teachers were encouraged to begin teaching in the dialect familiar to local children, in order to encourage their creativity.[48] Complementing the focus on the expressive arts was religious education, aimed at fostering the child's capacity for love and obedience toward something larger than itself. Originally, Lombardo-Radice had not equated this spiritual instruction with the dogmatic inculcation of the catechism--the form it came to assume in practice.[49] This distinctive, idealistic brand of progressivism would bear fruit again in the post-Fascist period, especially in the work of Ernesto Codignola and his Florentine coterie of reformers. History, geography, civics and science played a subordinate role in elementary schooling, but assumed greater prominence in the lower secondary curricula.[50] Administratively, the Gentile Reform treated secondary education in an authoritarian and traditional manner. Children continued to separate into tightly compartmentalized vocational and humanistic tracks after age eleven. Gentile took the greatest personal interest in upper secondary schooling, and reserved for himself the drafting of that portion of the 1923 reform text. A former classical lyceum professor, Gentile followed nineteenth century tradition when he reinforced that institution's role as the secondary school *par excellence*. By their mid-teens the best of the nation's youth would have matured intellectually enough to be trained in the highest form of knowledge, philosophy--and in particular Gentilian Idealism. Socialized in earlier grades to venerate Country, King and Duce, these adolescents would now be persuaded rationally that their freedom and self-realization required obedience to the State.[51]

Gentile imposed the greatest transformation of all on the old normal schools, now rechristened *istituti magistrali*. Given the spiritual and non-repeatable nature of each educational moment, Gentile had concluded that all attempts to define a science of teaching were not only futile, but pernicious. Thus he abolished the study of child psychology and didactics, and dispensed with student teaching.[52] At best, the aspiring teacher might prepare the way for the Spirit by his own cultural preparation. Thus the *istituto magistrale* curriculum centered on the study of ancient and modern languages and literature. The study of literary classics was to fertilize the future teacher's own imagination and to form his aesthetic taste. As a humanist, Gentile insisted that the

Italian language could be neither appreciated nor taught, even at the elementary school level, if the schoolmaster lacked a thorough grounding in the mother tongue, Latin. The introduction of Latin also promised *istituto magistrale* students a social status much closer to that of scholars in the classical and scientific lyceums. Unlike the lyceums, however, the *istituti* allowed their students only four, rather than five, years to cover a demanding range of subjects. This fact, coupled with the pressure to pass the newly instituted *esame di stato*, actually rewarded rote memorization and intellectual conformity, not independent thinking.[53]

In practice, the new teacher training institutions, with their elevated cultural aspirations, left their graduates poorly prepared for their work within the "schools of the people." The more conscientious young teachers sought out pedagogical and didactic assistance in their after hours. In particular, they turned to Lombardo-Radice's pre-war classic, the *Lezioni di Didattica*, for concrete suggestions and shrewd insights into the dynamics of the master-pupil relationship.[54] More frequently, new teachers simply fell back on the model of their secondary school experience, or the hazier recollections of their own, pre-Gentilian elementary schooling.[55] Most teachers simply drilled their charges for examinations at the end of the third and fifth grades. Such practices distorted or simply neglected the most progressive aspects of Lombardo-Radice's elementary curriculum.

The administrative side of the Gentile Reform also undercut Lombardo-Radice's conception of a sheltered *scuola serena*. Individual teachers had to keep increasingly detailed records of all classroom activities in a classbook, or *registro*, reviewed by their superiors.[56] They were constrained to select their texts from a list of titles which had passed preliminary ministerial screening. During the Giolittian era, principals had evolved from the role of petty bureaucrats and become didactic coordinators; now, they were to serve as political watchdogs for the central government. A series of ministerial circulars urged each principal to model his behavior on the nation's chief--in effect, to become principal and *duce* of his school. In secondary schools, principals reduced long-standing consultative faculty committees to rubber stamp bodies. At the provincial level, elective school councils, representing every grade of instruction, were scrapped.[57]

At the ministerial level, Gentile also reversed the pre-war trend toward teacher representation in the administration of public education. The Superior Council was reduced in membership to 24 persons, all to be nominated, as in the Casati law, by the king. Gentile also abolished the council's elementary and secondary subcommissions, on the grounds that they perpetuated the schoolteacers' already excessive "sectoral interests." In their place, Gentile allocated sweeping responsibility to his own unselfish, "higher" judgment.[58]

Incremental Fascistization

Gentile headed the ministry of education for little more than a year. Even before his resignation in mid-1924, he came under fire from several quarters. Despite its authoritarian qualities, militant Fascists found the 1923 reform too academic, too retrospective--too far removed from the dynamism of the Fascist revolution. The Italian petit-bourgeoisie which had contributed significant numbers to Mussolini's movement was incensed at Gentile's determination to reduce upper secondary enrollments.

When Gentile resigned and became editor of the *Enciclopedia Treccani*, Mussolini assured him that his reform would not be denatured by his successors. Yet by the end of the decade, the alteration of the Gentile Reform was well under way. In 1928 all of the laws and regulations pertaining to the operation of elementary schools and the supervision of personnel were consolidated for the first time into a single code, the *Testo Unico*. This code greatly assisted suceeding ministers in modifying the Gentilian legacy. The following year the regime renamed the Ministry of Public Instruction the Ministry of National Education, reflecting its ambition to shape the character of Italian youth, instead of merely imparting information.

In elementary schools, a reaction set in against what many saw as the "excessively aesthetic" emphasis of Lombardo-Radice's curriculum. In 1926 the *Opera Nazionale Ballila* (ONB) was established to promote the strictly Fascist physical and moral training of the young, by expanding physical education and promoting athletic competitions and other extra-curricular youth activities. In 1928, the national administration of the ONB was integrated with the Ministry of Instruction.[59]

In fact, the regular ministerial bureaucracy resisted political dictation at the hands of ONB militants. Like other civil servants, they mastered the rhetoric of the new regime, but already in 1927 it was clear that they and not party outsiders would continue to be the predominant influences in the life of Italian schools.[60] In 1934, the educational minister Cesare Maria De Vecchi di Val Cismon further centralized the already hierarchical structure of the ministry, without resolving the continuing rivalry between party and state personnel. De Vecchi made all responsibility for the content of study, the institution and inspection of schools, and the choice of teachers subject to the personal discretion of the minister. He also opened the streamlined *Consiglio Superiore* to the heads of the Fascist Party and the ONB, while retaining final decision-making authority in his own hands.[61]

Nothing could, of course, guarantee that the cascade of directives emanating from Rome would always be clearly understood or implemented by local administrators and teachers. At the classroom level, a much more effective guarantor of the orthodoxy of elementary instruction was the introduction of a uniform series of state textbooks in both public and private schools.[62]   Beginning in 1930-31, a comprehensive text was printed for each of the five primary grades; supplemental readers were also provided in the fourth and fifth grades.   The scale of this publication effort was striking; it dwarfed all subsequent Allied counter-efforts during the last years of World War II.   Of the 5.5 million texts printed in 1931-32, 1.7 were first grade *sillabari* (primers), while only 250,000 fifth grade texts and an equal number of fifth grade readers were produced.[63]   These figures suggest that, despite its totalitarian claims, the regime was content to accomodate itself to a rapid decline in attendance after the second grade, particularly among rural and southern children.

Under De Vecchi the Fascist *libri di stato* were revised, so as to dramatize the activities of Fascist youth groups and instill more effectively the ONB slogan "believe, obey, fight."   The very first word the child was taught to spell was "Eia," the Fascist war cry.   The first and second grade texts especially offered innumerable variations on the duty of the virtuous little Wolf-cub or Little Italian (*Piccola Italiana*) to love and obey the Pope, the King and, above all, the Duce.   In the fourth and fifth grades, geography lessons demonstrated Italy's "natural" domination of the Mediterranian.   History lessons celebrated the military, cultural, and spiritual superiority of Italians through the centuries. Despite scattered references to the loyalty and courage of the "common man"--notably in the trenches of the First World War--primary instruction focused overwhelmingly on heroes, whether mythical or historical.   "Ballila," the half-legendary boy who led an 18th century Genoese revolt which expelled Austrian occupation during the War of the Austrian Succession, figured prominently in reading selections.   But the greatest heroic figure by far was Mussolini himself.   As the 1930s progressed, and the Fascist regime evolved more and more into a personal dictatorship, the basic message of popular schooling became simply "the Duce is always right."[64]

At the secondary level, the state monitored, but did not attempt to monopolize the publication of textbooks.   Still, private authors and publishers found it prudent to provide chauvinistic and religiously orthodox treatments of history, geography, philosophy, Italian and even Latin.   After 1929 several changes were introduced which began to narrow the profound traditional differences between Italian primary and secondary schooling.   With the adoption of the Concordat, Catholicism returned to public secondary school curricula for the first time since the 1860s.   Its importance was underlined by a 1935 ruling, making proficiency in religion a prerequisite for promotion at the end of each school year. Secondary school curricula were also expanded to include instruction in the principles of corporativism and "class harmony," beginning in 1928. Mussolini's essay on the "dottrina del Fascismo" became required reading in the mid-1930s. Finally, in 1935 courses in military culture were added, as part of De Vecchi's campaign to "remake the school in the spirit of Empire."[65]

The Italian attack on Abyssinia and the ensuing condemnation by the League of Nations spurred a drive for cultural as well as economic autarky. The clerico-Fascist educator Nazareno Padellaro, and Luigi Volpicelli, one of Gentile's brightest disciples, founded the journal *Primato educativo*, devoted to "arming and defending Italy's pedagogical frontiers."[66] Idealist and orthodox Catholic approaches to teacher preparation, with their unyielding devotion to Latin and complete exclusion of psychology and other experimental sciences, had already cut off Italian education from significant currents of European and North American thought. Now an intensified spirit of xenophobia made itself felt, especially within the *istituti magistrali*. In 1935 the study of world literature was drastically curtailed: even Gentilian favorites such as John Stuart Mill, Victor Hugo, Leo Tolstoy and Henrik Ibsen disappeared from examination reading lists.[67]

Bottai and the Carta della Scuola

In late 1936, Giuseppe Bottai, former Minister of Corporations and among the most intelligent and capable of Mussolini's lieutenants, became Minister of National Education. Bottai asserted that in key respects the piecemeal process of Fascist *ritocchi* or revision--even as practiced by De Vecchi--had not adequately prepared Italy for its new national and international responsibilities. The nation was launching a concerted drive toward armament production and greater industrial productivity in general. Drawing on the expertise of Volpicelli and a number of other educators, Bottai insisted that the schools inculcate the ethical, social and cultural, as well as economic value of human labor in all of its aspects.[68]

At the same time, Italy's African adventure and its intervention in the Spanish Civil War dramatized its need for zealous, well-conditioned soldiers. Yet after a decade of steady organizing and propaganda, the activities of the Fascist para-military youth groups had still not been harmoniously integrated into the elementary schools--and still less in the secondary schools. Lack of coordination confused students and caused mutual resentment between local ONB officials and regular headmasters and teachers. In 1937 Bottai concentrated all paramilitary, physical education and social welfare activities (including all of those traditionally administered by the *patronati scolastici*) within a new body, the *Gioventù Italiana del Littorio* (GIL), directly administered by the Fascist Party. He then incorporated into his own sweeping, organic reform of Italian schooling, the *Carta della Scuola*, the obligation of Italy's youth to perform "scholastic service" from the ages of 6 to 14, and to belong to the GIL from ages 6 to 21.[69]

Bottai submitted his *Carta della Scuola*, or "School Charter," to the Fascist Grand Council in 1939. In a series of 29 solemn "Declarations," the School Charter set forth the basic values and institutional forms which would at last guarantee the "total education" of the new Fascist man. Bottai invited the family and Church to continue to provide their vital contributions to the formation of the young, in intimate and continuous collaboration with the state. Fundamentally, however, he insisted that only the interests of the state, and not the socio-economic aspirations of the family, would determine each pupil's scolastic training and his vocational future.[70]

Bottai proposed to recast the entire educational system in order to consummate a marriage of the traditionally antagonistic realms of culture and work. In order to eradicate a decadent and "bourgeois" contempt for manual labor still deeply rooted in Italian society, all Italians would engage in productive work as part of their school experience. The fourth and fifth primary grades were renamed the "School of Labor" to underline the importance of this new part of the curriculum. Eleven to fourteen year-olds were then promoted to one of three categories of intermediate schools. In rural areas, *scuole artigiane*, taught by elementary school teachers, would preserve the "love of the earth" and strengthen the agricultural skills of the peasantry.[71] In towns and cities, *scuole professionali* and *scuole tecniche* would prepare commercial and industrial workers. Students destined to continue their studies past age 14 attended a completely new *scuola media unica*; in theory, they too were to engage in some sort of productive labor. The School Charter also projected a number of changes in upper secondary schools, including the addition of a fifth year of in-school training to the *instituto magistrale*, which were never implemented due to the war.[72]

The centerpiece of the School Charter was the *scuola media unica*. Here the flower of the Fascist people would absorb the principles of a "new humanism," a synthesis of classical humanism and the dynamism of 20th century industry. Despite the equal pedagogical emphasis given to Latin and productive labor in the text of the School Charter, however, the Ministry of National Education offered very little advice or assistance to *professori* entirely untutored in the latter subject. Latin, on the other hand, continued to enjoy its traditional reputation as a peculiarly effective "factor of moral and intellectual formation." Furthermore, the literary elegance of the "mother tongue" was said to demonstrate the eternal greatness of the "Italic stock."[73]

The new "unified" middle school represented important progress over the separate lower secondary grades of the *licei* and the *istituto magistrale.* By consolidating the curricula of those schools, the *scuola media unica* postponed the vocational tracking of students until their capacities and personality had more fully emerged. At age 14 as compared to age 11, the career orientation of the student could meaningfully reflect individual differences, and not merely parental preferences.[74] This aspect of the School Charter also demonstrated a new, selective receptivity in prominent educational circles to basic insights in child psychology, and the possibility of applying them to secondary as well as primary education.

But the same sort of individualized consideration was denied to the worker and peasant student populations enrolled in the other types of intermediate schools. Only the *scuola media* offered Latin, and Latin continued to be required for entrance to all higher secondary schools. Bottai had promised to create a series of state-run rural boarding schools to prepare the very brightest poorer students for advanced studies; in fact, only a handful were ever built.[75]

Some of Bottai's advisors had urged the creation of a single, genuinely inclusive middle school to prevent continued socio-economic discrimination. The minister sided with those, like Ernesto Codignola, who argued that a completely unified system would "debase culture."[76]

For Bottai, "Fascist culture" was only in the process of being formed--it was not something to be taken for granted, but something to be earned. The Fascist educational minister boasted that the "school of the people" had nothing in common with the old democratic *scuola del censo* (literally, "school based on wealth"), an inferior, non-discriminatory school which had aspired, however inefficiently, to provide common instruction to the entire population.[77] Nor did Bottai intend the common educational esposure to labor and the "new humanism" to lead to any attenuation of class distinctions. Classes arose inevitably from the division of labor, and ultimately from genetic differences. Henceforth, Bottai simply wanted to guarantee that the Fascist state, and not, as in the past, individual wealth and status, separated those capable of higher studies from those "born for other tasks."[78]

In its Italian version of the *Arbeitdeinst*, and its campaign to preserve rural values and prevent an alarming depopulation of the countryside, the Fascist regime instituted policies reminiscent of cultural trends in Nazi Germany. The most direct consequence of the Rome-Berlin axis, however, was the implementation of discriminatory legislation against Italy's 50,000 Jewish citizens. In late 1938 all Jewish pupils were expelled from the GIL and all public and private schools. An exception was made for Catholic children of Jewish origin studying in ecclesiastical institutions; otherwise, Jewish pupils were forced to attend separate classes. Jewish teachers like other Jewish intellectuals now lost their posts, while a belated attempt was made to incorporate a vague "race-consciousness" into the nation's schools.[79]

How "Fascist" Were the Schoolteachers?

For all of the twists and turns of its educational policies, the regime consistently maintained a higher level of concern for the formation of Italian youth than had the preceding Liberal monarchy. In part, this is to be expected in any revolutionary state. In part, it was a consequence of Fascism's particular glorification of the natural strength and audacity of youth. But how did this youth worship effect the regime's attitudes towards the instructors of the young? How successful was the regime in winning the hearts of the nation's schoolteachers?

Several students of Fascist culture have portrayed primary schoolteachers--at least in the 1930s--as dedicated transmitters of the political ideology of the regime. The quality of elementary teachers' preparation in the *istituti magistrali* and the young age at which they began their teaching careers did leave them more vulnerable than the university-trained secondary teachers to the propaganda of the regime. Without question the regime singled out primary teachers for a great deal of rhetorical attention. Aside from involving them in youth group events and providing them with the *libri dello stato*, the Ministry of National Education carefully regulated even the teaching hints provided in schoolteachers' journals. As a result of such supervision, the Catholic journal *Scuola italiana moderna* sometimes exceeded even the lay publication *I diritti della scuola* in its jingoistic zeal.[80]

But it is difficult to gauge the degree to which Italian teachers internalized such political guidance. The relatively small number of teachers who have published memoirs since the Second World War are usually outspoken anti-Fascists with close ties to one of Italy's post-war political parties.[81] Such evidence, like the testimony provided in the personal profiles (*schede personali*) administered by Allied military officials during the war, surely under-represents the devotion of some teachers to Fascist ideals. Conversely, archival evidence originating in the Fascist Ministry of National Education may exaggerate levels of teacher militancy. The same bias may be expected in the colorful and detailed summaries of classroom activity prepared by schoolteachers in *registri*, which were reviewed by their didactic directors.

If it is difficult to reconstruct the specific political beliefs of schoolteachers under Fascism, it is easier to gauge their sympathy for the regime in a more general sense. Overall, teachers' sentiments turned on three sets of factors. Most important, probably, was the socio-economic treatment accorded them by the regime. A second factor was the appeal of a protean ideology of nationalism incorporating an impressive range of traditional values. In addition, the regime tried to imbue teachers with a new "virile spirit" by pressuring them to participate in a variety of Fascist organizations.

A well-established sociological interpretation of Fascism especially popular with Marxist historians emphasizes the large petit-bourgeois component among Mussolini's early supporters. There is no question that teachers--like other minor civil servants, shopkeepers, and many artisans and peasants--resented the significant socio-economic advances made by blue-collar workers before, during and immediately following the First World War. It is also true that elementary teachers' salaries, although modest, stayed ahead of inflation throughout the Fascist era, which they had failed to do previously--and would fail to do again after 1945.[82] Urban teachers in particular had reason to be pleased. In 1933 the regime established a five-step rating system for schools, according to which teachers in larger towns and cities received considerably higher pay than their small town and particularly their rural counterparts.[83]

In the late 1920s, a reduced number of *istituto magistrale* graduates only slightly exceeded the number of teaching positions available. No doubt this lessened elementary teachers' chronic sense of job insecurity, and may have strengthened a genuine sense of loyalty to the regime. But the restrictive Gentilian policy on secondary enrollments was intensely unpopular with Mussolini's wider lower middle and middle calss constituency. In 1929 and 1930 a much more liberal approach was adopted. By 1939, the pool of unemployed *istituto magistrale* graduates equalled the number of practicing teachers. This situation reinforced the external docility and conformity of teachers, but it bred greater dissension and a heightened sense of anxiety as well. Competition for teaching posts was especially fierce in the larger cities.[84]

On the other hand, the inferior pay of rural schoolteachers, in conjunction with new legislation restricting internal migration out of the countryside, created serious rural discontent by the latter 1930's. Bottai's introduction of a special rural series of *libri di stato* and the creation of the *scuole artiqiane* failed to mollify such feeling. Indeed, these measures were widely seen as confirming the separate and unequal status of rural schooling. In 1943, the Biggini ministry in the neo-Fascist Republic of Salò lost little time in discontinuing the rural textbook series, and granting uniform juridical and economic concessions to rural and urban teachers alike.[85]

Fascist police reports and Allied occupational records reveal, however, a tremendous variation in local teacher sentiment, which defies simple explanation based on urban-rural or regional distinctions. To cite but one example, the American educational officer Willis Pratt enjoyed such a cordial relationship with teachers in Avellino province, and elsewhere in Campania, that he depicted schoolteachers "as a group perhaps . . . the least affected by the Fascist doctrine."[86] Yet Carlo Levi, the writer exiled to Eboli during the *ventennio*, has left behind a scathing portrait of "Don Luigino," the arrogant village schoolteacher consumed by the rituals of the regime.[87]

A more reliable indicator of teacher sentiment is sexual difference: in general, female schoolteachers were less militant than their male counterparts.[88] The increasingly feminine composition of the nation's teaching force troubled the regime. The lack of men, above all in the elementary schools, deprived Italy's future soldiers of suitable role models. After the opening of the Ethiopian campaign, Mussolini promoted a high birth rate as an index of the vitality of the Italian nation, proclaiming that "maternity is to a woman what war is to a man."[89] In order to keep more women at home, and place more men in the classroom, authorities introduced a range of discriminatory juridical and economic measures between 1927 and 1938. Women students were assessed double fees in secondary schools and universities, while earning only half the salaries of men in work done for Fascist syndicates. In secondary schools they were banned from teaching certain subjects, or becoming principals. Finally, 1938 legislation restricted women to a maximum of 10% of civil service positions.[90] These measures failed to alter the ratio of male to female primary teachers, while causing resentment among the many *maestre* hoping one day to obtain more prestigious or higher paying work.

In its public pronouncements, the regime appealed not to schoolteachers' personal ambitions or pocketbooks, but to their idealistic sense of "vocation." In doing so, the Fascists took advantage of several favorable ideological developments. Gabriele D'Annunzio's antics in Fiume in 1919-20 had exacerbated longstanding popular longings for Italy's *terre irredente*. A new pope, Pius XI, was deeply committed to a tightly controlled and conservative *ralliement* of the Papacy to the nation-state. Chastened by their own ideological schisms of 1907, and proud of their newly-won status as national dependents, schoolteachers warmly embraced Credaro and Lombardo-Radice's non-partisan nationalism, through which they would forge the soul of a new Italy. By promising to elevate politics and culture to a new spiritual plane, and by presenting itself as a stern and impartial administrator of the nation, standing above all personal, class, and regional interests, the regime had initially exercised a powerful appeal to many Italians, including educators.[91]

For this very reason Mussolini refrained from lending his name to a positive Fascist ideology for as long as possible. Yet already in the early 1920's, he was forced to make concessions to party ideologues eager to politicize the nation's schoolteachers. As Director General of Elementary Education, Lombardo-Radice vigorously protested the first signs that the regime intended to pressure teachers into joining the Fascist party or its organizations. For Italy's schoolteachers to be effective agents of nationalism, Lombardo-Radice believed they had to devote themselves to the will of the state voluntarily. The more the politics of the regime turned from persuasion to coercion, the more Lombardo-Radice was convinced that Fascism would betray the "national party of the school."[92] Certainly the resignation of this influential figure from the ministry in 1924, in protest over the Matteotti murder, dimmed the appeal of Fascism in the eyes of many schoolteachers. By the mid-1920's, that very aversion to narrow "politics" which had turned so many educators toward Mussolini initially began to disenchant them with his regime.

The regime responded in 1925 by dissolving the *Unione Magistrale Nazionale* and the Catholic *Associazione Tommaseo*. Public school teachers were now herded into the successor Fascist syndicate, the *Associazione Fascista della Scuola*, while private school teachers were allowed to join the syndicate of intellectuals.[93] These were only the first of a series of measures adopted to legislate teacher conformity. Beginning in 1928, teachers not only had to swear loyalty to king and country, but they were threatened with permanent dismissal for any actions taken in or outside the classroom "incompatible with the general political directives of the government."[94] In 1931 Pius XI instructed Catholics who had to take the oath of allegiance for the sake of their careers that they might make the silent reservation that they would do nothing contrary to the laws of God or the Church. But later that year the pope raised no objection to teachers holding joint membership in Catholic Action and party organizations. After 1933, all *new* civil servants, including professors and teachers, had to be party members--unless they taught religion.[95]

However the regime never required that *all* practicing teachers belong to the party, perhaps due to powerful sentiments within the *Partito Nazionale Fascista* that any such regulation would undermine the party's elite nature. Instead, elementary teachers were informed that better appointments and advancement would depend on active extra-curricular involvement in the activites of the ONB. In rural areas, especailly, local teachers had little choice but to become leaders of local ONB and subsequently GIL chapters. By 1943, some 94,000 out of a total of 120,000 practicing elementary teachers belonged to the PNF, the GIL or one of several other Fascist cultural and social organizations.[96] Interestingly enough, the Republic of Salò placed little stock on these figures in assessing the loyalties of northern teachers. In the last few years of the *ventennio*, the regime had based teacher evaluation and promotion heavily on such superficial indicators as success in maximizing pupil enrollment in the GIL, preparing pupils to perform enthusiastically at public manifestations, and collecting the largest possible sums of money from families for various war-related drives. Ultimately, such policies rewarded a growing number of opportunistic individuals who were neither convinced Fascists nor effective teachers.[97]

A far more successful development for harnessing teacher enthusiasm to the objectives of the regime was the *rapprochment* between Church and State achieved in 1929. The Concordat of 1929 was a tremendous boost to the general political legitimacy of the regime. Shortly after signing the Lateran Accords, Pius XI described Mussolini as a "man of Providence" who had enabled him to "give God to Italy and Italy to God."[98] The regime enriched its educational materials, like all of its public propaganda, with religious phraseology. Fascism became a "sacred" or "holy struggle," and the service of the nation a "divine commandment." Crucifixes now appeared on the walls of public as well as parochial schools. Flanked always by a portrait of the Duce on its left and the king on its right, the crucifix served as the centerpiece of a new national trinity. The pope's praise contributed immeasurably to the construction of an aura of infallibility around the "man of Providence." In looking back on his own schooling in the 1930's, the writer Alfassio Grimaldi singles out this cult as the most compelling of all Fascist dogmas.[99]

As the Fascists proceeded to define the contours of a cultural ideal of "*italianità*," they drew upon and thereby strengthened the authoritarian aspects of the Roman Catholic tradition. Mussolini exulted "as an Italian" in the fact that 400 million faithful all over the globe looked to Rome for guidance. Through the 1930's, Fascism as the religion of the Italian state was emphasized at the expense of Catholicism as a universal faith. By the end of the *ventennio*, the regime inaugurated macabre "Fascist masses;" in one such celebration at the Campo Dux in 1938, the Fascist party secretary served as chief altar boy, and "at the elevation of the host the 15,000 young men present drew their bayonets and pointed them to the sky."[100]

The convergence of Fascist and Catholic values was delayed, but not ultimately prevented, by Mussolini and Pius XI's two year dispute between 1929 and 1931 over the role of Catholic Action's youth groups. A number of historians have noted how the dispute challenged Fascist aspirations for the totalitarian control over the nation's youth. In his encyclical *Non abbiamo bisogno* Pius XI did censor a "revolution that seduces the young from the Church and from Jesus Christ and teaches them hatred, violence and irreverence." Yet when party leaders responded by reviving traditional anti-clerical charges that the Church was insufficiently loyal, the pope hastened to reach a compromise with Mussolini, even at the cost of greatly weakening the Catholic Action groups.[101] Papal reservations about the extreme militarism of the regime receded greatly by the time of the African campaign, and disappeared altogether during Italy's crusade against the enemies of the Church during the Spanish Civil War.[102] Although the emergence of the Rome-Berlin axis and the new anti-Semitic legislation again caused friction between Mussolini and Pius XI, the latter's death and his replacement by the much more cautious Pius XII prevented this breach from becoming more serious. Only after Italy's entry into the Second World War were democratic Catholics, such as Alcide De Gasperi in Rome and Giorgio La Pira in Florence, able to convince many of their co-religionists of the final incompatibility of Fascist totalitarianism and Catholic social doctrine.[103]

The new brand of clerico-fascist nationalism which dominated the 1930s left its mark especially on very young teachers graduating from the *istituti magistrali* at the end of the 1930s. These were people whose schooling had taken place almost entirely after the 1929 Concordat. Even in 1943, this remained a distinct minority within a national teaching corps whose average age was 35.[104] Under the Republic of Salò, such young teachers often began their careers in rural areas where, according to ministerial reports, they carried out their duties faithfully, "despite hostile (partisan) propaganda and the suspicions of rebels and some of the local population."[105] Many older teachers, on the other hand, retreated as best they could in the late 1930s and early 1940s to the humble but honest ideal of imparting learning for its own sake. Perhaps the majority of teachers, however, found themselves in a demoralizing no-man's land, uncomfortable in their new found role as political cheerleaders, yet fearful of the censure of their superiors.[106]

In the end, it was the centralized restriction of didactic autonomy, and the authoritarian day-to-day operation of the schools, which constituted the most deeply-rooted legacy of the Fascist *ventennio*. Even during the "Years of Consensus" in the early and mid-1930's, the loyalty of schoolteachers to the regime was broad but superficial--the product less of faith than a well-developed instinct for self-preservation.[107] Thereafter, the unending parade of reforms, the proliferation of discriminatory socio-economic legislation, and above all the suffering brought on by the Duce's "redemptive war" left most schoolteachers, like most Italians, resentful and confused.[108] In 1943 it was far from clear whether, or when, they could place their trust in an alternative democratic order, let alone take an active role in shaping it.

ENDNOTES

[1] Dina Bertoni Jovine, *Storia della scuola popolare in Italia* (Turin: Einaudi, 1954), p. 37. Ida Zambaldi, *Storia della scuola elementare in Italia* (Rome: Libreria Ateneo Salesiano, 1975), pp. 31-33, 56-60. Owen Connelly, *Napoleon's Satellite Kingdoms* (New

38 *Progressive Renaissance*

York: Free Press, 1965), pp. 52-54.
    [2]Zambaldi, *Storia della scuola elementare*, p. 9.
    [3]*Ibid.* p. 105.
    [4]Denis Mack Smith. *Italy. A Modern History*, 2nd ed. (Ann Arbor: University of Michigan Press, 1969), p. 14.
    [5]Alfio Mastropaolo. "Elezioni," in *L'Italia Contemporanea*, ed. by Fabio Levi et. al. (Florence: La Nuova Italia, 1978), pp. 128-130.
    [6]After 1870 the North embraced the regions of Piedmont, Lombardy, Venetia, Liguria, Emilia and Romagna; the Center was comprised of Tuscany, Umbria, the Marches and Latium; and the peninsular Mezzogiorno included Abruzzi and Molise, Apulia, Lucania, Campania, Basilicata and Calabria. These statistics, drawn from the 1861 census, are cited by Pia Maria Tancredi Torelli, "Gli esclusi dall'alfabeto. Iniziative di scuola per adulti," in Tomasi, ed., *L'istruzione di base in Italia*, p. 85.
    [7]Denis Mack Smith, "Regionalism," in *Modern Italy: A Topical History*, ed. by Emiliana Noether and Edward Tannenbaum (New York: New York University Press, 1974), p. 127.
    [8]Elmiro Argento, "Continuity and Change in Italian Education, 1859 to 1923," *Canadian Historical Association, Historical Papers/Communications Historiques*, 1978, 94-95.
    [9]Canestri and Ricuperati, *La scuola in Italia*, p. 19.
    [10]Tracy Koon, "Believe, Obey, Fight. Political Socialization of Youth in Fascist Italy, 1922-1943" (Unpublished Revised Doctoral Disertation, 1982), chapter 2, p. 5.
    [11]On the traditional opposition of southern landowners to popular education, see A. Broccoli, *Educazione e politica nel Mezzogiorno d'Italia* (Florence: La Nuova Italia, 1968).
    [12]Benito Incatasciato, "Leggere, scrivere, far di conto. Per una storia della didattica nella scuola elementare," in Tomasi, ed., *L'istruzione di base*, p. 131.
    [13]For the full text of the Casati elementary curriculum, see Zambaldi, *Storia della scuola elementare*, pp. 603-615.
    [14]Simonetta Ulivieri, "I Maestri," in Tomasi, ed., *L'istruzione di base*, pp. 201-203.
    [15]Canestri and Ricuperati, *Scuola dalla legge Casati*, p.62; Minio-Paluello, *Education in Facist Italy*, p.16.
    [16]Ester De Fort, *Storia della scuola elementare in Italia*, vol. 1 (Milan: Feltrinelli, 1979), p. 84; Minio-Paluello, *Education in Fascist Italy* (London: Oxford University Press, 1954), p. 27.
    [17]Borghi, *Educazione e autorità*, p. 25. Canestri and Ricuperati, *Scuola dalla legge Casati*, pp. 84-87.
    [18]Tina Tomasi, *Massoneria e scuola dall'Unita ai nostri giorni* (Florence: Vallecchi, 1980), p. 58; Luigi Volpicelli, *Storia della scuola elementare a Roma* (Rome: Armando, 1963), p. 120. De Fort cites the comparative spending figures, drawn from a Chamber of Deputies report, in *Storia della scuola elementare*, p. 131.

An Authoritarian Heritage 39

[19]The phrase was coined by Pasquale Villari in 1872. Torelli, "Esclusi dall'alfabeto," p. 91.

[20]Socialist parliamentary addresses from the years 1896-1898 are reproduced in Canestri and Ricuperati, *Scuola dalla legge Casati*, pp. 100-104. See also Borghi's penetrating evaluation of socialist pedagogical assumptions, *Educazione e autorità*, pp. 96-103.

[21]Borghi, *Educazione e autorità*, pp. 19-20.

[22]S. William Halperin, *Italy and the Vatican at War. A Study of Their Relations from the Outbreak of the Franco-Prussion War to the Death of Pius IX* (Chicago: University of Chicago Press, 1939) p. 290.

[23]Carlo Arturo Jemolo, *Chiesa e Stato in Italia negli ultimi cento anni*. 2nd ed. (Turin: Einaudi, 1971), pp. 295-298; De Fort, *Storia della scuola elementare*, pp. 154-155.

[24]Dina Bertoni Jovine, *Scuola italiana dal 1870*, pp. 53-55, 63. On the Risorgimento origins of spiritualistic pedagogy, see Zambaldi, *Storia della scuola elementare*, pp. 175-202.

[25]Richard A. Webster, *The Cross and the Fasces. Christian Democracy and Fascism in Italy* (Stanford: Stanford University Press, 1960), pp. 12, 191.

[26]B. R. Mitchell, *European Historical Statistics, 1750-1975*, 2nd ed. (London: MacMillan, 1981), pp. 29-34. For comparative European elementary attendance figures, see pp. 787-804.

[27]Despite the Daneo-Credaro Law, teacher qualifications varied widely from area to area. In some rural communities, new teachers still were entering the classrooms after as little as six years of formal schooling of their own--as little as four years of elementary school followed by two years of normal school training. Zambaldi, *Storia della scuola elementare*, pp. 369-373, 411-412.

[28]Education Subcommission. *Politica e legislazione scolastica*, pp. 150-151.

[29]A first-hand account of the early years of the UMN is provided by Luigi Cremaschi, *Cinquant'anni di battaglie magistrali* (Rome: Ed. I Diritti della Scuola, 1952).

[30]Bertoni Jovine compares the reform efforts of UMN and FNISM in *Scuola italiana dal 1870*, pp. 127-138.

[31]*Ibid.*, p. 131.

[32]Tomasi, *Massoneria*, pp. 152-153.

[33]Zambaldi, *Storia della scuola elementare*, pp. 553-554.

[34]Bertoni Jovine, *Scuola italiana dal 1870*, p. 131.

[35]Remo Fornaca, "Scuola e politica nell'Italia liberale," in *Scuola e politica dall'Unità ad oggi*, ed. by Guido Quazza (Turin, Stampatori, 1977), pp. 41-42.

[36]As early as the 1880's, the socialist philosopher Antonio Labriola developed such an argument, emphasizing the necessity of transforming the school and its social environment simultaneously. Bertoni Jovine, *Scuola italiana dal 1870*, p. 179.

[37]Dina Bertoni Jovine, "Il maestro alle soglie della

borghesia," originally in *Il Politecnico*, 1946, n. 18, and now reproduced in Bertoni Jovine, *Storia della didattica dalla legge Casati ad oggi*, vol. II (Rome: Riuniti, 1976), 719-730.
   [38]Mack Smith, *Italy. A Modern History*, p. 258.
   [39]*Ibid.*
   [40]Pius X had established a precedent for the Gentiloni pact in 1904, when Catholic voters in certain northern districts were permitted to vote for the Vatican hierarchy's preferred anti-socialist candidates. Webster, *The Cross and the Fasces*, pp. 15-16. See also Smith, *Italy. A Modern History*, p.283.
   [41]Bertoni Jovine, *Scuola italiana dal 1870*, pp. 197-198; Charles Delzell, "Adolfo Omodeo," in Hans A. Schmitt, ed., *Historians of Modern Europe* (Baton Rouge: Lousiana State University Press, 1971), p. 128; Ninetta Jucker, *Italy* (New York: Walker, 1970), pp. 62-63, 66.
   [42]Renzo De Felice, *Mussolini il fascista; Vol. I. La conquista del potere, 1921-1925* (Turin: Einaudi, 1966), p. 762, cited by Koon, "Believe, Obey, Fight," chapter 2, p. 24.
   [43]Minio-Paluello, *Education in Fascist Italy*, pp. 65,66.
   [44]*Ibid.*, See also Canestri and Ricuperati, *Scuola dalla legge Casati*, p. 136.
   [45]Giuseppe Ricuperati, *La scuola italiana e il fascismo* (Bologna: Consorzio Provinciale Pubblica Lettura, 1977), pp. 6,7.
   [46]Minio-Paluello, *Education in Fascist Italy*, p. 64; Education Subcommission, *Politica e legislazione scolastica*, pp. 61,62.
   [47]Bertoni Jovine, *Scuola italiana dal 1870*, pp. 273-274.
   [48]Zambaldi, *Storia della scuola elementare in Italia*, pp. 512-515.
   [49]On the religious preparation of young teachers within the *istituti magistrali*, see Tina Tomasi, *Idealismo e fascismo nella scuola italiana* (Florence: La Nuova Italia, 1969), p. 49. The most recent general treatment of this subject is Luigi Ambrosoli, *Libertà e religione nella riforma Gentile* (Florence: Vallecchi, 1980).
   [50]Vittorio Masselli, *I programmi della scuola primaria* (Naples: Edizioni Morano, 1955), pp. 20-21. The full text of the Gentile elementary curriculum is reproduced in Zambaldi, *Storia della scuola elementare*, pp. 679-710.
   [51]This line of argument was already apparent in Gentile's speeches and publications of 1907 and 1908, and was developed most fully in his 1925 study *Che cos'è il fascismo?* Borghi, *Educazione e autorita*, pp. 175,186,190.
   [52]Gentile broke tradition by excluding from the 1923 primary curriculum all methodological instructions in order to protect "perfect spiritual freedom."
   [53]Lamberto Borghi, "Scuola e Chiesa in Italia," in *Stato e Chiesa*, ed. by Vittorio Gorresio (Bari: Laterza, 1957), p. 155.
   [54]Minio-Paluello, *Education in Fascist Italy*, p. 62.
   [55]Zambaldi, *Storia della scuola elementare*, p. 600.

[56]*Ibid.*, p. 570.

[57]Ricuperati, *Scuola italiana e il fascismo*, pp. 9, 16. Antonio Santoni-Rugiu coined the phrase *preside-duce* in his study *Il professore nella scuola italiana*, 2nd ed. (Florence: La Nuova Italia, 1968). For a discussion of the effect of the November, 1923 decree on the "hierarchical organization of all State administration," see Minio-Paluello, *Education in Fascist Italy*, p. 112.

[58]Ricuperati, *Scuola italiana e il fascismo*, p. 9.

[59]Bertoni Jovine, *Scuola italiana dal 1870*, p. 305. Zambaldi, *Storia della scuola elementare*, pp. 573-574.

[60]Alberto Aquarone, *L'organizzazione dello stato totalitario* (Turin: Einaudi, 1965), pp. 485-488.

[61]Excerpts from the legislation implementing De Vecchi's *bonifica fascista* (literally, "Fascist reclamation") are included in Canestri and Ricuperati, *Scuola in Italia dalla legge Casati*, pp. 170-175.

[62]Minio-Paluello, *Education in Fascist Italy*, p. 173.

[63]Howard R. Marraro, *The New Education in Italy* (New York: S.F. Vanni, 1936), p. 70.

[64]Koon, "Believe, Obey, Fight," chapter 1, p. 64; Minio-Paluello, *Education in Fascist Italy*, pp. 135,171. Ricuperati discusses the *libri di stato* and includes a lengthy appendix of direct citations in *Scuola italiana e il fascismo*, pp. 17-22, 47-106.

[65]Minio-Paluello, *Education in Fascist Italy*, p. 124; Borghi, *Educazione e autorita*, pp. 297-298; Jovine, *Scuola italiana dal 1870*, pp. 347-350. The legislation implementing *cultura militare* is reproduced in Maria Bellucci and Michele Ciliberto, *La scuola e la pedagogia del fascismo* (Turin: Loescher, 1978), pp. 323-336.

[66]Bertoni Jovine, *Scuola italiana dal 1870*, p. 339.

[67]Pius XI's encyclical *Divini illius magistri* reiterated and applied to pedagogy the spirit of Pius X's 1907 condemnation of Modernism. Borghi, *Educazione e autorità*, pp. 284-286. On De Vecchi's reforms within the *istituti magistrale*, see Ricuperati, *Scuola italiana e il fascismo*, p. 2.

[68]Volpicelli was indebted to John Dewey for much of his thinking regarding industrialization, technological change and their pedagogical implications. In attempting to extract specific insights from Dewey's writings while rejecting the American's general liberal biases, Volpicelli anticipated similar efforts by Catholic educators following the Second World War. Bertoni Jovine, *Scuola italiana dal 1870*, pp. 381-385.

[69]Giuseppe Bottai, *La Carta della Scuola*, pp. 21-22, as cited by Bellucci and Ciliberto, *Scuola a pedagogia del fascismo*, pp. 389-390.

[70]See especially Declaration VII, reproduced in Canestri and Ricuperati, *Scuola dalla legge Casati*, p. 182.

[71]Giorgio Gabrielli, *Principi, metodi e fini della scuola fascista secondo la Carta della Scuola* (Florence: La Nuova Italia, 1940), p. 136, as cited in Ulivieri, "I maestri," p. 195.

[72]The legislation of 1 July, 1940 authorizing the *scuola media unica* is reproduced in Bellucci and Ciliberto, *Scuola e pedagogia del fascismo*, pp. 414-423.

[73]Declaration XI, cited in Bellucci and Ciliberto, *Scuola e la pedagogia del fascismo*, p. 400.

[74]Bertoni Jovine, *Scuola italiana dal 1870*, pp. 374-379. On Bottai's general openness to the non-Fascist intellectual "opposition," see L. Mangioni, *L'interventismo della cultura. Intellettuali e riviste del Fascismo* (Bari: Laterza, 1974).

[75]Minio-Paluello, *Education in Fascist Italy*, pp. 217-218.

[76]Francesco Sisinni, *La scuola media dalla legge Casati ad oggi* (Rome: Armando, 1969), p.73.

[77]Bertoni Jovine, *Scuola italiana dal 1870*.

[78]G. Bottai, *La Carta della Scuola*, pp. 158-159, as cited in Bellucci and Ciliberto, *Scuola e pedagogia del fascismo*, pp. 364-365. See also Michel Ostenc, "L'ècole pendant le Fascisme," *Revue d'histoire moderne et contemporaine* XXX (July-September, 1983), 406-407.

[79]On the regime's rural policies, see Minio-Paluello, *Education in Fascist Italy*, pp. 189-191; Edward R. Tannenbaum, *The Fascist Experience. Italian Society and Culture 1922-1945* (New York: Basic Books, 1972), pp. 109-111, 173-174; Ricuperati, "Scuola e politica nel periodo fascista," in Quazza, ed. *Scuola e politica*, p. 102. On the anti-semitic campaign, see Borghi, *Educazione e autorità*, pp. 305-306; Minio-Paluello, *Education in Fascist Italy*, pp. 195-202.

[80]Tannenbaum, *The Fascist Experience*, pp. 160,164.

[81]An important memoir of this kind is Antonio Durante's *Memorie di un maestro* (Rome: Riuniti, 1974).

[82]Allied Commission. Education Subcommission. *Politica e legislazione scolastica*, pp. 206-209, and table, p. 301.

[83]Zambaldi, *Storia della scuola elementare in Italia*, p. 586 n.

[84]Marzio Barbagli, *Disoccupazione intellettuale e sistema scolastico in Italia* (Bologna: Il Mulino, 1974), p. 245.

[85]"Cronaca Retrospettiva," *I diritti della scuola*, XLV, 1-2 (September-October 1944), III-IV.

[86]Willis Pratt, Educational Officer to Regional Education Officer, Region III, June, 1944 Monthly Report, National Archives (hereafter NA), Records of the Allied Control Commission (Record Group 331), 10000/144/279.

[87]Carlo Levi. "Lo snobismo del conformismo," *Il Ponte*, 8, Nr. 10 (October, 1952), pp. 1476-1480, as cited in Tannenbaum, *The Fascist Experience*, p. 215.

[88]Zambaldi, *Storia della scuola elementare*, p. 591.

[89]Manlio Pomei, "Educazione virile," *Critica Fascista*, 15 April 1932, as cited in Koon, "Believe, Obey, Fight," chapter 1, p. 51.

[90]Maria Antonietta Macciocchi, *La donna "nera"; il "consenso" feminile e fascismo* (Milan, Feltrinelli, 1976), pp. 59-62. For a long-term overview of the comparative treatment of male and female schoolteachers, see Ulivieri, "I maestri," pp. 165-211.

[91]See Annibale Tona's candid admissions in his "Esame di Coscienza," *I diritti della scuola* XLV, 12 (Aug 1944), 109.

[92]Franz Neumann, *Behemoth* (London: Oxford University Press, 1946), p. 462; Jovine, *Scuola italiana dal 1870*, pp. 300-307.

[93]Ibid.; Canestri and Ricuperati, *Scuola in Italia dalla legge Casati*, p. 142; Minio-Paluello, *Education in Fascist Italy*. p. 115.

[94]Article 133, *Testo Unico*, 2 May 1928, n. 577, as cited in Zambaldi, *Storia della scuola elementare*, p. 580.

[95]Koon, "Believe, Obey, Fight," chapter 5, p. 41. Minio-Paluello, *Education in Fascist Italy*, pp. 161-162.

[96]Minio-Paluello, *Education in Fascist Italy*, p. 111; *I diritti della scuola*, XLV, 1-2 (Sept.-Oct. 1944), 27.

[97]"La restaurazione della scuola," anon, typescript, Archivio Centrale dello Stato (hereafter ACS), Segreteria Particolare del Duce, Carteggio Riservato/RSI, Busta 76, Fasc. 646, sottof. 13.

[98]Carlo Arturo Jemolo, *Chiesa e Stato in Italia negli ultimi cento anni*, (Turin: Einaudi, 1971), p. 485.

[99]Koon, "Believe, Obey, Fight," chapter 1, pp. 22,29. Ugoberto Alfassio Grimaldi, *Autobiografie di giovani del tempo fascista* (Brescia: Morcelliana, 1947), pp. 68-69.

[100]Koon, "Believe, Obey, Fight," chapter 1, pp. 22, 29; chapter 5, p. 41.

[101]Ibid.; Richard J. Woolf, "Catholicism, Fascism and Italian Education from the Riforma Gentile to the Carta della Scuola 1922-1939," *History of Education Quarterly*, 20, Nr. 2 (Spring, 1980), 18-23.

[102]Borghi, *Educazione e autorità*, pp. 290-294.

[103]Tannenbaum, *The Fascist Experience*, pp. 200, 202-203.

[104]*Ibid.*, p. 160.

[105]"Relazione sui rapporti fatti dai Provveditori agli Studi," June 6, 1944, ACS, Seg. Partic. del Duce, Cart. Riserv./RSI, Busta 76, Fasc. 646, sottof. 13.

[106]Franco Martino, "La scuola della sincerità," *I diritti della scuola*, XLV, 1-2 (Sept-Oct. 1944), 5-6. Zambaldi cites Padellaro's frank testimony on the "spiritual unease" of many schoolteachers during the 1930's, *Storia della scuola elementare*, pp. 590-591.

[107]Koon, "Believe, Obey, Fight," chapter 2, p. 25. The phrase "years of consensus" is used by Renzo de Felice in volume three, *Gli anni del consenso, 1929-1936* of his multi-volume biography of Mussolini.

[108]See Dina Bertoni Jovine, "La coscienza di classe nel maestro elementare," *Il Politecnico*, 1946, n. 2, 4, as reproduced in her *Storia della didattica*, vol. II, p. 725.

CHAPTER 3

THE SOUTH UNDER ALLIED MILITARY RULE

JULY, 1943 – FEBRUARY, 1944

> It is a generally accepted principle that we
> must banish the will to war from Italy and
> Germany, and this has been implanted by many
> years of perverted education. The immediate
> heart-sickness of the Italian people may have
> temporarily obscured the results of this
> teaching. But it is to be feared that with
> the rigors of war passing in to the background
> of memory the results of the ideological
> teachings of Fascism and Nazism will reassert
> themselves in some new and undesirable
> form....consequently we must set our hopes on
> re-education if we are to restore the peoples
> of Italy and Germany to political and social
> sanity.[1]

--George Robert Gayre,
AMG Educational Advisor,
September 10, 1943

Overview of the Allied Educational Mission

The first Allied invasion of Axis-held Europe commenced on
July 10, 1943, as North American and British armies breached
Sicily's southern and southeastern coastal defenses. Military
operations proceeded rapidly. Palermo fell to General Patton on
July 22, and by August 17, Axis forces lost Messina, their last
stronghold on the island. Three weeks later, the Anglo-Americans
crossed over to the mainland. They advanced steadily northward
through the fall, liberating Naples on the first of October and
reaching northern Campania and Molise before they were contained
for the winter months. In Sardinia, meanwhile, token opposition
was overcome by mid-September.

The Anglo-American attack precipitated a "palace *coup*" in
Rome. On July 25, a majority of the Fascist Grand Council, led by
Count Ciano and Giuseppe Bottai, prevailed upon the *Duce* to offer
his resignation to the king. Marshall Pietro Badoglio became
Italy's new prime minister, while Mussolini was promptly arrested.
On July 27, Badoglio surprised his collaborators on the Grand
Council by dissolving that body, along with the Fascist Party and
all of its subsidiary organizations, including the *Gioventù*

Italiana del Littorio. He replaced Bottai with Leonardo Severi as Minister of National Education. Severi voided most of the reforms of the 1930s, seeking to return Italian education to its status under Giovanni Gentile, whom he had served as a high military official.[2]

Meanwhile Badoglio's government had entered into secret armistice negotiations with the Allies. It took six weeks to reach an accord, allowing the Germans ample time to flood the peninsula with military reinforcements. Upon public announcement of the armistice on September 8, German troops seized Rome, ending the capital's forty-five days of freedom. King Victor Emmanuel III hastily fled southward to Brindisi, accompanied by Badoglio and a handful of ministers. In southern Apulia Badoglio reestablished a fragile government under Allied protection. Formal responsibility for schooling in this territory, known as "King's Italy," fell to Severi's Undersecretary of National Education, the elderly Giovanni Cuomo.

Allied plans drawn up on the eve of the invasion envisioned an integrated Anglo-American military administration of all occupied Italian territory. Such an Allied Military Government (AMG) was established in the wake of the advancing armies, with headquarters initially in Palermo and, after October, in Naples. After the signing of the armistice, however, the Allies modified their plans in order to allow a role for the new, "co-belligerent" Badoglio government. The Anglo-Americans agreed that "King's Italy" would not fall under AMG jurisdiction; instead, an Allied Control Commission (ACC), established in November, monitored the new regime's observance of the political and military terms of the armistice. The ACC also exercised a loose supervisory role over AMG in order to guarantee continuity of policy.[3]

As the campaign proceeded, AMG developed into a chain of administrative Regions. Eventually Italy would be divided into a baker's dozen of these zones, each one corresponding to one or more of the peninsula's pre-existing *compartimenti.* Every region was placed under an AMG Commissioner, with a staff of specialists (including a Regional Educational Officer) and Provincial Commissioners serving under him. By the winter of 1943, four AMG Regions had been established, stretching from Sicily to Campania and northern Apulia.[4] Southern Apulia and Sardinia remained apart, having been accorded to King's Italy at its inception.[5] Once physical and political reconstruction was firmly launched in the AMG Regions, the Allies planned to return them to Italian jurisdiction, thereby freeing AMG personnel to move north upon the liberation of additional territory. In February, 1944, Sicily, Calabria, Lucania and southern Campania were handed over to "King's Italy" under the Allied Control Commission, reducing AMG territory to a narrow band below the still impenetrable Gustav Line.

An Educational Advisor attached to the AMG central command formulated basic guidelines for educational reconstruction and coordinated the activity of the REOs in the field. George Robert Gayre, an anthropologist from Oxford, was the first of these advisors, serving from early September, 1943, through February, 1944. With the creation of the ACC in November, he became the Director of its Educational Subcommission, which now encompassed the existing AMG staff and a small liaison group in Brindisi. Until the beginning of January, when he was directly ordered to Naples, Gayre maintained his office in Palermo, a city whose people and traditions captivated him.[6]

From the outset, Gayre demonstrated a determined and at times colorful independence of mind. He had been chosen because of his general knowledge of European universities and his previous military experience in France in 1940. An Oxford physical anthropologist, Gayre had also achieved recognition in the interwar period as a spirited critic of Nazi racial theory. On the whole, he viewed Italian Fascism very much as he did National Scoialism, except that the latter had "gone a little deeper and been a little more efficiently organized."[7]

Gayre aspired to define not only the means but also the larger ends of the Allied educational enterprise. Prior to the invasion, neither British nor American military planners had developed a policy for educational reconstruction.[8] Gayre enjoyed the full confidence of his superior, Lord Rennell of Rodd, AMG's first Chief Civil Affairs Officer. Rodd found it easy to trust a man who shared not only his Tory and Anglican loyalties, but even his love of mead--albeit improvised with Sicilian ingredients.[9] But Rodd returned to England at the end of October. Thereafter Gayre enjoyed less freedom of maneuver within the ACC bureaucracy. As Director of the Education Subcommission, he was saddled with the responsibility of coordinating policy with Undersecretary Cuomo in King's Italy. Gayre complained that "merely administrative" chores now supplanted the "creative and recreative" aspects of his job.[10] At the end of February, he took a new position in London helping to plan England's re-education program for Germany.

The Education Director's three most important colleagues came from American ranks. Terence V. Smith, ex-Congressman from Illinois and philosophy professor at the University of Chicago, served as Gayre's deputy in Brindisi. Smith had been slated to head the Education Subcommission from its inception in early November, but had agreed to work under the more experienced Gayre until the latter's departure.[11] Carleton Washburne, the innovative former superintendent of schools in Winnetka, Illinois, shouldered major responsibility at headquarters for textbook revision and reform of the primary and lower secondary school curricula. Another progressive administrator, Robert Koopman of Ann Arbor, Michigan, assumed the sensitive post of REO in Sicily at the end of November. In different ways, all of these Americans espoused the pedagogy of John Dewey and the liberalism of FDR's New Deal.

By the end of November, the Education Subcommission numbered eight full-time officers--half of its eventual strength. Among the officers, only Gayre and Arthur Vessolo, REO for Calabria and Lucania, were Englishmen. The Subcommission also employed several enlisted men in clerical posts and Italian civilians as receptionists, translators and--most importantly--didactic and administrative advisors, both at headquarters and in the regional offices. Overall, it was among the smallest of the Allied subcommissions--though it faced an unusually complex task.[12]

Anglo-American educators had their hands full simply trying to undo the overtly destructive legacy of dictatorship compounded by war. Battle-damaged buildings required reconstruction. Textbooks and courses of study needed to be purified of Fascist and militaristic sentiments. Allied officials also had to initiate the long and necessarily painful process of vetting educational personnel, beginning with top administrators.

To consolidate "Defascistization," the Education Subcommission encouraged pedagogical and structural reforms aimed at rendering Italian schooling more efficient and "democratic." Ordinary teachers and school principals figured prominently on central commissions established to rehabilitate texts and curricula. Particularly in Sicily, the subcommission took steps to increase community initiative in the life of the school. Gayre was determined to restore an even-handed and untrammeled competition between state and private educational institutions. Washburne placed high hopes on introducing Italy's teachers to the insights of contemporary child psychology. Washburne and Koopman were also eager to begin adapting programs of study more closely to what they regarded as the requirements of an industrializing mass society.

British and American educators consistently denied any intention of imposing foreign models of education on prostrate Italy. Yet their assumptions and behavior bore the unmistakable stamp of their respective cultural traditions. Indeed, the persistent influence of distinct national educational experiences was to give rise to serious disagreements between members of the subcommission.

Differences in the two societies' perceptions of Italian education on the even of the Sicilian campaign foreshadowed such conflict. Though the Foreign Office took seriously the threat of rivalry with an expansionist Italy in the Mediterranean and in Africa, Britons displayed little interest in Italy or in Fascism.[13] Their country lacked America's history of Italian immigration, and harbored fewer anti-Fascist exiles than either France or the United States. In 1941, however, British scholarship did produce a first-rate study: D. A. Binchy's *Church and State in Fascist Italy*. For all its factual accuracy and attempt at objectivity, Binchy's study reinforced British dislike for Mussolini and sympathy for the Catholic Church. While the author did not ignore clerico-Fascism, fundamentally he portrayed the church as the defender and embodiment of Italy's "universalist and cosmopolitan genius" against the regime's nationalism and totalitarianism. Binchy criticized the anti-Fascist exiles for their anti-clericalism and "extremism."[14] These judgments may well have influenced G. R. Gayre while he was at Oxford.

Gayre certainly read the Political Warfare Executive's *Italian Basic Handbook*, published in May of 1943. That seminal British document reaffirmed Binchy's view that the predominantly ecclesiastical private schools made minimal concessions to the "Fascist atmosphere" around them. In general, the PWE handbook also emphasized how "indifference and skepticism" on the part of teachers and officials ultimately hindered "the full application of Fascist theories" even in state institutions. Indeed, this report asserted that

> there has been no Fascist revolution in the schools, but rather a long war of attrition between a school which had its own life and developed according to its own needs and a political movement without any definite views on education.[15]

Such remarks help explain the general British reluctance to take far-reaching educational reconstruction seriously in preparing for the Italian campaign--much to the dismay of the ambitious Gayre.[16]

Knowing little more than a repertory of Mussolini's more colorful slogans, Americans also lacked critical understanding of Fascism and Fascist education during the interwar years. One-sided studies such as Howard Marraro's *Nationalism in Italian Education* (1927) and *The New Education in Italy* (1936) contributed to the regime's popularity within and outside the Italo-American community. Only in the latter 1930s, as Italian foreign policy became increasingly bellicose, did many informed Americans begin to view Fascism as a serious political threat.[17]

Liberal educators now sharpened their definition of democratic schooling by contrasting it with inimical "totalitarian" systems of education in Italy, Germany and the Soviet Union. T. V. Smith authored one such study for use in high schools, contrasting Fascist statolatry and regimentation with America's toleration of individual difference and aptitude for compromise in political life.[18] In opposition to a statist *"Fuhrer-Prinzip,"* another author emphasized the lack of federal controls, the variety of curricula and textbooks and the multiplicity of autonomous educational associations and youth organizations prevailing in American and British society.[19] In addition Americans (unlike the British) generally supported a unified local public school system, inclusive of all social groups, and distrusted divisive private--especially parochial--institutions. This kind of concern for one or another structural remedy for partisan polarization or ideological hegemony was the hallmark of America's Progressive Reform tradition, and still dominated the thinking of most educational administrators. Pedagogues, on the other hand, concentrated on recasting the methods and content of instruction. The common goal of all progressive reformers was the development of minds that are

> free and resourceful, capable of applying logical reasoning to any situation and finding out the truth about it, and powerful always in resisting attempts of other minds to dominate them.[20]

This progressive ideology of "democratic education" inspired liberals within and outside of the Roosevelt administration to proselytize for the eventual cultural rehabilitation of each of the Axis nations. The fall of Mussolini in July of 1943 concentrated the attention of American educators and other intellectuals on Italy.[21]

How severely had decades of dictatorship crippled the moral and intellectual autonomy of individual Italians? Many Americans, including eventually the leading American members of the Educational Subcommission, were deeply skeptical. Certainly Gayre and his countrymen shared their concern. What separated the great majority of American progressive educators from men such as Gayre and Binchy was their fear that, particularly after the Lateran Accords, the Catholic Church had reinforced the oppression of individual conscience more than mitigating it.[22]

For its part, the Vatican opposed the liberal champions of cultural intervention from the outset. The Church accused the advocates of radical "democratization" of harboring anti-clerical and even "anti-Italian" prejudices. The American Catholic hierarchy also feared the reformist potential of American policy in Italy. Hoping to curb liberal influence, the Knights of Columbus passed a resolution in August of 1943 that American military government officials in liberated Italy be of the Catholic faith "in proportion to the Roman Catholic population of Italy."[23] More effective as allies of the Church were conservative officers within the traditionally Republican and isolationist State Department such as the prominent Irish-American diplomat Robert Murphy.[24]

Surprisingly, educational reconstructionists enlisted neither the approval nor the assistance of the most prominent Italian anti-Fascists who had found refuge in the United States. In comparison, anti-Nazi refugees at least contributed moderately to American proposals for educational reconstruction in their homeland. In the summer and fall of 1943, the New York journal *The New Leader* sponsored a series of symposia on the theme "What to do with Italy?," inviting the participation of a spectrum of anti-Fascist exiles, from the radical historian Gaetano Salvemini to the veteran Catholic leader Luigi Sturzo. In addition to sessions on such questions as the future of the Italian monarchy, one symposium confronted the possible re-education of Italian youth after the defeat of Fascism. Italian participants concurred that their countrymen would not have to be "re-educated" to the virtues of democracy. To some, the very question implied a deplorable American ignorance of Italy's earlier liberal heritage.[25]

Ideological preconceptions, nationalistic sensitivities and a paucity of up-to-date information on Italian social realities all obstructed a satisfactory evaluation of Fascism's educational legacy. The closest approximation to such a document was an Office of Strategic Services report of December, 1943. Prepared by Captain H. Stuart Hughes, the report included a detailed, balanced overview of Fascist educational legislation and practice, followed by a series of policy recommendations. In comparison to the PWE handbook of May, this report took more seriously the Italian regime's command over both schoolteachers and their pupils through its authority to dictate school curricula and textbooks.

In view of the delicacy of an issue touching on Italian cultural pride, Hughes felt that the United States should minimize its direct intervention. For its part, the post-Concordat Catholic Church had been too closely associated with the fallen dictatorship to lead the reconstruction of Italian schooling.[26] The Italian liberal intelligentsia, on the other hand, would have to play a central role in guiding the difficult "intellectual and emotional summersault involved in the transition from education for Fascism to education for democracy."[27] For all its sensitivity, however, the tardiness of the OSS report--a half a year after the initiation of the Allied educational effort--limited its impact in the field.

In any case, military government officers in the Italian theater had not been trained to engineer social changes in occupied territory. The curriculum at the American School of Military Government, established in Charlottesville, Virginia in May, 1942, like that at the English school for "civil affairs officers," or CAOs (as the British termed AMG personnel) at Wimbeldon, deliberately avoided ideology. Recruits learned that their primary duty was to safeguard the army's lines of communication by maintaining order among the civil population. It followed that "existing laws, customs and institutions" in occupied territory should be respected, as these had been created by local peoples and "were presumably best suited to them."[28] As warning against excessive political or social involvement, AMG trainees in Virginia were reminded of the purported excesses of post-Civil War Reconstruction. Only in early 1944 did intensive political and cultural orientation begin to earn equal billng with time-honored administrative techniques in AMG training programs, in belated recognition of what OSS Director William Donovan termed the unprecedented moral and ideological imperatives of the Second World War. By then, however, most personnel assigned to Italy, including educational specialists, were already on their way to Europe.[29]

Theoretically, the early contingents of AMG officers were to fortify their knowledge of pertinent languages and develop specialized policies following their arrival in the Mediterranean theater, at the combined Anglo-American centers located at Chrea and Tizi-Ouzou in Algeria.   Yet Washburne stayed in Tizi-Ouzou only for a one-week crash course in Italian before his departure for Sicily on October 8.   Smith spent two additional weeks at this center before he too was sent ahead.   Koopman joined the others at the end of November.   Meanwhile, Gayre had been recruited as AMG's first educational advisor only in July.   Delayed by red tape from reaching the Mediterranean Theater until the beginning of September, the quick-tempered Englishman flatly refused to tarry in North Africa before proceeding to Sicily.[30]

Thus the stage was set for a rocky fall and winter, as British, American and--increasingly--Italian actors competed to impose administrative and pedagogical order on a turbulent and often poorly understood social reality.

AMG Vetting of School Personnel

The purging of educational personnel presented AMG with its thorniest educational task.   No other school-related activity engaged as many Anglo-Americans, within and outside of the Educational Subcommision; none so stirred the hopes and anxieties of Italians.

The great political sensitivity of the issue prevented AMG planners from formulating clear advance guidelines on the general question of purifying the Italian civil service.   As one regional educational officer recalls, the questions raised by the purge of Italian Fascists were far from smple: What constituted a Fascist? How far down the line should one go in removing them?   And what precisely should "removal" be taken to mean?[31]   Compounding these substantive and procedural uncertainties was a jurisdictional one: who should be empowered to make such decisions?

The AMG educational advisor only managed to reach Palermo on September 9, two months after D-Day in Sicily.   In the interim, non-specialist civil affairs officers attached to Allied tactical forces initiated on their own a selective and individual vetting of notorious Fascist school administrators and teachers, with the understanding that their decisions would subsequently be reviewed by regualr AMG educational specialists.   After Gayre's arrival, there followed a period of confusion in which both Sicily's regional commissioner and the central AMG educational advisor claimed jurisdiction over insular educational policy, including the systematic screening of school personnel.   By the end of October, Gayre had finally acquired the experience and professional staff to establish his authority, and to standardize educational vetting procedures throughout AMG territory.   But the Education Subcommission remained subject to debilitating rivalries and political suspicions arising from within the new ACC bureaucracy and, increasingly, from Italians as well.   Overall, the absence of

clear, consistent Allied political and administrative direction
condemned southern Italian educators to a demoralizing, seemingly
endless state of uncertainty.

The reliability of the Italian civil service had been the
object of serious controversy between Allied political and military
leaders up until the very eve of the Sicilian campaign. In the
spring of 1943, Lord Rennell of Rodd had formulated an initial
blueprint for Allied Military Government in Sicily based upon
British military rule in the captured Italian colony of Tripoli.
Rennell proposed that the Anglo-Americans establish indirect rule
in Italy: under this arrangement, all policies—even when dictated
by the Allies—were to be announced and administered jointly by
Anglo-American CAOs and by Italian provincial and communal
officials.[32] Rennell, who had enjoyed close relations with members
of the regime before the war, recommended retaining incumbent civil
servants whenever possible.[33] He observed that sufficient numbers
of experienced Italian-speaking Allied administrators were
unavailable for a more punitive housecleaning. General Eisenhower,
overall commander of the Italian campaign, his deputy General
Harold Alexander, Prime Minister Churchill and Harold Macmillan,
Britain's top political adviser in the theater, agreed with
Rennell.

But President Roosevelt strongly disagreed. Stung by
widespread criticism of his earlier accomodation with Vichy
officials in French North Africa, he concurred with liberal members
of his kitchen cabinet that Italy required sterner treatment. As
a first step toward "democratization," he and his advisors called
for the removal of all Fascist-appointed officials and their
replacement by Allied personnel.[34]

Two weeks prior to the Sicily invasion, the American president
finally relented. On June 28, indirect rule became official AMG
policy. On this basis, General Eisenhower drew up his
"Proclamation to the Italian People," to be broadcast as the first
troops went ashore. Eisenhower compromised between liberal and
conservative approaches, proposing a forceful but narrow
intervention: the Anglo-American mission was to heal a sick
society, not create a new one. The Anglo-Americans promised to
"restore Italy as a free Nation," and stated that

> The Allied Forces have no intention of changing or undermining
> the traditional laws and customs of the Italian people. They
> will take all necessary measures, however, to eliminate the
> Fascist system in whatever Italian territory they occupy.
> Accordingly, the Fascist Party organization will be dissolved,
> and its appendages such as the Fascist militia and and the
> so-called Youth Organizations will be abolished. Fascist
> doctrines and propaganda in any form will be prohibited.[35]

While banning Fascist organizations and Fascist propaganda,

the "Proclamation to the Italian People" made no mention of the treatment which active party members might expect. On this subject Eisenhower was purposefully vague: like Churchill, he hoped that a conciliatory stance on vetting might yet tease Italy away from her German alliance.   In an immediate sense, the statement was couched in terms designed to elicit the most compliant behavior from the Sicilian population.[36]

The administrative guidelines issued to the first detachments of civil affairs officers offered little more detail.   The fundamental policy directive for the campaign, dated June 28, specified that "the entire Fascist Party leadership from the top down to the local secretaries should be removed from any post of authority." Such major officeholders as provincial prefects and mayors (the *podestà*) were subject to relief at the discretion of the local Allied military commander. Where did this leave other civil servants, including provincial and local school administrators, to say nothing of ordinary teachers?   AMG administrative directives from late spring and early summer mentioned none of these offices.   The June 28 directive simply encouraged civil affairs officers to concentrate on harmful party organizations, to be immediatly suppressed, and excluded those affiliated organizations (presumably including the *Dopolavoro* welfare and recreational groups) "which are of direct benefit to the people."[37] Educational institutions and their staffs evidently fell somewhere in between. Clearly they too performed a beneficial popular function; yet General Alexander's Directive No. 7 dictated that all universities and schools, along with all courts, be closed as soon as the Allies entered a new territory.[38]

Lord Rennell's Administrative Instruction No. 1 also indicated the need to proceed selectively, without offering any concrete instructions for such selections:

> The Fascist Party machine...cannot be broken up or Fascist influence eliminated in a day. Since also nearly all Italian administrative officials are, at any rate nominally, members of the party, it will not be possible to remove or intern all members   of   the   Party.   This   would   merely   cause   a breakdown...of   the   whole   of   the   Italian   administrative machine.[39]

In spirit, this directive might seem to shield such lower level civil servants as school personnel. But a more literal reading might produce the opposite interpretation: since Sicilian schools were already out for the summer, and traditionally reconvened only at the beginning of October, the expeditious vetting of educators could avoid subsequent administrative inconvenience.

Early civil affairs had little time to ponder the issue as they fanned out across the island. Simply guaranteeing adequate local sanitation and food supplies were only the most pressing of a bewildering array of problems confronting them. In the preliminary vetting of local civil servants, including school personnel, they relied upon the rapid investigations carried out by advance teams of political intelligence and field security officers. As a result, a number of provincial school officials, principals, didactic directors and, in a few cases, ordinary teachers lost their positions in July and August. The severity of this preliminary purge varied widely from area to area, as Allied officers employed neither a standardized procedure (they relied chiefly on the testimony of other local inhabitants) nor a consistent set of vetting criteria. In a number of cases they were taken in by enterprising former Fascists, and they wound up removing innocent persons from their posts. Even more frequently, they became embroiled in age-old inter-family rivalries connected only superficially with political ideology.[40]

In western Sicily, Charles Poletti, the liberal ex-lieutenant governor of New York and senior civil affairs officer attached to the American Seventh Army, initially had to administer the entire province of Palermo with but a single assistant. Throughout the summer he remained short-staffed, even after becoming the island's first regional commissioner. As a result, Poletti readily accepted the help of forthcoming "reputable non-Fascist civilians and educators," whom he organized as a provincial education committee. This body took stock of local conditions and advised Poletti on proposed revisions of textbooks and the removal of suspect teaching personnel. The resourceful New Yorker also relied heavily on the incumbent rector of the University of Palermo for assistance on educational matters.[41]

Outside of Palermo, early military government teams tended to find "publicly-minded" local citizens in short supply. Pre-invasion advocates of indirect Allied rule had assumed that the structures of Italian administration, staffed by competent civil servants, would survive the military phase of operations essentially intact. All too frequently, however, that local machinery had simply disappeared.[42] Some provincial and communal civil servants had fled or been evacuated to the mainland. Many of the middle or upper-class officials remained out at their country homes where bombardments were less likely and eggs, fruit and pasta plentiful. Others were reluctant to come forward for fear of being tainted as "collaborationists" should the Germans or the Fascists return.[43]

Among Sicilian educators, many *provveditori* and their staffs remained away from their posts until well into the fall. Their absence frustrated Gayre, who had arrived in mid-September committed to examine "the history of each teacher so as to exclude all ardent fascists."[44] Then and later, it was Allied policy to begin by purging officials in positions of greatest responsibility such as provincial superintendents and the rectors of state universities. Practically speaking, given his own limited resources and experience, Gayre could only proceed to a systematic screening of lower level administrators and instructors with reliable and cooperative *provveditori* in place. Unable to interview incumbent provincial superintendents and unprepared to replace them with other individuals of untested administrative ability, the educational advisor made little progress in purging the lower levels of Sicilian schooling until November. One positive step which Gayre did take in mid-September was to mandate establishing provincial education committees, similar to Poletti's in Palermo, to take stock of local educational resources.[45] The committees also represented reassuring counterweights to the authority of incumbent *provveditori* until the latters' reliability could be determined.

In September and October, the educational advisor focused his attention on purging Palermo's higher academies and its university. A dispute immediately arose between Gayre and Charles Poletti over the status of the rector of the University of Palermo, whom Poletti appointed as chairman of the textbook revision committee. Poletti stood by the incumbent, grateful for his assistance during the difficult summer months, while the educational advisor insisted on his dismissal. Not only was this individual a former member of the Fascist militia, but he had a penchant for making what Gayre considered "violently anti-British" speeches. Lord Rennell finally interceeded on behalf of his countryman, and the incumbent rector was removed from both committee chairmanship and rectorship.[46]

A clear definition of standards, formalization of vetting procedures and apportionment of responsibilities were now long overdue. In late September Aldo Raffa, the chief of the Allied Political Intelligence Section, took an important step when he devised a detailed, three-page personnel questionnaire (the *scheda personale*) to be used in screening all civil servants. These questionaires concentrated on individuals' dates of membership and positions of authority assumed in the *PNF, GIL, GUF,* or *Fasci Femminili*. Additional questions touched on membership in the various Fascist militia, paramilitary groups such as the *squadristi*, and "volunteer" service in the Spanish Civil War or the East or North African campaigns.[47] Allied educators did not hold mere party membership or a modest role in the GIL against teachers; rather, the objective was to isolate those individuals who had gone out of their way to engage in Fascist partisan activities, and had "profitted thereby." Such persons were summarily suspended--with the understanding, however, that all removals would eventually be annulled or confirmed by a democratic Italian government.[48]

Subcommission leaders professed to be satisfied with the results obtained from the *schede*. They maintained that the questionnaires were generally filled out "fairly honestly," for several reasons. The subcommission had access to school records in some areas, against which questionnaire responses might be checked--a fact which it advertised widely. Penalties for false

answers included the possibility of imprisonment. In many cases,
too, individuals attempting to disguise their pasts were informed
against by other teachers.[49] Arthur Vessolo, the REO in Calabria
and Basilicata, took a less sanguine view of the effectiveness of
Allied vetting, even after adoption of the *schede personali*:

> The problems were so involved, and so much of the evidence
> adduced by Italians was tainted, either by personal
> animosities on the one hand or by a sense of mass implication
> leading to an excessive tendency to find excuses for everybody
> on the other, that the probability of a genuinely satisfactory
> settlement seemed positively to recede as time went on.[50]

The arrival of a full complement of REOs for occupied southern
Italy in late October and early November prompted Gayre to devise
standard vetting procedures to be used throughout AMG territory.
These procedures he summarized in a general policy directive dated
November 4. The education advisor retained the authority to review
all university level appointments, while REOs supervised the
purging of secondary and elementary personnel on a region by region
basis. The regional educational specialists first confirmed or
suspended provincial *provveditori*, and then proceeded to evaluate
heads of secondary schools, elementary inspectors and didactic
directors. In his November 4 policy statement, Gayre still clung
to the hope that REOs would also be able to screen all classroom
teachers; in practice, regional educational specialists looked into
the credentials of individual teachers only when school
administrators or local AMG officers felt that their "non-Fascism
might be in doubt."[51] Physical education teachers were the most
likely to be removed, given the Fascist regime's notorious linkage
of physical exertion with aggression and militarism.[52] Newly
appointed or approved *provveditori* nominated replacements, subject
to confirmation by REOs, for persons dismissed by the
subcommission.

As 1943 drew to a close, it became clear that Gayre and his
colleagues were making a more determined effort at vetting than any
other branch of AMG. School personnel accounted for roughly half
of Sicily's 22,000 civil servants, but more than two-thirds of the
schede personali examined by the beginning of 1944.[53] Legal
specialists, labor officers and others may have been dissuaded by
the adsence of detailed, AMG-wide procedural instructions on use
of the *schede* until December 2. Whatever the explanation, Italian
teachers and administrators would increasingly complain as the more
lackadaisical or conservative approaches of other AMG offices
became widely known. Gayre himself resented the seeming
indifference of other AMG specialists; at the same time, he was
determined to continue his own rigorous approach. Any short-term
scruples over the fairness of AMG policy would not be allowed to

compromise the shielding of the next generation of Italians from the Fascist incubus.[54]
For all of Gayre's resolution, however, the vetting of southern educators proceeded slowly and haphazardly through the winter of 1943-1944. As of January 1, only 10% of Sicily's teachers and administrators had been screened.[55] By the end of that month, the figure was still under 5% in Naples province. In many provinces, *provveditori* procrastinated in distributing and retrieving *schede*. In the short run, the Anglo-Americans could do little about this. Ordinary civil affairs officers were much more thinly spread on the mainland than they had been in Sicily. For their part, REOs were too busy arranging the repair of schools, responding to complaints and requests of all sorts and conferring with AMG colleagues to many field surveys. Rough terrain, inadequate transportation and ongoing military operations all continued to pose practical obstacles on the mainland.[56]
The process of Allied-sponsored purging was also colored by the availability of acceptable substitutes. For teachers and school heads, this was not a significant concern, as there was an ample reserve of unemployed *istituto magistrale* graduates. Adding to this reserve were the many teachers and school administrators who had been discriminated against by Fascist legislation, notably non-party members and rural teachers prevented from transferring to urban areas. But the Anglo-Americans felt that the range of experienced alternative *provveditori* and elementary inspectors was quite limited, especially in the Mezzogiorno.[57]
Gayre's response was that, under the circumstances, "the most reliable elements" were "in the majority of cases officials who accepted fascism nominally in order to hold their appointments, but kept outside of active support of the regime." Some officials, he maintained,

> are far sounder, more respectable and more able characters than the political adventurers and scallywags whom we are likely to get otherwise. Where we can get the support of reliable anti-fascists of known probity we should of course use them, but they are bound to be few at all times.[58]

In principle, American REOs were much more favorably disposed toward what Washburne termed "antifascists with energy and inititative." Unfortunately, he concluded that in the south such men had "long since been disposed of by the regime." While admitting that "reasonably non-fascist civil service employees" generally had to be used instead, Washburne observed that

> they had for so long not dared to take any initiative, were so accustomed to obey orders servilely from above and to behave as petty dictators to those below, that they were not too satisfactory as leaders to open and direct educational

institutions under circumstances that would have made the
ablest and most experienced administrator quail.[59]

This difference of emphasis between the two educators, one a
liberal American and the other a British conservative, strikingly
mirrored the disagreements then heating up at the highest
policy-making levels over the relative merits of the first Badoglio
government and the Committees of National Liberation. This larger
issue will be discussed in chapter four.

The retention or reassignment of incumbent Sicilian and
southern *provveditori* and a considerable group of lesser
administrators, coupled with the generally slow course of
educational vetting, dismayed much of the wider Italian public.
Some regarded Allied performance in this area--to say nothing of
progress in vetting other categories of civil servants--as
criminally permissive.[60] Even the AMG's Chief Staff Officer, the
American C. M. Spofford, in reviewing the first six months of
Allied occupation in February, 1944, acknowledged that he and his
colleagues had squandered an important opportunity. He regretted
the small numbers and delayed arrival of Anglo-American educational
officers. Spofford recalled that

> In the early part of the occupation the civilian educational
> authorities were completely stunned and they expected drastic
> measures to be taken. These they would have accepted readily.
> But even mild measures carried out at a later period are much
> more difficult. By that time a spirit of resistance has
> grown up, a knowledge of the AMG machinery has been gained,
> and the possibilities of intrigue developed . . . .[61]

Probably the most important factor of all in conditioning the
depth of Allied educational vetting was the mounting pressure
through the fall and early winter to get children off the streets
and back into classrooms. According to Washburne's later
testimony, all administrators from the *provveditore* down to
individual school heads were vetted before schools in a particular
province reopened.[62] Yet the time frame allotted to different
geographical areas for completing this administrative purge varied
considerably. Although the vetting of teachers could be--and
was--continued after the first day of class, it became more
difficult in strictly human terms to remove school personnel after
that date. Complicating matters further was the widely known fact
that schools in "King's Italy" were beginning to reopen after very
little vetting at all.[63] These developments served only to deepen
Italian suspicions--within and outside of educational ranks--of the
equity of Allied policy.

Physical Reconstruction and Reopening of Schools

Upon occupying new territory, Allied military commanders immediately ordered the closure of all educational institutions, in compliance with General Eisenhower's July 10 ban on the promulgation of Fascist propaganda. Three to five weeks later, REOs arrived and shouldered the task of preparing schools for reopening. On the average, formal instruction resumed after an additional three months. Each regional commissioner was responsible for determining when schools could safely reopen in his own AMG region. Pragmatic and material considerations far outweighed ideological ones in such decisions.

Large numbers of schools had been demolished in the course of the fighting. The Sicilian campaign destroyed or severely damaged twenty-five percent of the island's schools; in Palermo, Catania and Messina destruction was even greater. Damage was also grave in Salerno and Naples. In areas adjoining the front lines and in strategic cities, schools were used as troop billets, hospitals and shelters for homeless civilians. Troops were particularly prone to vandalize school property, often burning desks, chairs, blackboards and even window and door frames in order to keep warm during the winter months.[64] Neither educational officers nor even the AMG leadership were authorized to remove such destructive occupants, however. Only local tactical army commanders could order school buildings cleared--a step they took strictly on the basis of military or administrative convenience. In Palermo and Salerno some schools were thus tied up for six to nine months; in Naples and in Apulia for as much as a year and a half.[65]

Yet the spectacle of hungry, ragged children living and working on the streets, in villages and towns as well as cities, struck AMG officials and visiting Anglo-American journalists as both immoral and unsafe. Lord Rennell's Chief Staff Officer, Lt. Colonel C. M. Spofford, recalled that in North Africa the prolonged closure of schools had become a serious source of "friction and discontent among the civil population," especially the "female half" which had to look after school-aged children at home or worry about their unsupervised activities on the streets. Wherever school buildings had not been razed by bombardments, or preempted for other uses, the AMG favored the earliest possible renewal of instruction consistent with public security.[66] Lord Rennell backed this resolution by providing for the purchase and transport of building materials, while Italian civilians volunteered their labor in repairing schools. For a long while, though, a great number of schools remained without heat, light or adequate sanitation, as these remained the responsibility of the impoverished and disorganized Italian communes.[67]

Despite such inconveniences, authorities established December

1 as the official opening date of the 1943-44 school year in
Sicily. On the peninsula, classes were to commence in January or
early February. But in many war-torn villages and towns, as well
as larger centers, classes commenced weeks or months behind
schedule. At the beginning of January, public schools had yet to
open in the eastern cities of Syracuse, Catania and Messina. In
Naples, a typhus epidemic delayed the resumption of classes in the
few unoccupied and undamaged structures available.[68] The absence
of classrooms was not necessarily an insuperable obstacle, however.
In the Campanian city of Avellino, scaled-back elementary lessons
totaling four to eight hours per week (as compared with the normal
schedule of 25 hours per week) began on December 1, held in
apartments and teachers' homes since not a single school building
was available. In several Sicilian communities, similar informal
classes had begun meeting in individual homes even earlier, using
pre-Fascist school books acquired from Malta or the Italian
community in Cairo. In order to encourage just this kind of
resourcefulness, CSO Spofford had decreed in late October that
well-organized single institutions might open early.[69] Meanwhile
pressures exerted by influential aristocratic and middle class
families, couples with the support of the educational advisor,
enabled private and parochial schools in Sicily and Campania to
open their doors several weeks ahead of most of their state
counterparts.[70]

But for the great majority of pupils, the Allies' rush
to reopen schools at the earliest possible date seriously
undermined the effectiveness of the instruction offered.
Throughout the winter, pupils' attentions centered more on the
warmth provided by the solitary classroom stove than on their
teachers' words. For their part, teachers had to inaugurate their
classes without knowing whether they would see them through until
the end of the school year. And in lieu of Allied-approved
textbooks, which would not become widely available until March,
elementary students had to make do with existing *libri di stato*,
in which offensive passages had been inked over or clipped out.
In many schools, even these tattered materials were unavailable at
first. That absence was serious indeed, in light of the
oft-remarked inability of many *maestri* to depart at all from
textual dictation as a method of teaching.[71]

Initiating Textbook and Curricular Reform

The absence of purified teaching materials, like the Allies'
faltering in vetting, originated in the lack of preinvasion
pedagogical planning and the continuing low priority of education
in the overall war effort. In September Gayre was incredulous that
liberal American educators had not earlier sought out New World
Italian exiles to help prepare non-Fascist textbooks.[72] Then, as

educational needs began to be acknowledged, the subcommission had to compete with other civilian and military agencies for access to scarce southern paper stocks and printing facilities. The first shipments of paper and notebooks from the United States would not arrive until the summer of 1944. Before then, the sheer material dislocations of war placed strict limits on any Anglo-American campaign for didactic reform.

Southern Italian educators were by no means reticent in making proposals both for textbook and curricular reform. On the morrow of Palermo's liberation, three diverse currents of opinion immediately attacked Fascism's pedagogical legacy. A formidable Catholic current headed by Palermo's Archbishop, Cardinal Lavitrano, concentrated initially on strengthening the position of parochial schools on the island. The Church's neglect of state institutions and their curricula would prove only temporary. On the other hand, a group of radical and socialist teachers, led by Gino Ferretti, Professor of Pedagogy at the University of Palermo, had met clandestinely since August of 1942, elaborating a wide-ranging philosophical assault on the spirit and subject-matter of traditional Italian schooling, both Fascist and pre-Fascist. Between the crusaders of left and right stood the incumbent provincial superintendent of Palermo, Dr. Albeggiani, who defended the educational heritage of Liberal Italy. Albeggiani claimed the close friendship and support of Benedetto Croce--as did a striking number of southern educators in 1943-44.

By the end of the summer, CSO Spofford and other AMG leaders in Palermo had convinced themselves that the "defascistization" of school books and programs would not be a difficult process. At Chrea, Henry Rowell, an American with extensive exposure to Italian affairs, had assured Spofford that both elementary and secondary level materials would need "little revision based on his familiarity with what schools were using several years ago." The British PWE's *Italian Basic Handbook* also downplayed the extent of Fascist penetration in Italian popular schooling.[73]

Robert Gayre upset that consensus upon his arrival on September 9. An impromptu visit to a Palermitan primary school convinced the Oxford don that the prevailing view on textbooks was "absolutely unfounded." After reviewing a complete set of the *libri di stato*, Gayre summarized his findings for Rennell as follows:

> Starting with the second class (for children of 7 years of age) we have such subjects as "The little sentry", "The little soldiers", an account of armoured weapons, and Italy's right to dominate the Mediterranean. All this is mixed up with "Tears of the Virgin" and "The sign of the Cross" in the best style of authoritarian propaganda. By the time we reach the third class (8 years) the indoctrination becomes even more intense, and more subtely interwoven with religious and moral

themes. We have "Exercises of Tomorrow", the "March on Rome", "Italy on the March", "The War of the People", "The Servants of Mussolini", "The Duce", "The Ballila" and much more.

Even arithmetic books were filled with pernicious story problems. For example, one stated that "A member of the *Ballila* is eight years old; in how many years can he become an *Avanguardia*?"[74]

Except for literary anthologies, modern histories and geography books, the Educational Advisor found secondary texts to be usable for the most part, at least for the coming school year. A short codex of proscribed works, along with lists of acceptable volumes and books to be expurgated, was soon compiled and sent out to the schools.[75]

The problem of the elementary *libri di stato* was less tractable. Gayre first ordered all elementary texts returned to Palermo. Short of staff, however, he realized that the AMG would have to settle for a "minimal disinfection" of these works, which excised and revised offending passages, with the promise of a more thorough revision by leading Italian educators at a later date. This compromise disappointed many *maestri*, who found their restriction to a single state series--unlike their secondary school counterparts--demeaning. In August, a group of Palermitan schoolteachers convened by Dr. Albeggiani had urged the complete abolition of the *libri di stato*, arguing that a "Fascist essence" informed the series throughout, and that in any case, it was a grave error to impose a uniform textbook regardless of the local environment.[76] On the other hand, senior AMG officials insisted that the schools had to reopen as soon as possible, and resources for printing newer texts were unavailable in Sicily.

Sustained progress in purifying textbooks and reforming the various official curricula commenced with the arrival of Carleton Washburne on October 8. After weeks of wrangling, Gayre had only then managed to establish the AMG educational office in Palermo's sumptuous Palazzo Costantini. In addition, he was deeply engaged in the rehabilitation of Palermo's university and its Royal Academy. Delighted with the arrival of his first staff officer, the overburdened education advisor readily granted the former school superintendent responsibility for textbook revision and curricular reform for both elementary and secondary schools.[77]

This division of labor in fact reflected fundamental philosophical and temperamental differences between the two men. Gayre regarded the "professional" or middle classes as the "foundation of any reasonable constitutional government." He preferred to concentrate his attention on advanced secondary and particularly university training of the Italian bourgeoisie. The fact that the universities of Palermo, Catania and Messina, with their deeply-rooted autonomous traditions, had resisted Fascist regimentation better than the island's popular schooling only confirmed the Englishman's vision of those institutions as the spearheads of democratic renewal. In particular, he looked forward to replacing Germanic with Anglo-Saxon scholarship as the chief model and inspiration for Italian humanistic and scientific endeavor.[78]

In contrast, the mundane world of the southern Italian schoolteacher had little to recommend it. Gayre especially disapproved of the steady stream of "place seekers" engulfing his office, seeking a teaching post or some other favor for themselves, their relatives or their town or village. He had to insist, "sometimes very rudely," that such patronage did not represent "a form of loyalty but corruption," and that "no one can receive an appointment except through the normal channels when merit alone will be the standard of judgment."[79]

The affable Washburne, with his "unsoldierly bearing," got along more readily with Italian teachers, if not always with higher-echelon military government officials. His Deweyian training and experience as superintendent of schools in Winnetka had convinced him that children from all class backgrounds should benefit equally form a truly democratic school system. In Italy, he was struck most of all by the inadequacies of popular education at the lower secondary and still more at the elementary levels.[80]

Washburne worked closely with Albeggiani, familiarizing himself with the provincial superintendent's summer initiatives. He recruited a local secondary school English teacher to complete the work of expurgating the *libri di stato* begun by Gayre and himself. The same English teacher then supervised a committee of Palermo elementary *maestri* which drafted substitute lessons. As December arrived, these revisions had been completed. But it took months to track down paper, ink, zinc, binding thread and glue; most of these were finally requisitioned in Naples. In March of 1944, some 200,000 purified *libri di stato* were finally printed in Naples and Palermo--hardly an adequate response to the needs of several million school-aged southern children.[81]

Like textbook reform, the revision of elementary and lower secondary curricula foundered through the fall and early winter, though the obstacles were chiefly ideological rather than logistical. Differences between pedagogical progressives on the one hand, and moderate liberals and Catholics on the other, forced Sicilian schools to open without approved programs of study. Approved elementary and middle school curricula were distributed during the month of December, and upper secondary curricula the following month. In Naples, only twelve thousand elementary and two thousand lower secondary *piani di studio* had been published by the end of January, 1944.[82]

During the previous August, a commission headed by the Palermo superintendent had produced a set of new, markedly idealistic elementary and secondary curricula for that province. The following month, Col. Gayre entrusted an enlarged version of that commission with the task of preparing new *programmi* for all of

Allied-occupied Italy. The commission was dominated by secondary school *professori*. The only member with first-hand primary school experience was the province's Chief Inspector of Ementary Schools.[83]

Following his arrival in October, Washburne empowered the inspector, and two elementary school teachers selected by him, to develop the new primary curriculum. Washburne expected this group to produce a document which was practical and would, at the same time, "move forward a little in the direction of a democratic and modern education." Instead, the subcommission's first proposals struck him as "rigid, over-academic and compulsory." At this point the American turned to "the one man in Palermo:" "familiar with modern psychology and pedagogy;" Gino Ferretti.[84]

Washburne had come to know and admire Ferretti's thought prior to the war through the meetings and publications of the New Education Fellowship, an international association devoted to the advancement of progressive education. In the 1920s and 1930s Ferretti had steadily modified an originally idealistic pedagogy under the influence of new international currents and a new appreciation for elements of Italy's positivist tradition.[85] Ferretti's scholarly eminence had enabled him, like Croce, to retain his university post throughout the *ventennio* despite his open anti-Fascism.[86] Washburne added him to the larger curriculum committee expecting that he would make an influential ally and interpreter both in intellectual circles and among ordinary schoolteachers.

As a socialist, however, Ferretti was the only representative of the political left on the larger curriculum reform committee. The predominant orientation in the committee appears to have been traditional Crocean liberalism, though it also included representatives of Cardinal Lavitrano, the Archbishop of Palermo. Notwithstanding these distinctions, certain changes were adopted quickly and smoothly, Commission members readily agreed that *cultura fascista* and *cultura militare* no longer belonged in secondary school programs of study. In the elementary schools, the pretense of "separate but equal" urban and rural curricula was eliminated, in favor of a unitary format. At the same time, physical education was relegated to a more modest position in the primary curriculum.[87]

But Ferretti's colleagues were scandalized when the Sicilian progressive proposed more far-reaching substantive and structural reforms. In primary and lower secondary schooling, Ferretti called for a new, investigative, problem-oriented schooling which would replace traditional dependence on uniform textbooks and rigid teachers' lesson plans. Even more controversial was his questioning of the propriety of religious instruction in state education, which challenged a Church perogative dating from 1929 in secondary schools and from the late 19th century at the primary level. Not surprisingly, Ferretti's elementary proposals in particular generated intense clerical opposition.[88]

At the end of October, Washburne attempted to resolve the conflict by inviting Ferretti to prepare a separate set of pedagogical recommendations, to be appended to the main text of the new elementary curriculum. The energetic Ferretti then produced a detailed discussion of the psychological assumptions, methods and instructional themes appropriate to each of the five primary grades. Washburne was delighted with the result, which he had published and distributed as part two ot the 1943-44 elementary curriculum. Ferretti's recommendations were presented to teachers as "tending to reorient instruction toward a more modern conception of culture closer to world-wide democratic tendencies." The AMG preface went on to invite "those teachers so inclined to experiment gradually with these new methods."[89] For the next month and a half, this compromise formulation was accepted by all parties on the commission.

Ferretti's most controversial proposals for lower secondary schooling concerned the continued utility of instruction in classical languages and the fate of Bottai's *scuola media unica*. Ferretti supported the retention of a unitary middle school as the best system for children of all classes. But he disparaged the Fascists' obsession with Latin and with *romanità* as the keystones of the midle school curriculum. A new, fully unitary middle school should now be constructed combining the experimental courses in "labor" from Bottai's School Charter with intensive preparation in the arts and sciences.[90]

But tenacious resistance on the part of the curriculum commission's liberal moderates as well as Catholics preserved for Latin and religion privileged places in secondary schooling. At the same time, traditionalist educators, within and outside of the commission, attempted to abolish completely Bottai's *scuola media unica*. In Sicily, as elsewhere, *professori* had found the School Charter's innovations unsettling. Many parents resented the *scuola media unica* as a curtailment of their right to shape their children's futures through the selection of a favorite form of lower secondary schooling.

Attentive as ever to local public sentiment, Charles Poletti, then Sicily's Regional Comissioner, announced on October 19 the abolition of the *scuola media unica* in Sicily and the reinstatement of the lower branches of the *ginnasio/liceo classico, liceo scientifico, istituto magistrale* and *istituto tecnico*.[91] Poletti must have regarded the decision as the logical extension of the Allied committment to "defascistization."

To others, however, his reform could be interpreted differently. Italian and Allied educational officials in recently liberated portions of the mainland had decided to retain the consolidated middle schools. A contradictory arrangement in Sicily would certainly complicate the eventual return of the island's schools to national Italian educational jurisdiction. Hence Poletti's decision might appear to encourage the island's rapidly growing separatist movement. Gayre strenuously objected to Poletti's decision as a political embarrasment, an administrative headache and a challenge to his own authority. Washburne opposed it on pedagogical grounds, concerned about the premature vocational tracking of youngsters which the Bottai reform had at least mitigated.[92]

Nonetheless the Italian curriculum commission chose to retain the full traditional gamut of lower and upper schools though it specified that the classical and scientific *licei* and the *istituto magistrale* curricula should share the same content over the first three years. On the mainland, however, ACC and Italian authorities agreed that students would follow this common program of studies, but within unitary *scuole medie*.[93] This denouement fully satisfied none of the Italian protagonists, while the whole experience placed a damper on subsequent Allied support for autonomous provincial or regional educational initiatives.

The furor over the *scuola media* also aroused the concern of Kenyan Joyce, the American general who succeeded Lord Rennell as ACC Chief Commissioner between November, 1943 and January, 1944. Joyce was particularly suspicious of any form of Allied social tinkering. During the second week in November he summoned Washburne to Brindisi to explain the furor over the *scuola media unica* and to review other aspects of the subcommission's work. Washburne's "eupeptic manners" and his reformist aspirations seem to have made a very disagreeable impresion on General Joyce. Enemy propaganda then flooding the south "frequently alleged Allied plans for indiscriminate interference" in Italian education. Fearful that Washburne and the Education Subcommission were indeed "bent on making Italian education over a certain American mold," Joyce "had eaten him up before he had a chance to say a word in his defense." It was not the last time the irrepressible Washburne would be accused of harboring such ambitions.[94]

Conclusion

G. R. Gayre had good reason to believe that the first eight months of Allied occupation--when AMG retained sole sovereignty over nearly all of the Mezzogiorno--might offer Anglo-Americans a unique opportunity to assist Italians in breaking with a deeply authoritarian educational past. In order to consolidate its hegemony, the Fascist regime had coopted, in one way or another, each of Italy's traditional loci of authority: the Church; the civil service (including the armed forces); and the privileged social classes. Now, the collapse of the regime and the humiliation of foreign occupation from both north and south had undermined, if only temporarily, the social control exerted by each of these traditional forces. Repressed personal resentments and political passions were let loose, converging in widespread popular support for a thorough purge of government as well as party officials. At long last schoolteachers who had languished under an increasingly arrogant and manipulative national educational bureaucracy were freed of its supervision. In Sicily, especially, educational specialists and local civil affairs officers enabled local populations to give voice to social and cultural aspirations through provincial education committees. In Sicily, too, capable educational statesmen were forthcoming with new pedagogical and administrative proposals. In contrast, Badoglio's undermanned government in Brindisi was unprepared to act, and still too weak to obstruct the initiative of others.

Yet the first Allied attempts to restore the social foundations of democracy while waging war proved to be profoundly contradictory. The military campaign which freed Italian schools from Fascism destroyed a great number, and requisitioned many more for non-educational purposes. The closing of primary schools silenced Fascism's most extensive agency of political indoctrination. But it also deprived southern Italians of the painstaking efforts of decades to extend a network of elementary schools throughout the countryside. The war also wrought havoc on transportation and communication systems, making it hard for many children to reach schools even after they had reopened, and delayed the production and shipment of new instructional materials for many months. In the Mezzogiorno, the results were especially tragic, as much of the progress since the turn of the century in lowering illiteracy was temporarily undone. At the same time, the material destruction of the war, followed by the uncontrolled influx of Allied military currency, especially via free-spending GIs, into the Italian marketplace, was economically catastrophic. The ensuing inflation struck hardest at lower level state employees, such as teachers.[103] The endemic southern specre of economic want now assumed menacing proportions: no wonder Allied educational officers so often found themselves distracted from their pedagogical mission by individual teachers seeking only a new *padrone*.

Such persons were hardly prepared to serve as catalysts of a new democracy. Furthermore, twenty years of Fascist sloganeering had left not a few school heads and teachers cynically deferential and conformist, incapable any longer of investing their faith in anything except their own advancement. Political surveillance and discrimination had left many others isolated, fearful of their superiors and of one another.[104] The Anglo-American purge of "committed Fascists" did not begin to address this deeper legacy of dictatorship.

From the beginning, Gayre and his associates had accepted the principle that "democratic education," by its very nature, could not be imposed. Yet in different ways, both Gayre and Washburne had been distressed to recognize on the Italian scene and in the policies of their own superiors so few of their own most cherished pedagogical principles. Already, it was becoming clear that in order to make even modest progress, education subcommission members might have to re-educate themselves as much as their Italian counterparts.

ENDNOTES

[1]Allied Military Government, Educational Division, "Review of Educational Activities," 4 Nov. 1943, U.S. National Archives (hereafter cited as NARA), RG 331, 10000/144/17.

[2]Remo Fornaca, *I problemi della scuola italiana dal 1943 alla Constintuente* (Rome: Armando, 1974, p. 63; Tommaso Filippi, *Un anno di scuola* (Rome: I diritti della scuola, 1945), p.6.

[3]Henry L. Coles and Albert K. Weinberg, *Civil Affairs: Soldiers Become Governors* (Department of the Army: Washington, D.C., 1964), pp. 217-222, 248-252. Charles R.S. Harris, *Allied Military Administration of Italy, 1943-1945* (London: Her Majesty's Stationery Office, 1957), pp. 106-109; an organization chart of AMG follows p. 32, and one for the ACC may be found following p. 126.

[4]Arthur Vessolo, "Italy: Education under Allied Military Government," *Yearbook of Education*, 1948, p. 579.

[5]Though granted to King's Italy by the terms of the armistice Sardinia was actually directly administered by Allied Force Headquarters out of North Africa until January, 1944. C.R. Harris, *Allied Military Administration*, p. 99-103, 122n.

[6]George Robert Gayre, *Italy in Transition: Extracts from the Private Journal of G.R. Gayre* (London: Faber and Faber, 1946), pp. 33, 112-113, 140.

[7]Typescript (Gayre?), n.d., "The Elimination of Fascism," p.1, NARA, RG 331, 10000/144/22; Gayre, *Italy in Transition*, pp. 18, 20.

[8]David W. Ellwood, *L'alleato nemico. La politica dell'occupazione anglo-americana in Italia, 1943-1946* (Milan: Feltrinelli, 1977), p. 261.

[9]Gayre, *Italy in Transition*, pp. 19, 47.

[10]Already in late October of 1943, Gayre could see this change in the nature of his work on the horizon. Directive, Gayre to CCAO of AMG, Sicily, NARA, RG 331, 10000/144/8.

[11]Gayre, *Italy in Transition*, p. 85.

[12]*Ibid.*, p. 124; Harris, *Allied Military Administration*, pp. 106-109; Gayre, *Italy in Transition*, p. 109; Ellwood, *L'alleato nemico*, p. 126.

[13]Charles Loch Mowat, *Britain Between the Wars. 1918-1940* (Boston: Beacon Press, 1955), pp. 473-475,480.

[14]Binchy, *Church and State in Fascist Italy*, pp. 434-436.

[15]British Political Warfare Executive (PWE), *Italian Basic Handbook* (May, 1943), pp. 4, 45.   NARA, Record Group 407, Box 2205.

[16]Gayre, *Italy in Transition*, p. 16.

[17]John Diggins, *Mussolini and Fascism: The View From America* (Princeton: Princeton University Press, 1972), pp. 276-283, 252-255.

[18]Terence Vernor Smith and Glenn Nagely, *Democracy vs Dictatorship: Teaching American Youth to Analyze and Understand Their Own and the Enemy's Way of Life* (Washington, D.C.: National Educational Association, 1942).

[19]*Education under Dictatorships and in Democracies.* Prepared by James F. Abell, Chief, Division of Comparative Education, U.S. Office of Education (Washington, D.C., 1942), p. 7.

[20]*Ibid.*, p. 25.   Two important studies of the evolution of American progressivism are David Tyack, *The One Best System* (Cambridge, Mass: Harvard, 1974) and George S. Counts, *School and Society in Chicago* (New York: Harcourt, Brace, 1928), p. 3-6.

[21]John P. Diggins, *Mussolini and Fascism*, pp. 365, 387-388.

[22]Americans participating in a United Nations conference on restructuring post-war education feared the prospects of Catholic hegemony in Italy.   J.P. Diggins, *Mussolini and Fascism*, p. 428.

[23]George Q. Flynn, *Roosevelt and Romanism, Catholics and American Diplomacy 1937-1945* (Westport, Conn.: Greenwood Press, 1976), pp. 115, 203-204; Diggins, *Mussolini and Fascism*, p. 394.

[24]A wide range of institutional and political actors within and outside of the executive and legislative branches of government influenced the creation of American policy towards Italy.   See David Ellwood, "Conflitti di potere e evoluzione dell'intervento americano in Italia," *Quaderni dell'Istituto Storico della Resistenza in Modena e Provincia*, Nr. 10 (1976), pp. 15-36.

[25]Tent, *Mission on the Rhine*, pp. 22-23; Diggins, *Mussolini and Fascism*, pp. 386-388, 429.

[26]U.S. Office of Strategic Services (OSS): Research and Analysis Branch.   *The Reform of Italian Education* (Washington, D.C., 1943), pp.3, 8-9, 15-17. NARA, RG 407, Box 2216.

[27]*Ibid.*, pp. 4, 21-22.   See also Diggins, *Mussolini and Fascism*, pp. 428-429.

[28]Merle Fainsod, "The Development of American Military Government Policy During World War II," in Carl J. Friedrich, ed., *American Experiences in Military Government in World War II* (New York, Rinehart, 1948), p. 30; George Benson and Maurice Neufeld, "American Military Government in Italy," in Friedrich, ed., pp. 120, 127; Carleton Washburne, "La riorganizazione dell'istruzione in Italia," *Scuola e Città* (1970), p. 273.

[29]John Brown Mason, "Lessons of Wartime Military Government in Training, *Annals of the American Academy of Political and Social Sciences*, Vol. 267 (1950), pp. 183-192.   A detailed record of the course of study at the School of Military Government during the

session attended by both Washburne and Smith is available at the University of Virginia Library Manuscripts Department, Frank Bane Collection, (#7280-a), Box 3. See in particular "School of Military Government, Fourth Course, Outline of Curriculum," May 15, 1943. In fact, this class completed only the first half of the curriculum before being flown to northern Africa to take up posts once the conquest of Sicily was completed. See T.V. Smith's rather upbeat account of his Charlottesville training, *A Non-Existent Man* (Austin: University of Texas Press, 1962), pp. 174-175, 179.

[30]Gayre, *Italy in Transition*, pp. 17-18; Washburne, "La riorganizzazione dell'istruzione," p. 273.

[31]Vessolo, "Italy: Education," p. 581.

[32]Harris, *Allied Military Administration*, pp. 2-4.

[33]James F. Miller, "*Epurazione Mancata*: The Failure of Defascistization in Italy," paper delivered at American Historical Association Convention, December 28, 1981, p. 4; Rennell offered a vigorous defense of his approach in his preface to Gayre, *Italy in Transition*, pp. 12-13.

[34]Flynn, *Roosevelt and Romanism*, pp. 203-204; Ellwood, *L'alleato nemico*, pp. 314-331; Diggins, *Mussolini and Fascism*, p.375.

[35]"Announcement to the Italian People," of Eisenhower, Commander in Chief, Allied Forces, 10 July 1943. Cited in Coles and Weinberg, *Civil Affairs*, p. 190.

[36]*Ibid.*, pp. 217-227; Harris, *Allied Military Government*, pp. 28, 37; Norman Kogan, *Italy and the Allies* (Cambridge, Mass.: Harvard University Press, 1956), pp. 20-21; Ellwood, *L'alleato nemico*, p. 52.

[37]CCS Directive "Organization and Operation of Military Government for HUSKY," 28 June 1943, reproduced in Coles and Weinberg, *Civil Affairs*, pp. 177-180.

[38]Harris, *Allied Military Administration*, p. 6.

[39]AMGOT GAI, p. 80, as cited in Coles and Weinberg, *Civil Affairs*, p. 186.

[40]Harris, *Allied Military Administration*, pp. 36-40, 49; Gayre, *Italy in Transition*, pp. 176, 198-200, 235.

[41]*Ibid.*, pp. 26-28, 36. Memo, Spofford to C.C.A.O., 6 September 1943, NARA, RG 331, 10000/144/8. Tina Tomasi, herself a young schoolteacher during the World War, notes that Poletti continued to play a primary role in initiating educational reconstruction throughout the campaign; see her *La scuola italiana dalla dittatura alla repubblica*, p. 14. John Diggins highlights Poletti's general commitment to "leave no stone unturned in his relentless effort to plant the seeds of grass-roots democracy," *Mussolini and Fascism*, pp. 424-425.

[42]On the reluctance of Italian local civil servants to reassume public responsibilities, see Ellwood, *L'alleato nemico*, p. 244; Robert M. Hill, *In the Wake of War. Memoirs of an Alabama Military*

Government Officer in World War II (University, Alabama: University
of Alabama Press, 1982), p. 12.
    [43]Typescript (Gayre?), n.d., "Problems of Education in Newly
Occupied Territory," p. 3, NARA, RG 331, 10000/144/8.
    [44]Gayre, *Italy in Transition*, p. 17; Memo, Gayre to Chief Staff
Officer, 18 Sept 1943, NARA, RG 331, 10000/144/8.
    [45]Review of Educational Activities, 4 Nov. 1943, NARA, RG 331,
10000/144/17, partially reproduced in Coles and Weinberg, *Civil
Affairs*, p. 400.
    [46]Gayre, *Italy in Transition*, pp. 46, 138.
    [47]Benson and Neufeld, "American Military Government in Italy."
pp. 122-123; "Review of Educational Activities." 4 Nov. 1943, NARA,
RG 331, 10000/144/17. A sample *scheda personale* is located in
NARA, RG 331, 10000/144/19.
    [48]Smith, *A Non-Existent Man*, p. 192; Vessolo, "Italy:
Education," p. 581.
    [49]Memo, Gayre to R.C.A.O. III (Attn. Dir. E & FA), 4 Nov. 1943,
NARA, RG 331, 1000/144/8; Washburne, "Education under Allied
Military Government in Italy," *Educational Record*, XXVI, 4
(October, 1945), p. 263.
    [50]Vessolo, "Italy: Education," p. 581.
    [51]Review of Educational Activities, 4 Nov 1943, NARA, RG 331,
1000/144/17, reproduced in part in Coles and Weinberg, *Civil
Affairs*, pp. 400-401; Washburne, "Education under Allied Military
Government," p. 264.
    [52]Memo, Willis Pratt to Provincial Commissioner, Avellino
Province, 6 May 1944, NARA, RG 331, 1000/144/216.
    [53]Rennell, preface to Gayre, *Italy in Transition*, p. 12.
    [54]Gayre, *Italy in Transition*, p. 235; The vetting record of a
range of AMG specialists is discussed in Benson and Neufeld,
"American Military Government in Italy," pp. 122-126. See also
Maurice Neufeld, "The Failure of AMG in Italy," *Public
Administration Review*, VI, 2 (Spring, 1946), pp. 137-188.
    [55]*Schede* of Sicilian educators comprised 1,100 out of 1,676
questionnaires processed by Major Raffa's staff by the beginning
of the year. Gayre, *Italy in Transition*, p. 235.
    [56]Memo, Asst. REO, Region III Sam Noe to Poletti, Regional
Commissioner, 24 Feb 1944, NARA, RG 331, 10000/144/216; Hg AMG
Rept. for October, 1943, NARA, RG 331, 10000/144/501, as cited in
Coles and Weinberg, *Civil Affairs*, p. 384.
    [57]Sicily Regional Headquarters, "Special Orders and
Authorizations for Opening and Functioning of Schools," 14 Dec.
1943, NARA, RG 331, 10000/144/8; Washburne, "Education under Allied
Military Government," p. 262.
    [58]Gayre, *Italy in Transition*, p. 222.
    [59]Washburne, "Education under Allied Military Government," pp.
262-263.

⁶⁰Muriel Grindrod, *The New Italy* (London: Royal Institute of International Affairs, 1947), p. 51; Diggins, *Mussolini and Fascism*, pp. 424-425.

⁶¹Educational Division and Subcommission, AMG/ACC, Rept., September to February 1944, Spofford Report, ex. Y-14, reproduced in Coles and Weinberg, *Civil Affairs*, p. 402.

⁶²Memo, "Defascism of Educational Personnel," Washburne to Vice President, Civil Affairs Section, Hq. Allied Commission, 5 Dec. 1944, NARA, RG 331, 10000/144/Box 4.

⁶³Memo, Vessolo to Major General Solodovnik, 17 April 1944, NARA, RG 331, 10000/144/124.

⁶⁴Harris, *Allied Military Administration*, p. 16; "Resconto delle attività svolte dal governo alleato e dalla commissione alleata di controllo" (Rome: Città universitaria, 1945), p. 22, as cited in Tomasi, *Dalla dittatura alla repubblica* p. 15; Washburne, "Education under Allied Military Government," p. 269.

⁶⁵Memo, Smith to Vice-President, Administrative Section, ACC, 21 Feburary 1944, NARA, Rg 331, 10000/105/709; reproduced in Coles and Weinberg, *Civil Affairs*, p. 402; Memo, Washburne to Vice-President, Civil Affairs Section, 15 Dec 1944, NARA, RG 331, 10000/144/Box 4; Monthly Report, Naples Zone Education Office, December 1944, NARA, RG 331, 10000/144/219.

⁶⁶Memo, Spofford to C.C.A.O., 6 September 1943, NARA, RG 331, 10000/144/8; on the role of journalists in the early stages of the campaign, see Diggins, *Mussolini and Fascism*, pp. 362-365, 386n.

⁶⁷Gayre, *Italy in Transition*, pp. 67-71; Educational Survey, Avellino Province, 23 March 1944, NARA, RG 331, 10000/144/216.

⁶⁸Report on Educational Activities, 4 November 1943, NARA, RG 331, 10000/144/8; Monthly Report, Educational Advisor, Education Subcommission, Feburary 1944, NARA, RG 331, 10000/144/709, reproduced in Coles and Weinberg, *Civil Affairs*, p. 403; Monthly Education Report, Region III, January 1944, NARA, RG 331, 10000/144/216.

⁶⁹Educational Survey, Avellino Province, 23 March 1944, NARA, RG 331, 10000/144/216; Letter, Spofford to Regional CAOs, 26 October 1943, NARA, RG 331, 10000/100/999, reproduced in Coles and Weinberg, *Civil Affairs*, p. 400.

⁷⁰The opening of Sicilian parochial schools is discussed at greater length in Chapter 4. For Campania, see Monthly Education Report, Region III, December 1943, NARA, RG 331, 10000/144/216.

⁷¹Washburne, "Education under Allied Military Government," pp. 265-266. In his review of Educational Activities of 4 November, Gayre remarked the "The Italian teacher virtually cannot teach without a textbook, so reliant has he become on this method," NARA, RG 331, 10000/144/17. George Geyer, the REO in Region III, corroborated this fact for Naples' schools: See also Tent, *Mission on the Rhine*, pp. 27-28.

⁷²Gayre, *Italy in Transition*, p. 20.

[73]Rowell had briefly been designated AMG Education Advisor early in the summer, but was soon transferred to another post: Memo, Spofford to C.C.A.O., 18 Aug 1943, NARA, RG 331, 10000/144/8: *Italian Basic Handbook*, p. 45, NARA, RG 407, Box 2205.

[74]Memo, Gayre to Chief Staff Officer, 18 Sept 1843, NARA, RG 331, 10000/144/8.

[75]A. Vessolo, "Italy: Education," pp. 584-585; Washburne, "Education under Allied Military Government in Italy," pp. 265-267.

[76]"Relazione della sottocommissione per i libri di testo R. Provveditorato di Palermo," N.D., NARA, RG 331, 10000/144/490.

[77]Gayre, *Italy in Transition*, p. 60; Washburne, "La riorganizzazione dell'istruzione in Italia," p. 273.

[78]Typescripts (Gayre?), "Difficulties Planning Education in Italy," n.d., p. 4 and "Problems of Education in Newly Occupied Territory," n.d., p. 4 NARA, RG 331, 10000/144/22; Gayre, *Italy in Transition*, pp. 40, 45, 114.

[79]Typescript (Gayre?), "Difficulties Planning Education in Italy," n.d., p.1, NARA, RG 331, 10000/144/22.

[80]The description of Washburne's appearance is Gayre's: see *Italy in Transition*, p. 60; Carleton Washburne, *A Living Philosophy of Education* (New York: John Day, 1940), pp. xvii-xviii; Washburne, "La riorganizzazione dell'istruzione in Italia," p. 273.

[81]A. Vessolo, "Italy: Education," pp. 584-585; Washburne, "La riorganizzazione dell'istruzione in Italia." pp. 273-275.

[82]"Monthly Report on Education," Education Division, Dec 1943, NARA, RG 331, 10000/144/12; Monthly Report, REO, Region III, Jan 1944, NARA, RG 331, 10000/144/216.

[83]Copies of these *programmi* are located in NARA, RG 331, 1000/144/490; Memo, "Religion in the Schools," Washburne to Dir, Ed Sub, 29 Feb. 1944, NA, RG 331, 1000/144/157.

[84]*Ibid.*, p. 2. Like many contemporary educators in the United States, Ferretti and his colleagues in the *Associazione Libera Scuola* refused to regard elementary education as culturally inferior to secondary or higher schooling in any sense. See the untitled 4-page typescript accompanying the "Manifesto della Libera Scuola," NARA, RG 331, 10000/144/8; on American attitudes, see also Tent, *Mission on the Rhine*, p. 117.

[85]V. D'Alessandro, *Gino Ferretti e il rinnovamento della pedagogia* (Florence: La Nuova Italia, 1959), p. 307.

[86]Memo, "Religion in the Schools," Washburne to Dir, Ed Sub, 29 Feb 1944, NARA, RG 331, 10000/144/157.

[87]"Programmi di Studio ed indicazioni didattiche per le scuole elementari per l'anno scolastico 1943-44. Parte prima, programma base." A copy of this official AMG elementary curriculum is located in NARA, RG 331, 10000/144/489.

[88]"Abbozzo schematico di nuovi programmi generali di Riforma Scolastica," Aug 1943 and " Manifesto della Libera Scuola," n.d., NARA, RG 331, 10000/144/8; Gayre, *Italy in Transition*, pp. 136-138.

[89]D'Alessandro, *Gino Ferretti*, pp. xi-xix; Fornaca, *I problemi della scuola italiana dal 1943 alla Constituente*, pp. 66-68. A copy of Ferretti's proposal, as published by the Educational Division, is located in NARA, RG 331, 10000/144/489.

[90]Gino Ferretti, "Per la riorganizzazione della scuola secondaria media unificata nel primo grado," NARA, RG 331, 10000/144/490.

[91]Fornaca, *I problemi della scuola italiana dal 1943 alla constituente*, p. 61.

[92]Gayre, *Italy in Transition*, pp. 81-82, 87.

[93]"Piano di studio per le scuole secondaria-media unificata nel primo grado," NARA, RG 331, 10000/144/490; see also AMG Sicily Regional HQ, "Special Orders and Authorizations for Opening and Functioning of Schools," 14 Dec 1943, p. 2, NARA, RG 331, 10000/144/8.

[94]Washburne, "Education under Allied Military Government," p. 268. On Joyce's rigidly "orthodox" administration, see: Gayre, *Italy in Transition*, pp. 82-84, 86; Harris, *Allied Military Administration*, pp. 113, 386; Ellwood, *L'alleato nemico*, pp. 229, 251. T. V. Smith, "Swan Song from the Ex-Director of the Education Subcommission, Allied Control Commission," p. 3; OSS, "The Reform of Italian Education," Dec 1943, p. 21, NARA, RG 407, Box 2216.

[95]Vessolo, "Italy: Education," pp. 581-582.

[96]The teachers of the *Associazione Libera Scuola* in Palermo described the majority of their fellow *insegnanti* in just such terms: see the 4-page untitled statement accompanying the "Manifesto della Libera Scuola," n.d., NARA RG 331, 10000/144/8.

CHAPTER 4

RETURN OF THE REPRESSED:

POLITICS AND EDUCATION, FEBRUARY - DECEMBER, 1944

> We do not hold ourselves responsible for the
> poverty, illiteracy, dense population, the
> undervision and over-pride of these tired
> peoples of a dazed land. Nor without sympathy
> but with a touch of mature realism, we cannot
> but observe that for others too easily to save
> the foolish from the consequences of their own
> folly (even if they could), is one sure way to
> fill the world with fools.[1]

--T. V. Smith
ACC Education Director
July, 1944

Introduction

In late February of 1944, T. V. Smith succeeded Gayre as head
of the ACC Education Subcommission. During Smith's half-year
tenure in that post, the territory of liberated Italy nearly
doubled. Rome fell on June 5th. By September of 1944, the
Anglo-Americans had pressed northward along the Adriatic beyond
Ancona, and had liberated both Florence and Pisa further west.
Strong German defenses along the Gothic line would prevent the
Allies from breaking into the Po Valley untill the spring of 1945.
Still, the rapid advances of the late spring and summer had placed
northern Abruzzi and Lazio, Umbria and most of Tuscany and the
Marches under direct AMG rule.

While Allied responsibilities expanded in the north, they were
shrinking in the southern half of the peninsula. From Rome south,
the entire peninsula (save the AMG enclave surrounding Naples) was
restored to Italian jurisdiction after mid-summer. Then in late
September, Roosevelt and Churchill announced from Hyde Park the
gradual phasing out of ACC liason personnel from the Mezzogiorno.
Reflecting that development, the word "Control" would henceforth
be omitted from the title of the Allied Commission. After reaching
a maximum strength of 18 officers in May and June, the Education
Subcommission staff contracted by one-forth by the fall of 1944.
Smith's own return to the United States to help train civil affairs

officers for Germany and Japan coincided with the Hyde Park Declaration. After the brief interim directorship of Henry Rowell, Carleton Washburne assumed the subcommission's helm in early October, 1944.

In the course of 1944, the Education Subcommission leadership collaborated with three increasingly powerful Italian educational ministers: Giovanni Cuomo, Adolfo Omodeo and Guido De Ruggiero. In February, Prime Minister Badoglio and his staff moved from Brindisi to Salerno, which became the seat of a new, expanded government--the so-called "Cabinet of Undersecretaries." Giovanni Cuomo was one of the former undersecretaries who now found himself promoted to ministerial rank, as Minister of National Education. Despite his new title, Cuomo's resources and his freedom of action remained limited. His actions were scrutinized not only by the Allies, but also by resurgent anti-Fascist politicians who resented their continuing exclusion from the Italian government.

In April, after months of agitation, the six anti-Fascist parties which composed southern Italy's Committees of National Liberation (CLNs) won the support of the Allies for a new, genuinely "political" government. Proceeding roughly from left to right, the cabinet included Communists, Socialists, a moderate leftist Action Party, the Labor Democrats, the Liberals and the Christian Democrats. On April 22, Adolfo Omodeo of the Action Party became the new educational minister. The following month, Omodeo restored the traditional designation of Ministry of Public Instruction to his office, as part of a stepped-up defascistization campaign. With the liberation of Rome, he looked forward to reoccupying the old ministerial palace in Trastevere.

But another governmental crisis intervened in mid-June. Upon assuming the powers of the highly unpopular King Victor Emmanuel III, Crown Prince Umberto was compelled to replace Badoglio with Ivanoe Bonomi, the Chairman of the Central Committee of National Liberation in Rome. In the ensuing negotiations, the controversial Omodeo lost his post to a fellow historian and Action Party leader, Guido De Ruggiero. On July 15, a full year after the initial Sicily landings, the neophyte Bonomi government moved north from Salerno to reclaim Italy's capital. De Ruggiero kept his post at *La Minerva*--as the Trastevere ministry was often called--until a new round of political infighting in turn brought down the first Bonomi government in December.

In reflecting on the character of his three Italian ministerial counterparts, T. V. Smith described them as enacting "a sort of Hegelian pedagogical dialectic:"

> Cuomo was old and tired, but tolerant and shrewd--and did well on nothing, the nothing that was to be done in the first inevitable floundering toward a cabinet under Badoglio. Omodeo was in truth his antithesis. He was younger and dynamic; he was imperious and precipitate; but he was

unyielding and characterful. (In friends we call it "character" in enemies "stubbornness.") De Ruggiero is for a fact the fine synthesis of the two. He is full of strategy but without guile; he is patient and conciliatory; but he is also resolute and full of decision and frictionless in operation.[2]

In his memoirs, Smith implies that Allied counsel predominated in the selection of each of these educational ministers. After "using" Cuomo as best he could, Smith recalls, "we set him aside" for Omodeo, "a better man, but not the best." Then, once Rome was taken, the Allies turned to De Ruggiero, "whom we had reserved for the hour, for a more fruitful hour than any before."[3]

In fact, Smith overstates the role that the Control Commission chose to play in the selection of individual cabinet members throughout the first half of 1944. The foreign offices of each Allied government, and the leadership of the ACC itself, did engage in protracted, heated negotiations over the retention of Prime Minister Badoglio, as well as the larger and related problem of the fate of Italian monarchy. But domestic influences increasingly predominated in the disposition of the cabinet posts. In February, the ACC chose not to block Badoglio's promotion of the lackluster Cuomo in the interests of strengthening the legitimacy of the newly-expanded Italian government. Aside from Smith's subsquent testimony, evidence is lacking of an Education Subcommission role in the cabinet negotiations of April and June. As Italian educational ministers grew more self-confident and self-reliant, their relationship with the Education Subcommission evolved unevenly but unmistakably from suspicion and procrastination toward fruitful cooperation. De Ruggiero recalled how his early impatience with Anglo-American "interference" gave way in time to appreciation for the balanced and "disinterested" advice he received from Smith and Washburne. In an article written after his departure from government, De Ruggiero described Smith as a man of "philosophical perspective and great diplomatic sensitivity."[4]

Both Allied and Italian government officials certainly had need of diplomatic tact in the Italy of 1944. Militant new schoolteachers' confederations, embracing for the first time a full range of educators from primary school to university, emerged alongside older lay and Catholic associations of *maestri*. Associated in some cases with the Italian Resistance movement, these groups did not hesitate to insist on ideological as well as socio-economic change. Counterbalancing such grass-roots organizations was a sizeable army of ministerial functionaries, who posed an increasingly formidable barrier to academic reform of any kind after July 15. All of the anti-Fascist parties, as well as interested teachers and administrators, watched closely as the Education Subcommission turned over to Italian authorities its preliminary findings on the vetting of school personnel.

Catholics, liberals, moderate leftists and Marxists all monitored
the gradual progress of pedagogical reconstruction.

The Church and the Allies

The Catholics were particularly well-organized and
influential. Within the Ministry of Public Instruction, Christian
Democrats would occupy the key administrative post of
Undersecretary of State from the first "political" cabinet of 1944
until July of 1946, when one of their number would finally become
Minister. On a different plane, as a sovereign state, the Vatican
brought pressure on the American and British governments to
preserve the clerical privileges negotiated in the 1929 Concordat.
The Sicilian clergy carefully courted the Allies from the
beginning of Anglo-American occupation. Cardinal Lavitrano, the
Archbishop of Palermo, refused to quit the city despite intense
bombardment so as to welcome the Seventh Army upon its arrival.
In early discussions with General Alexander and Lord Rennell, he
broached the question of opening "free church schools" on the
island. As Gayre subsquently observed, his British compatriots
were hardly likely to deny Catholic Italy a liberty enjoyed by
parochial schools in England.[5]

They appear not to have realized that, except for seminaries,
the Church had never been able to operate schools completely free
of Italian state supervision. Since 1870, all parochial schools
had been subject to some state inspection and evaluation. The
Gentile Reform of 1923, the creation of the *Ente nazionale per
l'istruzione media e superiore*(National Administration for Private
Intermediate and Higher Education) in 1938 and the School Charter
of 1939 increased the scope and efficency of state regulation. Had
the School Charter been completely implemented, the only surviving
parochial schools would have been the so-called *scuole parificati*,
in which the Church supplied the building and the teachers, and the
state the curriculum and inspectors.[6]

But Allied authorities accomodated Cardinal Lavitrano in early
September, granting recognition to fourteen small independent
Catholic primary schools, to be opened in the diocese of the Bishop
of Mazara del Vallo on the western end of the island.[7] Church
officials felt that this decision established their right to
organize similar primary or secondary institutions elsewhere.
Within the next month clergymen sought authorization for schools
in Agrigento, Catania and Syracuse.[8] Before long, this trend
elicited vehement protests from the provincial superintendents in
the island.

Gayre himself sympathized with these Church initiatives for
several reasons. He was impressed by the cleanliness and order of
the Catholic *collegi* as compared with the state schools that he
visited. As he confided in his private journal in October, he was

inclined to believe that the Church schools gave a "sounder and better education," which explained why "the better class people" preferred them. Furthermore, the reopening of parochial as compared with state institutions posed fewer practical obstacles for hard-pressed Allied officials. Unlike state employees, the nuns or priests teaching in ecclesiastical schools would not have to be reviewed on political grounds before being allowed back into the classroom. The Church was also prepared to repair its own school buildings without any financial assistance from the Allies.[9]

Among the first schools permitted to open on the island were, in fact, the parochial schools in Mazara del Vallo. Gayre granted the Bishop permission to begin classes on November 10, three weeks before the official opening date of Sicily's state schools. The Bishop pressed the Educational Advisor to attend the elaborate opening day ceremonies. Gayre declined, but sent a warm message, which was read on the occasion and subsquently broadcast over Radio Palermo. In that message, Gayre described the first opening of completely independent parochial schools as an important demonstration of the Allies' belief in the freedom of all to live according to the dictates of their own conscience.[10]

Gayre assured the Bishop that his schools would not be placed under the jurisdiction of the superintendent of studies of Trapani province. Instead, the Educational Advisor hoped that a joint committee representing the superintendent and church authorities could be formed to regulate the new schools' curricula and exams. In this way, parochial school certificates would come to have the same validity as those of other schools. But the superintendent soon protested what he viewed as an unprecedented infringement on his authority, and urged that the new "independent" schools be closed.[11]

By Christmas, Gayre concluded that his original proposal for a joint commission was "far too English," as it involved a "degree of compromise" impracticable in Sicily. In lieu of direct negotiations at the provincial level, Gayre then endorsed Cardinal Lavitrano's offer to establish a Church directorate for the entire region, composed of three clerics, which would consult with Allied authorities regularly and would pass down instructions to the bishops, just as the Allies' Educational Division oversaw the activities of the provincial superintendents. Gayre urged his countryman, Major Vessolo, to make a similar arrangement with "a Cardinal or leading Archbishop" in Region II (encompassing essentially the heel and toe of the Italian boot). Until his departure from Palermo in early January, 1944, Gayre in fact treated the Sicilian directorate "as on a national level," since he had "no other means of sounding Church opinion."[12]

Gayre realized that this was one of several actions which exposed him to charges of showing undue favoritism towards the Church. He took comfort in the thought that at least he was defending the rights of what he felt was the "weaker party."

Throughout his tenure, he was determined not to take any action which might offend the sizeable Roman Catholic population of the United States or the "great sympathy felt for the Church in England." When asked to refer the whole question of the "independent schools" to higher Allied authorities, Gayre also forwarded a comprehensive, forcefully written brief presented him by the Bishop of Mazara del Vallo in late December, which catalogued international, British and American laws and customs paralleling clerical aspirations in Italy.[13]

The American members of Gayre's staff took the state's side in the controversy, noting that it would simplify the Allies' administrative tasks if the new schools were abolished. Nor was Undersecretary Cuomo prepared to accept the status quo. In February Col. Smith, the educational liason officer in Brindisi, reached a compromise agreement with Cuomo which was confirmed under Cuomo's successor, Adolfo Omodeo: the free parochial schools sanctioned by Allied Military Government during the 1943-44 school year would remain open, but beginning the following year they and all other schools would be subject to ministerial regulation.[14]

By the end of 1943 another controversy involving the Catholic Church came to a head: the suitability of Gino Ferretti's "Recomendations for the Modernization of the Elementary School." Aware that Ferretti was considered "notoriously anticlerical,"[15] Washburne had instructed him in October to avoid the subject of religion in his document. But Ferretti could not resist explaining in a preliminary note to the "Recommendations" that moral and ethical instruction (*l'educazione morale*) would now assume the central place previously held by para-military GIL activities and instruction in religion in the Fascist elementary curriculum.[16]

Ferretti's explanation seemed unexceptionable enough to Washburne. Like the great majority of Americans, Washburne believed that the effectiveness of his nation's common ethical code, based on vague Judeo-Christian principles, depended on its separation from any particular sectarian affiliation. And as a Quaker, Washburne hesitated to regulate or codify spiritual truths, least of all within public schools.[17] Indeed the Americans in the Educational Division even considered strengthening Ferretti's foreward with the following instruction:

> Religion should not be the subject of instruction or of grades or examinations. It should be left solely to the churches and to persons connected with them, without any connection with the schools.[18]

Ferretti's document and the general approach of the American members of the Educational Division engendered violent clerical opposition, within and outside the elementary curriculum commission. Cardinal Lavitrano and his representatives were incensed at Ferretti's rhetorical juxtaposition of militarism and religion.   Ferretti's frank empiricism and his reference to scientific knowledge as "doing away with superstition" in the body of his proposal were seen as covert attacks on the Church.   The Sicilian churchman also took exception to the placement of the word *facoltativa* ("elective") following the title "religion" in the Allies' new curriculum for the secondary schools.[19]   Haunted by the discriminatory record of the Liberal monarchy, they feared that the term would be employed not as a reminder of the individual student's right of exemption, but as an excuse for entire schools to cease offering religious instruction.   Fundamentally, Catholic doctrine disputed the very possibility of religiously neutral education: not only the dogmas of the Church, but all subjects should be taught to Catholic children from a Catholic perspective.[20]

Gayre himself had not seen Ferretti's proposals before they were distributed to the provincial superintendents.   But by late December he found himself engulfed in "the most unholy storm" surrounding their continued application in primary schools.   After intensive conferences with Washburne and Koopman, and with the Cardinal's representative, Gayre imposed his own settlement.   The word *facoltativa* would remain in the lower secondary school curricula already printed, but would be omitted in subsequent editions prepared for more northerly regions.   On the other hand, Gayre scrapped Ferretti's elementary "recommendations" on the grounds that "Italy was not ready" for such "so-called progressive notions," and that "in any case, by the time she is, they will be out of date."[21]   Any undistributed pamphlets still in the hands of provincial superintendents were to be returned to the Education Division and destroyed.   However, Gayre agreed with Washburne that a demand on every teacher to give back the copy he might have would be unreasonable and "would give undue emphasis to the pamphlet."[22]

In his diary, Gayre recorded that Washburne "nearly cried" at the decision, while Ferretti, he predicted, would "dance with rage."   But the Englishman had already exposed himself to vociferous Catholic protests by appointing Ferretti as Dean of the University of Palermo's Faculty of Arts and Sciences.   In return Gayre was inclined to grant the Cardinal and the Sicilian Christian Democratic leaders a favorable resolution to the curriculum dispute.[23]

In the late winter, a new commission began to meet in Naples to re-draft the pamphlet on "Advice for Modernizing the Elementary School."   In this second draft Professor Guido della Valle of the University of Naples offered his "authoritative collaboration."   Cardinal Lavitrano's Secretary was entrusted with writing a section on religious education, which was given first place in the new document.   The Allies secured clerical approval of "every detail" of the remainder of the document.   A revised pamphlet differing only marginally from the 1923 elementary curriculum was then published in Naples in February, and distributed throughout the South the following month.[24]

In the meantime, another controversy had been building in Calabria and Basilicata. The British Regional Education Officer for those regions, Captain Arthur Vessolo, had been surprised to discover Fascist texts, complete with portraits of Mussolini, still in use in a church seminary in Potenza during a visit there in mid-December. Education officers had tended to leave such institutions alone, given Col. Gayre's assumption that they had defied the regime prior to the war. Now, however, Gayre agreed that Vessolo should send instructions on non-religious subjects to all the seminaries in his jurisdiction. In Reggio Calabria, a local civil affairs officer mistakenly sent these instructions on to the local Archbishop, Antonio Lanza, via the provincial superintendent of schools. As a result the Archbishop, widely suspected of clerico-fascist tendencies, refused to implement any of the suggested changes. Ironically, he justified his stance on the grounds that article 39 of the Concordat forbade any secular interference with church seminaries. In such cases, Allied education officers simply renewed their requests for voluntary compliance.[25]

By the end of 1943 Cardinal Lavitrano found the drift of Allied educational activity sufficiently alarming to alert his colleagues in Rome. The Vatican's first expressions of concern reached Washington even before Gayre's December 30 decision on the elementary curriculum.[26] A month later, Monsignor Walter Carroll of the Vatican Secretariat of State, accompanied by Bruce Mohler of the North American Bishop's Welfare Conference, confronted Gayre and Koopman in Palermo. The Vatican was disturbed by reports that copies of Ferretti's pamphlet remained in circulation, despite the agreements of late December. Bishop Carroll also protested the retention of Omodeo at the University of Naples and the appointment of "Communists," allegedly including Ferretti, at the University of Palermo. Carroll frankly regarded "the whole incidence [sic] of Gayre's administration as anti-clerical." For the future, Carroll wished to be assured that "there were no educational affairs in which the Church would not be consulted," and that no non-Catholic would be appointed to public offices as prominent as the rectorship at Naples.[27]

In response Koopman reiterated the Allies' commitment to "freedom of religion," and insisted on their right to name any qualified person--"even an atheist"--as rector of an important university. In a subsequent memorandum, Koopman described Bishop Carroll's attitude as "the most dangerous threat to our policies that I have encountered in military government."[28] The pugnacious American's remark about employing atheists circulated widely and contributed to Allied educators' reputation for insensitivity to Catholicism in other branches of AMG and ACC.[29]

Col. Gayre adopted a much more accomodating tone in the January 31 meeting with Carroll and Mohler. He pointed out that his university appointments had in fact "balanced all elements, ranging from one communist and one socialist to several liberals, many Christian Democrats and several Sicilian separatists." By the end of their consultations, Gayre had also convinced Carroll that Ferretti's pamphlet had been handled "fairly."[30]

Carroll left Sicily with new respect and sympathy for the English Educational Advisor, and new suspicions of the principal American members of his staff. On the whole, however, the Church was now disposed to view the immediate course of Allied educational efforts with greater optimism. Soon the Vatican Secretary of State himself, Cardinal Maglione, visited the Palermo educational office. He was "much impressed with the progress made," while voicing continuing concern over the "suitability of the religious and political beliefs" of persons being given posts in the schools.[31]

One can imagine the Archbishops of Naples' and Palermo's consternation when, early in February, they learned that Gayre was slated to leave the Italian theater shortly in order to assist with educational planning for the occupation of Germany. They immediately dispatched Bishop Carroll to Washington to obtain formal guarantees of a sympathetic Allied educational policy in Italy. On February 14, Archbishop A. G. Cicognani, the U. S. Apostolic Delegate, presented the State Department with a sharply worded summary of the "actual situation" in southern Italy, written by Carroll. Carroll was convinced that the English Educational Advisor had succeeded only with great difficulty in preventing his chief American subordinates from carrying out a perilous and oppressive "de-Christianization" of popular schooling. In Italy, Carroll asserted, Washburne, Koopman and Smith "are regarded as extreme doctrinaires and superficial educational experimentalists." In order to prevent any further erosion of the goodwill of the Italian people, not only should Gayre be retained, but the misguided American personnel should be withdrawn at once.[32]

The Church's intervention prompted a thorough Allied review of educational policy, if not of personnel. The Combined Civil Affairs Committee obtained guarantees from the ACC leadership that religious instruction in Allied-controlled territory respected the terms of the 1929 Concordat, and that all new textbooks conformed to Catholic priciples. The Vatican also sought reassurance that "present southern Italian teachers" were not hostile to the Catholic Church or to religion in general. Although the ACC could scarcely launch a formal investigation, its executive commissioner pointed out that since the proportion of teachers replaced by the Allies had been small, "the general body of teachers may be assumed to hold the same religious beliefs as they did before Allied occupation."[33]

The State Department's concern extended beyond the issue of religious instruction, and addressed the general scope of Allied educational initiatives. The ACC was now queried to what extent "the elimination of Fascist teachings and characteristics" in fact required curricular revision. Bishop Carroll's description of "superficial educational experimentalists" may well have prompted this broader line of inquiry. Secretary of State Cordell Hull himself felt that "it would be unwise for the U. S. government to undertake to apply, much less impose a foreign educational program in liberated countries."[34] In December of 1943 the OSS had urged such restraint in the case of Italy. Certainly the State Department's alarm now reflected the increased influence of two of that organization's more conservative officers. James Dunn, newly appointed head of the Office of Europian Affairs, and Robert Murphy, the American political representative with the Supreme Allied Command and the ACC, were both skeptical of the exportability of American-styled democracy, and fearful of weakening the forces of social order on the continent, including the Catholic Church. A staunch Catholic, Murphy was a long-time personal acquaintance of Pope Pius XII.[35]

By mid-March, a comprehensive, two-part report on Educational Division and Subcommission activities since September, 1943 was dispatched to Washington. In his March 23 summary of that report, ACC Chief Commissioner Noel Mason MacFarlane took pains to stress that the Educational Subcommission had endeavored to pursue a policy of "scrupulous fairness" to the Catholic Church. This policy had been "approved by eminent Church authorities on the ground, including Cardinal Lavitrano of Palermo, Bishop Ballo of Mazara del Valle, Father Gliozzo of the Society of Jesus and Cardinal Ascalesi of Naples."[36]

Glossing over the personal nature of Gayre's initial rapport with those dignitaries, MacFarlane asserted that Allied policy "was accepted and has been and is being furthered by British and American officers with identity of viewpoint as touching the educational rights of the Church in a predominantly Catholic country and with common determination to observe these rights as defined by the prevailing treaty and concordat." The chief commissioner went on to express his "regret and resentment" at the "insinuations that the policy of one of my subcommissions is affected by the nationality of its chief or members." Smith's replacement of Gayre in February had in no sense changed the "direction of effort accepted by both and furthered by them in entire accord."[37]

The whole rancorous history of the controversy would leave Smith little opportunity to alter his predecessor's relationship with the Church. Despite MacFarlane's denials, differing national perspectives had contributed to a substantive dispute within the Educational Subcommission. In early 1944, a more generalized form of Anglo-American rivalry had emerged within the ACC. Once MacFarlane succeeded General Joyce, Americans within and outside of the ACC began to protest the predominance of British leadership at the apex of ACC and among its subcommissions.[38] Smith's appointment was one of several MacFarlane made to right the balance, a fact which rendered the continuity of policy within the subcommission all the more necessary.

As a Jamesian pragmatist, Smith was sharply critical of the philosophical grounding of Catholicism and Catholic pedagogy. When diversity is valued less than commonality in religious experience, he had written in 1941, religion ceases "to affirm divine creativeness through human hands," and becomes "sordid superstition exploited in the name of bogus control."[39]   Once in the Mediterranean Theater, however, Smith displayed a keen appreciation of the importance of sound relations with the Vatican.   As he reflected on the eve of his departure from Italy in the fall of 1944:

> The minimum of our duty, internationally defined, was to uphold during the period of our interim sovereignty the maximum advantage diplomatically wrestled by the Church from Fascism. Moreover, it would have made no sense at all for us to fail to appreciate as fully as possible the influence of the greatest Agency of Order perhaps on earth, when the primary job of military government is to keep order among conquered peoples.[40]

The Problem of Politics

The winter crisis with Church authorities had challenged a fundamental axiom of the Anglo-American re-education effort: the supposition that the subcommission could eliminate Fascism's educational legacy without substituting an alternative ideology, and without favoring one or another of Italy's non-Fascist political currents. In response to clerical inquiries, ACC leaders steadfastly asserted the non-partisan nature of Allied intervention.   In March, the State Department reiterated American intentions to do no more in Italy "than eliminate the teaching of Fascism." At the same time, the U. S. government "reaffirmed the policy of leaving the formulation of a new positive program to the Italians themselves."[41]

Rather than reexamine this simple formula in light of the practical difficulties it had encountered, the ACC leadership criticized its educational specialists in Sicily for having failed to steer clear of the cross currents of domestic Italian politics. Within ACC circles, the controversy with the Vatican served only to depress the standing of the subcommission and the individual educators involved. If Cardinals Lavitrano and Ascalesi bemoaned Gayre's departure, many ACC officials did not.[42] On the other hand, Washburne and the predominantly American subcommission were now saddled with an anti-clerical reputation which would dog them through the rest of the occupation.[43]

Why were the Anglo-American so loath to admit that educational reconstruction did not and would not proceed in a perfect political vacuum? Fear of offending the Church was an important reason, but not the only one. A second answer may be found in the Allies' own educational traditions. Americans in particular assumed that partisan politics had no place in either the administration or the content of popular schooling. The United States had just emerged from a forty-year Progressive crusade to rescue the nation's growing urban school systems from selfish "bosses," and to entrust them to non-partisan school boards and "professional" administrators, counselors and pedagogues.[44] Increasingly, public schools emphasized "life adjustment skills," from personal and social hygiene to good sportsmanship. Such skills underlay all forms of American associative and civil life: at most, they might be described as "pre-political." No wonder Americans were dismayed at the eruption of ideological hatreds which the 1930's brought to the classrooms not only of Italy, but of Germany and Russia as well. Surely the first order of business in Italy would be to drain the peninsula's classrooms of all ideological venom, Fascist and non-Fascist alike.

On a more pragmatic level, the blanket exclusion of politics from the schools simplified Allied educators' tasks, and reduced the likelihood of conflict between Englishmen and Americans, and between liberals and conservatives. Furthermore, the policy reflected AMG's overriding purpose, which was to secure and protect the combat forces' lines of communication and supply. In this sense, Anglo-American educators were no different from other AMG specialists. From the outset, all civil affairs officers were warned against allowing either "local personalities or organized political groups, however sound in sentiment" to have any part in determining their course of action. As non-partisan experts, AMG officers' job was to "administer military government and not to frame policy . . . [or] discuss either political or religious matters." Instead, all political questions were to be referred back through several intermediate bureaucratic levels to an Anglo-American Combined Civil Affairs Committee (CCAC) in Washington. The corrollary of these warnings had been a stiff prohibition on public assembly and political agitation by local populations, which was only lifted in the south by stages after the beginning of the new year.[45]

Through the winter of 1943-44, Allied civil affairs officers' chief concern was to establish the Brindisi and Salerno governments on a sound footing. Anglo-American military leaders justified this support on practical rather than ideological grounds: having signed the armistice with Marshall Badoglio, they prefered to keep him and his associates in positions of responsibility, so as to assure continued Italian observation of the terms of that documant. For his part, Badoglio had carefully composed his staff of "apolitical technicians" ever since the beginning of the Forty Five Days in the summer of 1943, though almost all, including Cuomo, were staunch conservatives and monarchists. Regardless of their own sentiments, Allied specialists found themselves in the increasingly frustrating situation of supervising Italians in the forging of an orderly and competent administrative structure, without being able to offer any political guidance whatsoever.[45]

As education liason officer in Brindisi, and then subcommission director after February of 1944, T. V. Smith conscientiously sought to perform this delicate role. While still in North Africa in the fall of 1943, he had assured his AMG superiors that he would not "propose in a single season to try to straighten Italy's old Leaning Tower of Learning--but only to clean it of the poison ivy of fascism." Indeed, by "nursing an Italian Ministry of National Education into being," his goal would be to "work the Subcommission out of work."[46]

But in educational matters, as in so many other fields, the Italian government had to "be made to stand on its own."[47] In his first day-long meeting with Gayre and Smith on November 25, 1943, Cuomo confessed that he had no immediate plans to reestablish a functioning ministry. An ex-deputy and secondary school principal, Cuomo had returned to public life under Severi, despite his advanced age, out of a patriotic desire to "serve his King and Country."[48] When pressed to define his educational objectives, he could only state that "his purpose would be to reestablish the honest character of education, to get rid of Fascist influence, and to return to where education would have been had Fascism not intervened." Practically speaking however, Cuomo felt sure that it would be better if the Allies retained control over education until Rome had been retaken, in order to give him time to reorganize a functioning administration.[49]

Despite his modest initial demeanor, Cuomo became more assertive in time. But his performance also departed increasingly from Anglo-American preferences. In his zeal to distribute local favors and conduct propaganda in favor of the none-too-popular monarchy, Cuomo neglected physical and pedagogical reconstruction.[50] Even more serious was his obstructionist attitude toward vetting, which is discussed separately in the next subsection. By April, Cuomo had exhausted the tolerance of both the Allies and the great majority of his countrymen.

Educational Subcommission staff members hoped that Cuomo's successor would be committed anti-Fascist who nonetheless shared their own fundamentally non-political conception of culture. Initially, they looked to Benedetto Croce. Like many Anglo-Amercians, they were particularly attracted to Croce's insistence on preserving the fundamental liberal distinction between the private and public spheres of human activity. In the decade following the First World War, Croce warned his contemporaries against letting their political loyalties eclipse the autonomous use of their intellect and conscience. On this basis Croce had frankly criticized Fascism's aspiration to subordinate every level of schooling and culture to the collective needs of the nation. He had opposed the 1929 Concordat as another, equally disturbing threat to individual autonomy.[51]

The British and the Americans had sought Croce's counsel on cultural reconstruction from the first months of Allied occupation. H. Stuart Hughes, the OSS educational specialist, may well have had Croce in mind when he urged in December of 1943 that the Italian Minister of Education should be a man of "universally recognized Liberalism, integrity and practical realism."[52] Even before his departure from England in the summer of 1943, Robert Gayre had received instructions from Sir Alfred Zimmern, head of the Foreign Office Research Department, to "bring Croce in" as soon as possible. In early September, Gayre wished to call Croce down to Palermo to head up his new curriculum reform commission on the grounds that the Neopolitan was "the greatest living Italian scholar, of whose democratic views there is no doubt."[53] Chief Staff Officer Spofford cautioned against taking this step until the Allies had agreed on a common political line to adopt toward Italian authorities. The request was referred to General Eisenhower, who felt that Croce's advanced age precluded his direct involvement, but who concurred that Croce might be "useful" on the mainland later.[54] When Gayre reached the Campanian capital in January of 1944, he found Croce ill, and therefore unable to take an active role in educational reconstruction.

In April of 1944, Anglo-American authorities and several southern CLN leaders, among them Omodeo, urged Croce to take over from Badoglio as prime minister in the new coalition government. But Croce's frustrating experience as Minister of Public Instruction under Giovanni Giolitti in 1920 had convinced him that he was better suited to the role of political advisor and moral teacher than that of governor. Nonetheless, Croce played a key role in the politcal negotiations to allot cabinet posts among the various anti-Fascist parties in early and mid-April. Omodeo credited him with overriding vehement Christian Democratic opposition in securing for him the educational ministry.[55]

Indirectly, Croce's influence on the direction of academic defascistization was greater still. Both De Ruggiero and Omodeo had intimate and long-standing ties with the renowned Neapolitan philosopher. Initially among Giovanni Gentile's most devoted followers, both men had turned to Crocean liberalism at critical stages of their personal and intellectual maturation. De Ruggiero had served under Croce in the Ministry of Public Instruction in 1920-21. Croce in turn arranged for many of De Ruggiero's philosophical and historical writings to be published by Laterza. During the 1930s, Omodeo virtually became Croce's alter ego on the editorial board of Croce's journal *La Critica*.

Omodeo's and De Ruggiero's individual quests for a satisfactory brand of reform liberalism eventually carried each of them to points further left on the political spectrum than that occupied by their mentor. Nonetheless each approached his

ministerial duties in fundamentaly Crocean terms. Both men
aspired, as Croce had, to restore a non-ideological brand of
culture to Italy's schools. As Omodeo insisted in a ministerial
circular, "before the child and the adolescent, the teacher must
rein in his own beliefs," and indeed must refrain from "coercing
their assent even to liberal or democratic doctrine."[56] Yet, like
the leaders of the Educational Subcommission, Omodeo and De
Ruggiero would find it impossible to purify Italian education
without enmeshing themselves in intense political controversy.

The Evolution of the Purge

The vetting of Italian educators passed through several stages
in the course of 1944, reflecting the shifting balance of domestic
political forces in liberated Italy. As undersecretary and then
minister, Giovanni Cuomo refused to wage a purification campaign
that would jeopardize the King's base of political support within
the Italian civil service. Indeed, the elderly educational
minister went out of his way to reemploy and otherwise protect
Italians who had been removed or were suspected by Allied
officials. In mid-April, however, the anti-Fascist parties entered
a new government under Badoglio, opening the way for a vigorous
purge of educational personnel. Adolfo Omodeo made a gallant
beginning with the limited resources and staff available to him in
Salerno.[57] Once Rome had been reoccupied, his successor Guido De
Ruggiero established the central and provincial machinery to review
systematically the political suitability of all educators under
Italian jurisdiction. Acting on the basis of the Bonomi
government's definitive purge legislation (Law No. 159 of 27 July,
1944), De Ruggiero sought to balance respect for Italian legal
precedent and the rights of the individual with a thorough and
expeditious procedure. But by fall, the precarious anti-Fascist
consensus which had permitted the vetting initiatives of the late
spring and summer began to unravel. Within the educational system,
and within the government as a whole, resentments at perceived
excesses and inequalities in the purge strengthened the position
of Liberals, Christian Democrats and, to some extent, Communists,
at the expense of De Ruggiero's Action Party and the Socialists.
After mid-December, the vetting of school personnel slowed
considerably under the ministry of De Ruggiero's successor, the
Liberal Arangio Ruiz.

The waxing and waning of the purge in AMG territory paralleled
its progress in King's Italy. As they learned more about the
structure of the Italian state, civil affairs officers gradually
refined and expanded the scope of the *scheda personale*. Beginning
in January, local anti-Fascist legal experts such as Arangio Ruiz
in Naples were recruited to regularize administrative procedures
and methods for appeals. After the penetration of the Gustav Line,

Allied leaders stiffened vetting criteria in the expectation that a larger percentage of dedicated Fascists would be found in areas newly wrested from the Republic of Salo. In June the Regional Commissioner in Rome drafted particularly severe guidelines to be applied to the central government. But the adoption of Law No. 159 and fears of unduly disrupting orderly governance led to a more permissive Allied stance in the late summer and fall. By the winter of 1944-45, a renewed military stalemate in the north and a more conservative educational ministry in Rome nearly brought purification under Allied auspices to a halt.

The subcommission's ability and inclination to influence the conduct of the purge in Italian-administered territory had been curtailed sharply since mid-February, 1944. The return of much of the Mezzogiorno to Italian jurisdiction transformed the role of ACC officials there from "immediate control" to "advice and circumspection." Henceforth Regional Educational Officers would be constrained to recommend rather than order the dismissal of secondary principals, elementary inspectors and didactic directors. The vetting of classroom teachers was now left entirely up to local Italian educational officials. It was up to the *provveditori* to submit names and corroborative evidence relating to persons already suspended by AMG, accompanied by their own recommendations for confirmation or reversal, to the minister for final disposition.[58]

From their first meetings, the conduct of the purge was a source of rancor between Cuomo and the Anglo-American subcommission. The Undersecretary felt that riding the heel of the Italian peninsula of Fascist influence required the removal of very few incumbent educators. In February of 1944, all four of southern Apulia's original provincial superintendents remained in office, despite the fact that three of the four were reputed to have long Fascist records. More disturbing still, in Allied eyes, was Cuomo's practice of staffing his own office in Brindisi with *provveditori* and other school personnel previously removed by the Educational Subcommission in AMG territory. When Cuomo named the former provincial superintendent of Messina province, "a notorious squadrista," to a high post in his secretariat, Gayre beseeched his ACC superior to ask the Undersecretary "if he is deliberately attempting to reduce me to a non-entity by these methods?"[59]

What accounted for Cuomo's recalcitrant behavior? Like virtually all secondary school principals, he had held a Fascist party card. As the ACC liason officer in daily contact with Cuomo in Brindisi, Smith felt that the Underscretary had never been more than a nominal party member. Croce, who had known Cuomo since 1920, regarded him as a confirmed anti-Fascist.[60] Gayre harboured greater suspicions. By the beginning of 1944, however, he concluded that like many and perhaps most southerners, Cuomo was motivated less by political belief than by extensive ties of family and friendship which ignored ideological boundaries.[61]

Nonetheless, Gayre was determined to seek Cuomo's dismissal

prior to the February 11 expansion of King's Italy. Lord Stansgate, Gayre's superior and Vice President of the ACC, agreed to pursue the matter.[62] Ironically, however, it was Gayre who was replaced by the end of the month, while Cuomo was promoted by Badoglio to the rank of Minister of National Education.

The new Educational Subcommission Director, T. V. Smith, concluded that too much energy had been wasted in trying to secure Signor Cuomo's resignation. Instead, he wrote the new Minister a carefully-worded letter inviting his continuing collaboration, but insisting that "persons discharged by the Allies for political reasons must not then assume important offices with the support of the Minister."[63]   Smith's letter succeeded in restoring civil relations between the Education Subcommission and the Italian Ministry, but it did not reverse Cuomo's lenient approach toward politically suspect *provveditori* and other educators.

The subcommission leadership was slow to recognize objective differences between AMG vetting guidelines and the Badoglio governement's first purge decree, RDL No. 29/B of December 28, 1943. The most serious of these differences concerned school heads and teachers who had doubled as local party secretaries. Many of the educators suspended by the Allies fell into this category. In King's Italy, the Badoglio government exempted ex-secretaries in communes of less than 50,000 from vetting. But AMG regulations recognized no such population limit elsewhere in the Mezzogiorno. This discrepancy became an issue after the expansion of King's Italy in mid-February. Despite subcommission pleas, Cuomo insisted on reconsidering all AMG findings in light of the Italian government's criteria. At the end of his term in office, as many as three fourths of the persons removed by Anglo-American REOs in some provinces had been reinstated by the Ministry of National Education.[64]

On two occasions at least, Cuomo's obstructionism drove frustrated subcommission staff members to approach Soviet diplomatic representatives in the Italian theater, as a means of prodding not only the educational minister, but also the ever-diplomatic Smith. At the beginning of 1944, Andrei Vyshinski, the Russian political representative on the Allied Council for Italy, requested permission to visit the Italian schools to see whether the Anglo-Americans "were getting rid of the Fascists." Vyshinsky took a "large retinue" with him, leaving behind detachments at Bari and Brindisi while he completed his tour of the South.   The Soviets found plenty of ground for criticism, especially in Apulia. They cataloged Italian complaints, and even recorded a case of "disaffection" on the Education Subcommission staff. As a result, Smith began receiving reports from the field alleging "damage" to the Anglo-Americans' "reputation among the Italians."[65]

Major General Mestor Solodovnik, who represented the Soviet Union on the Control Commission after the beginning of January, also took an interest in the progress of the purge. In mid-April, he received a frank letter from Arthur Vessolo, cataloging Cuomo's continuing negligence in the field of vetting.[66] In particular, the English REO described a longstanding controversy over the status of Dr. Lelio Rossi, *provveditore* of Brindisi province, just then coming to a head. Prior to the Italian government's move to Salerno, Rossi had served as Undersecretary Cuomo's Chief of Staff, despite the fact that two of the *provveditore's* history and civics texts published during the *ventennio* had been banned by AMG in Sicily. According to the Brindisi Port Security Section, Rossi was "unsympathetic with the Allies," and should therefore be removed from office and transferred out of Brindisi. As REO in the area, Vessolo had repeatedly made the same recommendation, to no avail. Now Solodovnik lodged inquiries of his own.

Even so, Smith refused to demand Rossi's removal. As he wrote to the educational minister on April 19, he was "content for the time" to leave the case to Cuomo's conscience. Rossi did not fall into any of the *scheda* categories (such as *sciarpa littorio* or local party secretary) which "automatically called for action against him." Smith noted that the *provveditore's* banned books might well have contained "praise of Fascism in order to get published rather than being published in order to praise Fascism," and that in any case, it did not appear that "Rossi profitted from Fascism, beyond his ability, either financially or professionally."[67]

The uncertainty surrounding the purge took its toll on classroom morale throughout the south. From Matera province Arthur Vessolo reported on the contents of a letter intercepted in the local post, in which a schoolboy spoke "contemptuously" of the fact that the teachers "who are now preaching democracy are the very ones who previously preached fascism."[68] To a degree, such disenchantment on the part of the more astute pupils was inevitable. But there is no doubt that Cuomo's obstruction of the purge magnified a sense of cynicism among Italians while it dismayed and angered subcommission staff members.

Most disturbing of all were signs of a Fascist resurgence, particularly in Catanzaro province. Initially some 60 provincial school personnel had been suspended there by the Allies. Subsequently, however, the *provveditore* recommended but three names to the minister for disciplinary action. Then in March, pro-Fascist demonstrations, involving schoolteachers among others, broke out in the *provveditore's* home town of Nicastro. Yet the provincial superintendent was willing to oust only one of the *maestri* involved. The Nicastro disturbances attracted widespread publicity in the Italian and Anglo-American press. Finally the Subcommission was compelled to call for the *provveditore's* dismissal. But the Anglo-Americans obtained satisfaction in the case only with Cuomo's successor.[69]

Adolfo Omodeo's inaugural address as the new educational

minister on April, 22 restored the purification of school personnel to the top of the Italian ministry's agenda. As Rector at the University of Naples, Omodeo had already instituted an orderly but severe purge the preceding fall. That effort had attracted favorable attention in both Allied and Italian educational circles. Vessolo confirmed at the beginning of May that in Apulia and Basilicata, Omodeo was "better viewed" than his predecessor "owing to his good academic qualifications and reputation for independent thought."[70] In his seven weeks as educational minister, Omodeo suspended more than 100 educators, and was preparing to act against almost 100 more by the time he left the cabinet in early June.[71]

This liberal intellectual aspired to restore a Mazzinian devotion to the commonweal and an ascetic standard of disinterested public service not only for educators, but to all civil servants. Thus, in addition to his educational responsibilities, he agreed to chair a multi-party commission to draw up new guidelines for the vetting of all public servants below the grade of VI. In comparison with the Badoglio decree law of the previous December, the Omodeo commission's recommendation of May 26 greatly expanded the classes of Fascists subject to automatic dismissal. For the first time, the commission called for retroactive criminal liability, including imprisonment, to be imposed on prominently placed supporters of the fallen regime. In order to break cleanly with the Fascist past, long-standing traditions of Italian jurisprudence had to be modified. But in Omodeo's eyes, only a rapid, broad-brushed "political" purge could forestall endless litigation, which would otherwise poison the national atmosphere for decades.[72]

The coalition Badoglio government fell, and Omodeo lost both his ministry and the presidency of the vetting commission, before the May 26 decree could be fully implemented. Still, it established the juridical pattern for subsequent legislation. More immediately, the commission's deliberations had stimulated the adoption of a stiffer policy in AMG territory.[73]

After penetrating the Gustav Line, the Allies expected to find a larger percentage of dedicated Fascists in areas newly wrestled from the Republic of Salo. At the same time, Chief Commissioner MacFarlane hoped that as the Allies moved north, the possibility of finding "suitable anti-fascist personnel should become much greater than hitherto."[74] On the basis of these projections, Allied Military Government policy in May and June called for the automatic dismissal of all local officials who had served that Fascist Republic. At T. V. Smith's initiative, the new directive was modified as it applied to local Italian teachers, who had been induced to swear their loyalty once again to Mussolini during the winter of 1943-44. "Since teachers are in general not so much wielders of power as molders of influence," Smith urged that they not be arrested or interned along with other "senior Fascist officials." Doubtless many would have to be dismissed, but "only after individual examination of their public records."[75]

Nonetheless, overall AMG policy toward Italian civil servants continued to be hardnosed in the weeks preceding and immediately following the Allied liberation of Rome. In anticipation of the occupation of the capital, Charles Poletti was brought north from Naples Zone, where he had served as Regional Commissioner since January. On the basis of his own repeated visits to Italy during the *ventennio*, the ex-lieutenant govenor had become convinced that the Fascists had manufactured much of their popular support by expanding the portion of the population which derived its income wholly or partially from an enormous civil service. They had created a monstrous labyrinth, in which efficiency, corruption and favoritism had multiplied even beyond the control of the Fascist leaders themselves. The liberation of the Italian capital now provided an unparalleled opportunity to break the stanglehold of the government bureaucracy over civil society. Following his arrival in Rome, Poletti called for the immediate dismissal of some 33 categories of persons, including *provveditori* and university rectors, within the confines of the capital and its immediate hinterland. Nor was Poletti predisposed to deal leniently with "minor Fascists." The lower levels of the state apparatus were also to be investigated and purged, even at the cost of increasing the government's inefficiency.[76]

Upon liberation of the city, AMG officials found that local anti-Fascist organizations had launched their own vetting investigations. One of these was the *Associazione italiana degli insegnanti* (AIDI), a well-organized group of Roman schoolteachers and professors representing every level of schooling and a broad spectrum of anti-Fascist poltical opinion. During the long months of German and Republican Fascist occupation, the association had resisted the revival of Fascist educational practices, from the use of the *saluto romano* to the study of Nazi racial doctrine and the reimposition of a loyalty oath. AIDI members also documented the collaboration of fellow educators, particularly in administrative posts, with the German and Fascist enemy. During the summer of 1944, the Roman anti-Fascist group called for the automatic suspension, pending examination of their political and moral conduct, of all incumbent school heads in the capital.[77] Allied officials refused to countenance such a drastic step, but they did incorporate evidence collected by AIDI in identifying "notorious Fascist school personnel."[78]

The month of July brought a more circumspect approach to purge activity in the capital. Daunted by the specter of administrative chaos and by the adverse reactions of conservative Roman opinion, the new Acting Chief Commissioner, Captain Ellery Stone, issued a new AMG vetting directive to supplant Poletti's earlier decrees. Executive Memorandum 67, which appeared on July 5, backed away from the automatic suspension of whole classes of civil servants.[79]

The Education Subcommission's own plans for the reoccupation of the Italian capital reflected this more cautious approach. These plans focused on placing "trustworthy personnel" in the "key positions--Ministry, Rectors and *provveditori agli studi*." On the other hand, the plans neglected any long term role for Rome's organized anti-Fascist movement. Instead, the Ministry of Public Instruction was to be assisted in taking charge of the purge at the earliest possible moment. To this end it would be important to secure the Trastevere building immediately, to safeguard its records and to put ministerial functionaries back to work after a "quick screening."[80]

De Ruggiero proceeded accordingly. He immediately dismissed all incumbent divisional directors and central inspectors. Yet instead of bringing in a clean slate of politically trustworthy outsiders to replace them, he promoted experienced technicians from within the ministry. These persons served in an acting capacity; after a probationary period, their performance was reviewed, and only two were confirmed.[81] De Ruggiero and Smith also purified that "plum of a Fascist place," the University of Rome. Some twenty-five professors were expelled, including Luigi Volpicelli, the Gentilian idealist who had contributed so prominently to the drafting of Bottai's School Charter.[82]

But the new educational minister was willing to proceed more deliberately in vetting secondary and elementary personnel. In his inaugural address in late June, De Ruggiero had sought to reassure the classroom teachers and school heads of liberated Italy. Certainly the "opportunists" and "petty tyrants" among them would be shown the door. But the new minister expressed every confidence that these constituted but a "marginal minority of the *classe magistrale*."[83]

De Ruggiero's approach was consistent with the philosophy of Count Carlo Sforza, Italy's new High Commissioner for the Purge. Upon accepting his post, Sforza announced the intention to *far presto, colpire in alto, perdonare in basso* ("act quickly, strike at the big shots, and let the small fry go").[84] Sforza's instrument was Royal Decree Law No. 159, Italy's first comprehensive purge legislation. The new law, which went into effect on July 27, shied away from Omodeo's proposed political reconstruction in favor of an elaborate sequence of judicial hearings. RDL No. 159 aimed "as far as possible at penalizing individuals rather than whole categories." The decree identified a broad range of persons liable to dismissal, including

> any person who had "participated actively in the political life of Fascism" or been a consistent apologist of Fascism," or obtained appointment or promotion through favoritism of the Party or its officials, or had been guilty of Fascist bias, incompetence or corrupt practice."[85]

In accordance with liberal Italian and Anglo-American juridical principles, the new law carefully respected the rights of the accused. Prior to dismissal, proof of responsibility had to be established, and the accused retained the right to appeal. RDL No. 159 stipulated that each ministry was to be purged by means of its own vetting commissions. By autumn, De Ruggiero had established separate commissions for primary, technical secondary, classical secondary and university instruction, as well as a commission assigned to oversee the purge of the central educational administration, the *provveditori* and their chief inspectors. Each commission established detailed procedures and criteria to be followed in vetting its branch of the nation's educators. The actual purge deliberations were conducted by sectoral subcommissions located in each province. In addition, a central appeal commission was created in Rome.[86]

Members of vetting commissions and subcommissions were drawn from Sforza's High Commission for the Purge, from the Italian court system (the *magistratura*), and from the central and the provincial educational bureaucracies. In the case of the commission assigned to *La Minerva* itself, a representative of the Vatican, Domenico Rosati, supplanted the ministerial functionary.[87]

The new legislation and administrative arrangements encouraged greater flexibility and greater moderation in the conduct of the purge. Ever since the occupation of Sicily, *maestri* had complained forcefully at Allied reliance on the single punishment of suspension from office without pay for all persons suspected of excessive Fascist involvement. In King's Italy, Omodeo had convinced T. V. Smith on humanitarian grounds of the propriety of restoring salaries to at least some of the school personnel whom the Allies had dismissed without pay, and whose cases lingered unresolved for months on end.[88] The Royal Decree Law of July 27 permitted dismissed civil servants to retain their pensions and, in certain cases, granted a small allowance. Finally, on September 4, Prime Minister Bonomi ruled that all vetted civil servants could continue to collect their pay until the final disposition of their cases. By November, Allied authorities were also allowing suspended Italian personnel to retain their salaries.[89]

In another important step restoring traditional Italian disciplinary practices, the Royal Decree Law of July 27 permitted the new provincial vetting subcommissions to select from a range of sanctions, calibrated to the severity of the offense committed. In the case of *maestri*, sanctions varied from outright dismissal for the most serious offenders to such reprimands as disqualification from administrative promotion, or transfer to a new province in less serious instances. Suspect school administrators were often pensioned off early.[90]

Such reforms only began to mitigate schoolteachers' anxieties and resentments over the purge. In many provinces, political and jurisdictional rivalries, often pitting the *provveditore* against the High Purge Commission representative, delayed the formation of the new vetting boards for months.   Even in Grossetto province, where local officials, including a vigorous new *provveditore*, and Allied specialists had attracted widespread attention for their efficient preliminary vetting through the summer and fall, delays in forming the appropriate Italian review subcommission created "great unrest" among suspended *maestri*.[91]

In Rome, the vetting of the central ministry faced obstacles of its own.   De Ruggiero was determined to complete the purge at *La Minerva* by the end of the year, despite a "wall of passivity and even ill-will" which he encountered among all but a few of the functionaries in Trastevere.[92]   When De Ruggiero left the ministry, the central vetting commission had nearly completed its task. Provincial superintendents did not fare well: of the 38 incumbents in provinces under Italian government supervision, only 12 remained in office as of the end of 1944.   But at *La Minerva*, the commission's findings were circumspect: even among civil servants of grade IV (the highest grade represented in the ministry), 90 percent of the incumbents were retained at their posts.[93]

When the second Bonomi government took office, many of the civil service purge commissions' functions were transferred to the prime minister's own office, or to the very conservative Italian judiciary.[94]   In such fora, even the relative handful of highly placed officials singled out for dismissal, suspension or early retirement stood a good chance of reversing those judgements on appeal.

Over the winter of 1944-45, the lull in the purge of the higher reaches of the Italian state, coupled with persisting discrepancies at the provincial level, kindled new outcries by local *maestri* and *direttori didattici*.   As one schoolteacher protested in the pages of *I diritti della scuola*:

> Vetting is well and good.   We were promised a policy of "severity at the top and indulgence below."   Why then begin with so many teachers and school heads?   Are these then the "big shots?"   What bitter irony!   Meanwhile the leaders and chief sustainers of Fascism--the very ones, perhaps, who forced those unfortunate educators to compromise themselves--remain undisturbed.[95]

In AMG-occupied Naples and in Allied-administered territory north of Rome, still vigilant REOs came under severe local criticism of their own.[96]   The Hyde Park Declaration of September, with its promise of greater autonomy, prompted Italian authorities to call for the exclusion of Anglo-American specialists from all purgative activity, even in the north.

Subcommission officers criticized such a change on both practical and ideological grounds.   They predicted that allowing Italian committees to carry out preliminary vetting would delay the reopening of schools by an extra two months or more.   Even then, they feared that many dedicated Fascists would retain their posts, particularly in light of the dilatory approach being adopted by the Arangio Ruiz ministry. Willis Pratt, the energetic REO in Emilia-Romagna, was particularly outspoken. In a December 10 letter to a senior AMG official, he wrote that

> to deny us the right of giving to liberal Italians control of
> the educational system "while we are here" is to defeat the
> very purpose for which the Education Division of Allied
> Military Government was created.[97]

Reluctantly, Allied Commission authorities agreed. In the impending liberation of the Po Valley, the Education Subcommission would retain a role in the preliminary purge of local civil servants, on the condition that the Italian vetting machinery spelled out in Decree Law No. 159 be created as soon as possible.

Beneath the clash of personalities and the ebb and flow of events, three distinctive conceptions of the purge coexisted uneasily in 1944 and early 1945. To many Italians, particularly in the Action and Socialist parties and in anti-Fascist groups such as AIDI, the purge represented an invaluable instrument for thoroughgoing political reconstruction. A similiar, frankly ideological approach had dictated Gayre's policies in the fall of 1943, and continued to figure in the attitudes of educational specialists such as Vessolo and Pratt. This approach singled out Italy's educators for severe vetting, based on their influence, for good or for ill, on the long term political socialization of the nation.

Moderately progressive Italians such as De Ruggiero and many Anglo-American specialists preferred to view the purge as a method of administrative reconstruction. They were less concerned with a relatively small number of ideological Fascists than with the large number of opportunists and incompetents who had established themselves throughout the civil service during the preceding *ventennio*. As Poletti's performance in Rome demonstrated, this approach to vetting was capable of producing as many victims, at least in the higher civil service ranks, as an openly ideological purge.

Beginning in July of 1944, however, a very different assumption came to the fore: purification should be treated as an extended series of legal investigations based on traditional Italian criminal and civil jurisprudence. Most Allied Commission leaders preferred this approach, as it guaranteed that they would be able to deal with a centralized administration of experienced bureaucrats.[98] The Liberal, Labor Democrat, Christian Democrat and (by the end of 1944) Communist parties endorsed a traditional, legalistic approach as well, making it a cornerstone of the second Bonomi government.

Administrative Reform

In the course of 1944, important strides were also made in curbing authoritarian administrative arrangements in Italian classrooms and within the educational hierarchy. Prior to April, Allied officials and educational minister Cuomo had been too preoccupied by jurisdictional conflicts with the Church, and by their own differences over the conduct of the purge, to give this area much attention. But Adolfo Omodeo lost no time in introducing a number of procedural reforms aimed at restoring greater dignity and greater liberty to the world of the school.   He abolished loyalty oaths and ended all forms of political surveillance.   In particular, school heads were forbidden to listen in on or to intervene capriciously in classroom proceedings. All commemorative assemblies, rallies and subscription drives, regardless of their nature, were excluded from the school calendar.   In Omodeo's view, Fascist classroom collection drives for wool, metal and other war materials had served only to mortify the more impoverished pupils. In general, all "bureaucratic formalities" would hereafter be minimized, in order that "everything within the school might contribute to that sober concentration and hard work" which alone could redeem a "disgraced land."[99]

To his dismay, Omodeo found that there was only the shadow of a functioning ministry in Salerno to implement these cardinal reforms.   The Allies' refusal to sanction pay increases for Italian state employees (out of fear of exacerbating inflation) made it difficult for the various ministries to retain the support staffs they needed.   The new educational minister struggled unsuccessfully to obtain even a single automobile for the use of his inspectors in outlying areas. He lacked the most rudimentary academic records for many southern provinces.[100]   In his ministerial addresses and circulars, his naturally emphatic mode of expression became still more forceful, as if the moral impact of his rhetoric might somehow compensate for the paucity of physical resources at his command.

Omodeo and his skeletal ministry confronted a chaotic and difficult social reality.   Throughout the Mezzogiorno, physical and economic distress and social dislocation had engendered a pervasive yet largely unfocused political disillusionment among all social classes.   At the same time, "liberation" still held out the long term promise of prosperity, opportunity and upward mobility for Italy's younger generations. For the petit-bourgeoisie especially, the expansion of educational opportunity and an easing of academic standards represented a vital means of advancing from a disheartening present to an inspiring future.

Omodeo's determination to restore the decorum and severity of Italian schooling clashed directly with such aspirations.   The educational minister became a lightening rod for much of the socio-political discontent in the air when he vetoed any

enlargement of the Italian university system, and insisted that
secondary school examinations previously suspended due to the
upheaval of war be reinstituted at the end of the academic year.
Encouraged by anxious parents and by Omodeo's clerical and
monarchist political foes, secondary students staged protest
strikes and demonstrations. Vicious political and personal attacks
on the minister covered city walls throughout the South.
Provveditori and school heads threatened by Omodeo's commitment to
the purge did little to restrain the escalating unrest. The
educational minister had to insist that school principals again
gather the reins of authority tightly in their own grasp. As a
result, students returned to classrooms and to their exams. But
Omodeo's *maniera forte* had made him widely unpopular, and his
replacement at *La Minerva* was only a matter of time.[101]

As the controversy surrounding the educational minister
deepened, T. V. Smith urged him to adopt a more conciliatory
stance. The Education Subcommission director even staged a staff
meeting in Omodeo's presence to illustrate the dynamics of "mutual
accomodation." But the strong-willed Italian responded that "such
compromise methods might work in America, but that in Italy one
must be stern."[102] Smith coolly concluded that Omodeo was "too
energetic for the lethargic times," adding that the minister "was
given enough rope and he proceeded to put it to its proverbial and
proper use."[103]

Guido De Ruggiero shared Omodeo's commitment to recasting the
spirit of Italian education through procedural reform. But he had
inherited a highly polarized situation, and therefore proceeded
cautiously. His first step in June was to mollify students,
teachers and parents by relaxing his predecessor's rigid schedule
of secondary school examinations.[104]

De Ruggiero felt obliged to adopt a firmer attitude with the
Educational Subcommission. Despite laudable intentions, the
Anglo-Americans had made many decisions which De Ruggiero regarded
to be contrary to Italian legal tradition. The new minister found
the subcommission to have been most remiss in Sicily, where Gayre
had freely hired and fired university professors, and granted so
many concessions to new parochial schools. Through such actions
as well as growing traffic in Italian honorary degrees for Allied
officers--a practice abruptly halted by Smith in late
February[105]--the minister felt that Gayre had naively perpetuated
some of the most corrupt practices employed under Fascism. In
intensive summer consultations with Smith, De Ruggiero agreed to
let stand most of what had been done in the south, while the Allies
promised to heed Italian laws and standing ministerial procedures
as they commenced educational reconstruction in AMG territory to
the north.[106]

In order to prevent further irregularities in their standards
and behavior, De Ruggiero clamped down on parochial schools in a
number of ways. After the signing of the Lateran Accords, the

Fascist regime had progressively relaxed its scrutiny over the content of parochial education and the performance of parochial students on their graduation examinations. De Ruggiero curbed the widespread practice of sending but a single state commissioner to participate in these examinations. He rescinded official recognition (*parificazione*) of those schools which had permitted the most scandalous abuses of intellectual discipline. To guarantee closer state vigilance in the future, he also proposed that a new ministerial division assume responsibility for supervising both parochial and non-sectarian private schools. Under De Ruggiero's successor such an *Ispettorato per l'istruzione media non governativa* legally supplanted the more autonomous Fascist-created *Ente nazionale per l'insegnamento medio e superiore.*[107] As a liberal intellectual, De Ruggiero believed in the principle of untrammelled competition between state and private educational institutions. As an educational minister, however, his concern for the integrity of the newly reconstructed state apparratus and his fears of the Church's own history of illiberalism induced him to adopt these restrictive measures towards parochial schools.

If De Ruggiero felt compelled to defend the authority of the ministry as a whole vis-a-vis the Allied subcommission and the Church, he was also determined to liberalize the inner spirit of *La Minerva.* In the past, the *Consiglio Superiore della Pubblica Istruzione* had represented the nation's local teachers and school heads within the central ministry. But the *Consiglio* had lost its independence in 1935, when its functionaries were made to depend "solely on the will of the Minister." In June of 1939, the council ceased to exist as a distinctive organ, having been merged into a new *Consiglio Nazionale dell'Educazione, delle Scienze e delle Arti.* In October of 1944, De Ruggiero dissolved that artificial and overly centralized amalgam and reconstituted the *Consiglio Superiore.* Most of the new council's members were university professors appointed by the educational minister and concerned largely with rehabilitation of Italy's universities.[108]

The Fascist emasculation of the *Consiglio Superiore* had removed a key check on the intiative and authority of the minister's office. To concentrate control still further, successive Ministers of National Education had made heavy use of their prerogative to set aside normal operating procedures in any division of the ministry when they felt particular situations warranted such action. As a result, even after the overthrow of Fascism, Italian educators continued to court the minister's favor with abandon. De Ruggiero was appalled by the sea of personal appeals which soon engulfed him.[109]

Determined to emphasize standard administrative procedures and professional competence in place of personal and political patronage, in October he forbade ministerial functionaries to appeal over the heads of their direct superiors to his own

"discretionary power."[110] In a parallel ruling, petitioners from
within or outside the ministry were forbidden to approach the
Educational Subcommission except via the appropriate channels.[111]

At the local level and at the apex of the central bureaucracy,
Omodeo and De Ruggiero had made a start at overturning the
widespread tendency of Italian educators to identify their own
wellbeing with submission to a *padrone*. But a key manifestation
of the "duce principle" remained at the nexus between the central
ministry and individual teachers.

Giuseppe Bottai's incorporation of primary schoolteachers
within the national civil service had sharply limited their
opportunities for promotion. The law of July, 1942 established
stiff quotas (known as *ruoli chiusi* or "closed rolls") on the
numbers of schoolteachers who could advance from a base civil
service grade at grade XII towards a maximum grade of IX. As a result,
half of the nation's 120,000 primary schoolteachers found
themselves frozen at the base grade, while less than 8,000 could
reach grade IX. The personnel division of the central ministry
selected the fortunate minority of *maestri* who would be promoted.[112]

In De Ruggiero's view, this arrangement led to several baneful
consequences. It undermined the cooperative spirit of the *classe
magistrale*, encouraging instead insidious competition for the favor
of personnel division officials in Rome. The system rewarded
political conformity rather than professional competence. Many
teachers fled the classroom for other positons offering greater
dignity or more liberal advancement opportunities. A favored
avenue of escape was appointment to a "temporary" post in the
central bureaucracy in Trastevere. Such appointments, or *comandi*,
bypassed the usual procedure of announcing and conducting
competitive examinations for openings, and might be prolonged
indefinitely. During the waning years of the Fascist dictatorship
a sizable number of such recruits accumulated in the personnel
division itself. These astute and obsequious former *maestri*,
having engineered their own release from instructional
responsiblities, brokered the promotion of favored colleagues from
the hinterland.[113]

Early in his ministry, De Ruggiero halted the recruitment of
ministerial functionaries by means of *comandi*. Then late in the
fall he called for the opening of the *ruoli* and the creation of an
automatic system of seniority-based promotion. This reform aimed
to boost morale of the entire *classe magistrale* while streamlining
the Leviathan in Trastevere. Such a step would necessarily burden
the state treasury. But De Ruggiero believed it was essential if
the nation's discontented *maestri* were to become a noble "army of
democracy," uniquely capable of transforming Italy's civil
conscience due to their "diffusion" throughout the country's social
fabric.[114]

Notwithstanding Washburne's support, De Ruggiero's proposal
foundered on the hostility of fellow Italians. The Ministry of the

Treasury resisted the opening of the *ruoli chiusi* on the grounds that the attendant increase in teachers' salaries would cost the state half a billion lire. The reform also encountered fierce opposition from the recesses of *La Minerva* herself. The educational minister now paid the price for his earlier refusal to replace veteran bureaucrats with loyal "outsiders" during the summer high tide of the purge. The reform was shelved for the duration of the war. Deeply discouraged by this defeat, De Ruggiero submitted his resignation in early December.[115]

Adolfo Omodeo and Guido De Ruggiero had each assumed the post of educational minister eager to free Italy's teachers from the excessively heavy hand of local and central bureaucratic control. Both men believed that a robust and independent-mined citizenry could only emerge in Italy if her teachers were equally self-reliant. But in 1944 each had to face a badly demoralized teaching corps and an administrative system near collapse after many years of insatiable Fascist tinkering followed by the chaos of war. The local and national bureaucratic apparatus would have to be reconstituted on a sound footing before it could be reformed. For twenty years Mussolini had grandiloquently promised Italians a new Roman Empire. In 1944, Omodeo and De Ruggiero settled for the simple restoration of a republican Roman legacy: the rule of law.

Conclusion

From the outset, the Anglo-American reeducation effort had been predicated on the assumption that the subcommission could eliminate Fascism's educational legacy without depending on, or favoring, any one of Italy's intensely competitive non-Fascist political currents. Under the disinterested supervision first of the Education Subcommission and then a rejuvenated Ministry of Public Instruction, educational reconstruction would proceed, ensconced in its own serene and apolitical milieu until one day it emerged in full democratic dress. At that point, the school system would be the very template of a reasonable and tolerant style of domestic politics and international behavior. T. V. Smith prophesied that some day, each of Italy's political campaigns would become "an education in social issues, and every election an exemplification of moral choice."[116]

In the short run, Allied authorities were loath to grant Italian "partisan" interests any influence over the course of educational reconstruction. In Sicily, Washburne's and Gayre's difficulties in steering between Scylla and Charybdis in the winter crisis over elementary religious instruction had only strengthened the ACC leadership's insistence that the subcommission remain completely insulated from the cross currents of domestic Italian politics. True, the Church obtained the right to review both curricula and textbooks. But it garnered this privilege as a sovereign international power, not a domestic actor.

In fact, the Allies' original commitment to the forcible "reeducation" of an enemy nation had been undercut by the creation of King's Italy and the restoration of indigenous political liberties between November 1943 and April, 1944. The Allied task now became one of identifying like-minded Italians to implement congenial educational reform on their behalf.

With the creation of the first anti-Fascist coalition government in April, 1944, the Anglo-Americans turned to Benedetto Croce for advice, given the closeness of his political and cultural values to American and particularly British traditions. Though Croce refused to serve directly in the new government, he played a key role in placing the educational ministry in liberal Italian hands.

Though Omodeo favored a more radical purge than did Croce, both he and De Ruggiero approached their educational responsibilities in fundamentally Crocean terms. In their own ways, each of these ministers focused their energies on removing unwarranted political influence from Italy's classrooms and from her administrative structure. Like Croce and the Allied educational specialists, they believed that the school should inculcate tolerance and mutual respect, and not a single, exclusive ideology.[117]

Given their non-ideological orientation, it is perhaps not surprising that political miscalculations figured prominently in both Omodeo's and De Ruggiero's fall from office. The former lacked both the patience and the charismatic personality to rally the schoolteachers of the war-torn Mezzogiorno to his own ascetic and disinterested vision of post-Fascist education. De Ruggiero, on the other hand, probably failed to act decisively enough in breaking with incumbent staff and established procedures at *La Minerva*. His early decision to retain experienced bureaucrats, rather than his own external appointees in major ministerial posts returned to haunt him when he tried to prune the ministry late in the fall. Despite their own progressive intentions, the apolitical approach of Allied and Italian liberals alike paved the way for the conservative reaction to come.

ENDNOTES

[1] Monthly Report, Education Subcommission, July 1944, NARS, RG 331, 10000/144/165.

[2] Smith, "Swan Song from the Ex-Director of the Education Subcommission," p. 4.

[3] Smith, *A Non-Existent Man*, p. 196.

[4] Guido De Ruggiero, "Esperienze di un ministro," *Idea* I (Jan 1945), reproduced in Giovanni Spadolini *L'Italia dei laici*

(Florence: Le Monnier, 1980), p. 111.

⁵Gayre, *Italy in Transition*, p. 74.

⁶Binchy, *Church and State in Fascist Italy*, pp. 473-477.

⁷Gayre, *Italy in Transition*, pp. 77, 133.

⁸*Ibid.*; Letter, Bishop of Agrigento to Lord Rennell, 5 Sept 1943, and Memos, Lt. Col. Wellesly to AMGOT HQ, 25 Sept 1943, and Gayre to SCAO, Syracusa, 9 Oct 1943, all in NARA, RG 331, 10000/144/10.

⁹Gayre, *Italy in Transition*, pp. 58, 65, 75, 96; Memo, Poletti to Mason Hammond, 3 Sept 1943, NARA, RG 331, 10000/144/8.

¹⁰Letters, Monsignor Ballo to Gayre, 27 Oct and 1 Nov 1943, and Letters, Gayre to Monsignor Ballo, Bishop of Mazaro del Vallo, 6 and 10 Nov 1943, all in NARA, RG 331, 10000/144/10.

¹¹See Washburne's summary of these developments in his letter to Minister of Public Instruction, 6 April 1945, NARA, RG 331, 10000/144/157.

¹²Gayre, *Italy in Transition*, p. 134; Memo, Gayre to RCAO, Region II (Attn. Ed. Director), 4 Jan 1944, and Memo, Gayre to HQ, Region I (for the Ed. Director), 10 Dec 1943, both in NARA, RG 331, 10000/144/10.

¹³Gayre, *Italy in Transition*, p. 135; Memo, Gayre to Major Bergin, 16 Feb 1944, NARA, RG 331. 10000/144/157; Typescript, "Scuola Cattolica Libera," n.d., located in NARA, RG 331, 10000/144/10.

¹⁴Memo, Gayre to Major Bergin, 16 Feb 1944, and Letter, Smith to Minister of Public Instruction, 26 May 1944, RG 331, 10000/144/157.

¹⁵Memo, "Religion in the Schools," Washburne to Dir. Ed. Sub., 29 Feb 1944, NARA, RG 331, 10000/144/157.

¹⁶Tomasi, *Scuola italiana dalla dittatura alla repubblica*, p. 17.

¹⁷Flynn, *Roosevelt and Romanism*, pp. xi, xii. In his study *What is Progressive Education?*, Washburne carefully attempted to distinguish "religiously inclusive" values which he considered admissible to public schooling from exclusive dogmas and rituals which were not. See the Italian edition *Che cos'è l'educazione progressiva?* (Florence: La Nuova Italia, 1953), pp. 58-59, 106-107. For an interesting critique of Washburne's religious thinking by an Italian Catholic scholar, see Diega Orlando, *Carleton Washburne e l'esperimento di Winnetka* (Brescia: La Scuola, 1971), pp. 160-161.

¹⁸Fornaca, *I problemi della scuola italiana*, p. 67; Orlando, *Carleton Washburne*, pp. 164-166.

¹⁹Memo, "Religion in the Schools," Washburne to Dir. Ed. Sub., 19 Feb 1944, NARA, RG 331, 10000/144/157.

²⁰On Catholic pedagogical doctrine at the end of the war, see Arthur J. May, *Europe Since 1939* (New York: Holt, Rinehart and Winston, 1966), p. 608.

²¹Gayre, *Italy in Transition*, pp. 80, 136-137.

[22]Memo, "Religion in the Schools," Washburne to Dir. Ed. Sub., 29 Feb 1944, NARA, RG 331, 10000/144/157.

[23]Gayre, *Italy in Transition*, p. 137.

[24]Washburne, "La riorganizzazione dell'istruzione in Italia," 275; Tomasi, *Scuola italiana dalla dittatura alla repubblica*, p. 19; *I Diritti della scuola*, XLV, 1-2 (Sept-Oct 1944), iv.

[25]Memos, Vessolo to Ed. Advisor, 31 Jan and 15 Feb 1944, all in NARA, RG 331, 10000/144/158.

[26]Memo, "Religion in the Schools," Washburne to Dir. Ed. Sub., 29 Feb 1944, NARA, RG 331, 10000/144/157.

[27]On Gayre's allegedly "anti-clerical administration," see his *Italy in Transition*, pp. 195-197. The remainder of this account is based on Memo, Koopman to Regional Commissioner, 3 March 1944, NARA, RG 331, 10000/144/157. See Appendix II.

[28]Memo, Koopman to Regional Commissioner, 3 March 1944, NARA, RG 331, 10000/144/157.

[29]See for instance Maurice Neufeld's comment in his article "The Failure of Allied Military Government in Italy," *Public Administration Review*, VI, 2 (Spring, 1946), 1944.

[30]Gayre, *Italy in Transition*, p. 197.

[31]"Monthly Report on Education," Education Division, February 1944, NARA, RG 331, 10000/144/157.

[32]Letter, Cicognani to Stull, 14 Feb 1944 with attached Carroll Memorandum, NARA, RG 331, 10000/144/157. See Appendix I.

[33]Letter, Major T. B. Jackman to HQ, ACC, 21 Feb 1944, NARA, RG 331, 10000/157; Letter, Lush to MGS, 23 Feb 1944, NARA, RG 331, 10000/144/157, partially reproduced in Coles and Weinberg, *Civil Affairs*, p. 404.

[34]Letter, Jackman to HQ, ACC, 21 Feb 1944, NARA, RG 331, 10000/144/157; Hull's remark is cited in Smith, Final Report on Education, Mission to Mideast, Nov 1944, NARA, RG 331, 10000/105/709, cited in Coles and Weinberg, *Civil Affairs*, p. 404.

[35]Flynn, *Roosevelt and Romanism*, pp. 203-204; OSS, "The Reform of Italian Education," Dec 1943, p. 22, NARA, RG 407, Box 2216; Robert Murphy, *Diplomat Among Warriors* (New York: Doubleday, 1964), pp. 19, 68.

[36]Letter, MacFarlane to MGS, 23 March 1944, NARA, RG 331, 10000/144/157.

[37]*Ibid.*

[38]Fisher, "American Military Government in Italy," p. 116.

[39]T. V. Smith, *The Democratic Tradition in America* (New York: Farrar and Rinehart, 1941), p. 49.

[40]Smith, "Swan Song," p. 10.

[41]Post-War Programs Committee Report PWC-177, "Italian Education Under Allied Military Government," 30 May 1944, University of Virginia Library Manuscripts Department, Edward P. Stettinius Papers, Box 379.

[42]For Smith's scathing remarks, see his *A Non-Existent Man*, p. 187.

⁴³Neufeld, "The Failure of Allied Military Government," p. 144.

⁴⁴Tyack, *The One Best System*, pp. 185-186.

⁴⁵AMGOT GAI no. 1, 1 May 1943, cited in Coles and Weinberg, *Civil Affairs*, p. 186; Fainsod, "The Development of Allied Military Government Policy," in Friedrich, *American Experiences*, pp. 30, 33-34; Harris, *Allied Military Administration*, pp. 136-137.

⁴⁶Smith, "Swan Song," p. 3.

⁴⁷Coles and Weinberg, *Civil Affairs*, pp. 158, 275-279; Ellwood, *L'alleato nemico*, p. 241.

⁴⁸Gayre, *Italy in Transition*, pp. 100, 113, 118.

⁴⁹Minute of Conference Between Italian Under Secretary for Education and the Education Advisers of ACC, 25 Nov 1943, reproduced in Coles and Weinberg, *Civil Affairs*, p. 290.

⁵⁰Tomasi, *Scuola italiana dalla dittatura alla repubblica*, p. 15.

⁵¹See Cecil Sprigge, *Benedetto Croce: Man and Thinker* (New Haven: Yale University Press, 1952), pp. 50-85.

⁵²OSS, R&A Branch, "The Reform of Italian Education," p. 22, NARA, RG 407, Box 2216.

⁵³Memo, Gayre to CSO Spofford (with Spofford's handwritten response), 22 Sept 1943, NARA, RG 331, 10000/144/9.

⁵⁴*Ibid.*, see Spofford's handwritten response; Memo, Eisenhower to CQ, 7th Army, 29 Sept 1943, NARA, RG 331, 10000/144/9.

⁵⁵Tomasi, *Scuola italiana dalla dittatura alla repubblica*, p. 24.

⁵⁶Omodeo, Circular, 16 May 1944, cited in *Libertà e Storia*, p. 518. On broader political differences, see Marcello Gigante, ed., *Carteggio Croce-Omodeo* (Naples: Istituto italiano per gli studi storici, 1978), pp. 205-214, and David D. Roberts, "Benedetto Croce and the Dilemmas of Liberal Restoration," *The Review of Politics* 44, 2 (April, 1982), 235-240.

⁵⁷Roy Domenico, "Sanctions Against Fascism: The Politics of Purges in Italy, 1943-1948" (Ph.D. Dissertation, Rutgers University, 1986), p. 76.

⁵⁸Gayre, "Directive to Chiefs of ACC Regions," NARA, RG 331, 10000/144/23.

⁵⁹Monthly Report, REO, Region II, March 1944, NARA, RG 331, 10000/144/23. Gayre, *Italy in Transition*, pp. 113-114; Memos, Gayre to Vice President, Economic and Administrative Section, ACC, 9 and 18 Feb, NARA, RG 331, 10000/144/124.

⁶⁰Smith, *A Non-Existent Man*, pp. 195-196; Croce, *Scritti e discorsi politici*, pp. 220-238.

⁶¹Gayre, *Italy in Transition*, pp. 100, 176; Lamberto Mercuri, *1943-1945: Gli Alleati e l'Italia* (Naples: Edizioni scientifici italiani, 1975), p. 179.

⁶²Gayre, *Italy in Transition*, p. 225.

⁶³Smith, "Swan Song," Appendix B (Letter to Undersecretary Cuomo, February, 1944).

⁶⁴Memo, Vessolo to Ed. Sub. HQ, 8 April 1944, NARA, RG 331, 10000/144/Box 4.

⁶⁵Smith, *A Non-Existent Man*, pp. 185-187. While Smith does not date Vyshinsky's excursion, it is known that Vyshinsky and other Allied Council members toured the Mezzogiorno in mid-January to evaluate ACC performance there. *Foreign Relations of the United States*, 1944, III, pp. 1000-1012. See also Harris, *Allied Military Administration*, p. 148.

⁶⁶Memo, Vessolo to Major General Solodovnik, 17 April 1944, NARA, RG 331, 10000/144/124.

⁶⁷Smith reproduces the text of his April 19 letter in his *A Non-Existent Man*, pp. 183-184.

⁶⁸Monthly Report, REO, Region II, March 1944, NARA, RG 331, 10000/144/Box 4.

⁶⁹*Ibid.*

⁷⁰Inaugural message, 23 April 1944, reproduced in Omodeo, *Libertà e storia*, p. 517; Monthly Report, REO, Region II, April 1944, NARA, RG 331, 10000/144/Box 4.

⁷¹Smith, Memo on Conference with Minister of Public Instruction, 10 June 1944, NARA, RG 331, 10000/144/124; Domenico, "Sanctions Against Fascism," p. 71.

⁷²Aldo Garosci, "Adolfo Omodeo III. Guida morale e guida politica," *Rivista storica italiana* LXXVIII, 1 (March, 1966), 140-183; Omodeo, "Le vicende politiche del periodo napoletano," in his *Libertà e storica*, pp. 329-330; Harris, *Allied Military Administration*, pp. 151, 173.

⁷³Harris, *Allied Military Government*, p. 173.

⁷⁴Directive, MacFarlane to SCAO 5th and 8th Army, and Regional Commissioner, Regions IV and V, 24 May, 1944, NARA, RG 331, 10000/144/62.

⁷⁵Memo, Smith for Administrative Section, attached to MacFarlane Directive, 24 May 1944, NARA, RG 331, 10000/144/62.

⁷⁶Benson and Neufeld, "Allied Military Government in Italy," 124. Domenico, "Sanctions Against Fascism," pp. 109-110. See also text of Poletti's address at the Teatro Massimo in Palermo, 8 Jan 1944, CP Papers, File S-5, and the newspaper clipping "Poletti Reveals Evils of Fascist Civil Service," *Albany Kniokorbocker News*, 3 Oct 1944, CP Papers, File S-47.

⁷⁷Bertoni Jovine, *Scuola italiana dal 1870*, pp. 390-397; Daniela Colombo, "Gli insegnanti tra impegno antifascista e sindacalizzazione della categoria. Le vicende del AIDI attraverso la rivista "La Voce della Scuola 1943-1945" (Unpublished Tesi di Laurea, University of Rome, 1979-80), pp. 91-92.

⁷⁸Edgar Erskine Hume, *Report to the Army Commander. Allied Military Government Under the Fifth Army 5-15 June 1944* (Rome, 1944), p. 127, copy contained at NARA, RG 207, Box 2215.

⁷⁹Executive Memo 67 is cited in part in Coles and Weinberg, *Civil Affairs*, pp. 387-388.

[80]Washburne, "Summary of Plan," AMG Educational Division, n.d., NARA, RG 331, 10000/144/281.

[81]De Ruggiero, "Esperienze," p. 114; Monthly Report, Educational Subcommission, July 1944, pp. 12-13, NARA, RG 331, 10000/144/Box 3.

[82]Smith, *A Non-Existent Man*, p. 196; Serant, *I vinti della liberazione*, p. 255; Domenico, "Sanctions Against Fascism," p. 112.

[83]"Il ministro agli insegnanti e agli alunni," *I diritti della scuola*, XLV, 1-2 (Sept-Oct 1944), 3; De Ruggiero, interview, *Italia Libera*, 14 Oct 1944.

[84]Grindrod, *The New Italy*, p. 53.

[85]*Ibid.*, Harris, *Allied Military Administration*, pp. 207-208.

[86]Grindrod, *The New Italy*, p. 53.

[87]*Ibid.*

[88]*I diritti della scuola XLV, 1-2 (Sept-Oct 1944), 27 and XLV, 4 (Dec 1944), 46.*

[89]Serant, *I vinti della liberazione*, p. 255; Harris, *Allied Military Government*, p. 148; Bonomi's September 4 circular is cited in *I diritti della scuola* XLV, 4 (Dec 1944), viii.

[90]*I diritti della scuola*, XLV, 4 (Dec 1944), 46-47; See also Cremaschi, *Cinquant'anni di battaglie magistrali*, p. 207.

[91]*I diritti della scuola*, XLV, 6 (Feb 1945), xxvi.   On Grosssetto province and Tuscany, see Hill, *In the Wake of War*, pp. 60-112 and Monthly Report, REO, Region VIII, March 1945, NARA, RG 331, 10000/144/320.

[92]De Ruggiero, interview, *Italia Libera*, 14 October 1944.

[93]Memo, Executive Officer J. V. Vella, Ed. Sub. to Civil Affairs Section, Allied Commission, 9 Jan 1945, NARA, RG 331, 10000/144/171; *I diritti della scuola* XLV, 4 (Dec 1944), 47.

[94]Douglas Charles Day, "The Shaping of Postwar Italian Politics: Italy 1945-1948" (Unpublished Ph.D. Dissertation, University of Chicago, 1982), p. 21; Miller "Epurazione mancata," p. 8.

[95]*I diritti della scuola*, XLV, 6 (Feb 1945), 63, xxvi-xxvii.

[96]Monthly Report, REO, Naples Zone, Feb 1945, NARA, RG 331, 10000/144/279.

[97]Memo, Pratt to Lt. Col. H. H. S. Hartley, 10 Dec 1944, NARA, RG 331, 10000/144/Box 4; see also Memo, Washburne to Vice President, Civil Affairs Section, 5 Dec 1944 in same file.

[98]Day, "The Shaping of Postwar Italian Politics," p. 21.

[99]Omodeo, "Per il rinnovamento della scuola," (inaugural greeting), 23 April 1944 and circular, 13 May 1944, both cited in Omodeo, *Libertà e storia*, pp. 516-520; Tomasi, *Scuola italiana dalla dittatura alla repubblica*, p. 24.

[100]Omodeo, "Le vicende politiche del periodo napoletano," in his *Libertà e storia*, p. 327.

[101]*Ibid.*, p. 327, 520-524; De Ruggiero, "Esperienze," p. 108.

[102]Smith, "Swan Song," p. 8.

[103]Smith, *A Non-Existent Man*, p. 196.
[104]Smith, "Swan Song," p. 8.
[105]*Ibid.*, pp. 3-4.
[106]De Ruggiero, "Esperienze," pp. 108-109; for Gayre's perspective, see *Italy in Transition*, p. 135.
[107]See Ministerial Circular 3557, 8 Nov 1944, reproduced in Prot. 3575, Reggente Bubbico, Dir. Gen. Affari Generali e del Personale, 15 Nov 1944, in the Ministry of Public Instruction, Archivio Deposito (hereafter Min PI, AD), Records of the Consiglio Superiore; De Ruggiero, "Esperienze," p. 115; Collaltino Collalto et. al., *Ordinamento della pubblica istruzione* (Rome: Grismondi, 1947), p. 21.
[108]De Ruggiero, "Esperienze," pp. 126-127.
[109]Guido De Ruggiero, interview, *I diritti della scuola* XLV, 4 (Dec 1944), 41.
[110]Prot. 2482, 23 Oct 1944, Regente Bubbico, Dir. Gen. Affari Generali e del Personale, Records of the Consiglio Superiore, Min PI, AD.
[111]See Prime Minister Ivanoe Bonomi's Circulars of 16 Oct and 9 Nov, 1944, cited in Prot. 3104, 3 Nov 1944 and Prot. 3709, 24 Nov 1944, Reggente Bubbico, Dir. Gen. Affari Generali e del Personale, Records of the Consiglio Superiore, Min PI, AD.
[112]"Interessi magistrali," *I diritti della scuola*. XLV, 4 (Dec 1944), 42-43; see also Zambaldi, *Storia della scuola elementare*, pp. 370-371; Cremaschi, *Cinquant'anni di battaglie magistrali*, p. 199; Guido De Ruggiero, "Problemi della scuola. La scuola elementare," *Realtà politica*, 5 Jan 1945, 5-6.
[113]De Ruggiero, "Esperienze," pp. 117-118.
[114]*Ibid.*, 114, 117-118; Smith, "Swan Song," p. 12. On decentralization, see the lay moderate Giovanni Ferretti's unpublished piece of 1943-44 entitled "Aspetti di una riforma," reproduced in his *Scuola e democrazia* (Turin: Einaudi, 1956), pp. 46-50.
[115]De Ruggiero, "Esperienze," pp. 113-115.
[116]Smith, "Swan Song," p. 16.
[117]Roberts, "Benedetto Croce," p. 240.

CHAPTER 5

THE MATURATION OF DIDACTIC REFORM

Introduction

In December, 1944 dissension over the uses of the purge and other issues brought down the first Bonomi coalition government. During the ensuing negotiations the British vetoed the nomination of Count Sforza, an outspoken anti-monarchist, as prime minister. FDR and top American policymakers decried Great Britain's action, but were unprepared to dictate a political alternative.[1] Consequently Bonomi proceeded to organize a new coalition. The Action and Socialist parties refused to participate out of resentment over Bonomi's weakness and his inability to resist British pressure.[2] Although the Communist party remained within the cabinet, this second Bonomi government was considerably more conservative in its complexion and behavior than had been its predecessor.

At the ministry of Public Instruction, Vincenzo Arangio Ruiz replaced De Ruggiero. A professor of Roman Law at the University of Naples, Arangio Ruiz had assisted Benedetto Croce in founding the Liberal party. This Neapolitan had also served as Minister of Justice during the second Badoglio government in the spring of 1944.[3] In that post and as Minister of Public Instruction, he advocated a cautious and legalistic approach to the purge. Arangio Ruiz willingly collaborated with Allied educators in revising Italy's various national curricula and opening the door to new cultural influences. Yet Arangio Ruiz' own pedagogy and politics were highly traditional. A philosophical idealist, Arangio Ruiz' fundamental aim was to restore to Italy's schools the "noble temper" of the Risorgimento.[4]

In the meanwhile, Carleton Washburne had become head of the Education Subcommission in early October, 1944. Of the subcommission's four directors, Washburne was to leave the greatest mark on Italian schooling. De Ruggiero described him as a "born educator, motivated by a missionary zeal to improve Italy's schools."[5] Unlike Robert Gayre or T.V. Smith, he achieved a working command of the Italian language, which permitted him to establish a wide range of contacts with Italian educators. He enjoyed a close rapport with De Ruggiero and Arangio Ruiz, and continued to regard both men as friends even after they had departed from *La Minerva*.[6]

During his nineteen-month tenure as director, Washburne gradually shifted the Education Subcomission's focus from the short term rehabilitation and relief of Italian popular schooling to the longer term work of positive reconstruction. In newly liberated areas of the center and north, REOs continued to work with provincial superintendents clearing and reopening schools and purging local educational personnel. In Rome, committees of Italian educators collaborated closely with Washburne as they progressed from the cleansing of existing texts and programs of study to the preparation of definitive post-Fascist instructional materials. The new elementary curriculum was approved by the educational minister on February 9, and formally implemented with Decree Law No. 459 of May, 1945. Guidelines for new textbooks were also issued during the spring. Then on September 18, 1945, the ministry released a new curriculum for the teacher training institutes.

In Washburne's eyes, these achievements marked only the beginning of a democratic renaissance of Italian education. As he explained in a comprehensive memorandum of mid-November, 1944, the subcommission was committed to

> assisting the Italian government in its attempt to organize its schools in a way which will foster healthy living, good citizenship, decent world attitudes and economic efficiency, while preserving the best cultural traditions.

As a foundation for systematic reform, Arthur Vessolo undertook a unprecedented and comprehensive study of the Italian educational system, encompassing its pre-Fascist background, its metamorphosis under Fascism and its contemporary condition. In place of the Fascist youth organizations, Washburne championed the revival of the Boy Scout and Girl Guide Movements, as well as "democratic," non-partisan associations and clubs in secondary schools and universities. In order to break down Italy's two decades of cultural isolation, he arranged for the translation of leading international works of education and social science. He also encouraged the minister to set up "local discussion groups of teachers," which would "discuss the practical problems confronting the Italian schools" and would recommend possible solutions to the central ministry.[8]

His blueprint for reconstruction got Washburne into trouble even before he became Educational Director. While still in Naples in the spring of 1944, he drew up a detailed, three-page "Outline of Basic Inprovements Needed in the Italian Educational System" for T. V. Smith's consideration. Irritated especially by Washburne's promotion of scouting, Smith told his deputy to "forget the fads," and to concentrate on "opening and furthering the schools."[9]

More serious was a controversy which sprang up just as Washburne was assuming the helm at the subcommission. An interview appearing in the *New York Herald Tribune* attributed to him the aim of pioneering a reform of Italian education "along the lines of his previous work in the United States." The article dismayed Washburne. As he confided to his superior officer in a letter of

October 10, it seemed "to justify a fear that some people (presumably Italian Catholics and conservatives, and perhaps senior Allied civil affairs officers as well) have had as to my work and intentions in Italy." Based in his own firsthand study of education in many parts of the world, he knew very well that

> nothing is more fatal than for a foreigner to try to impose his ideas, or more futile than for a nation to try to model its social structure on that which arose in another nation of widely different history and tradition.[10]

Nonetheless, conservative Italian and Anglo-American critics of the work of the ACC, including its Education Subcommission, believed that the time had come to circumscribe its influence. The Hyde Park Declaration of late September, 1944 had promised Italy greater self-determination. Italian government leaders felt that their "democratic apprenticeship" under ACC tutelage was nearly completed. Influential American journalists such as Edgar Ansel Mowrer concurred.[11] On November 16, the Bonomi government urged the elimination of those ACC agencies, such as the Legal and Education Subcommissions, whose functions "were not immediately connected with the war effort."[12] Failing that, the Italian government requested that the Education Subcommission "cease to supervise schools and universities within Italian government territory."[13]

Washburne responded with a comprehensive defense of both the short and long-term missions of his agency. Among other points, he noted the continuing reluctance of local Italian authorities even to clear and repair local schools unless prodded by the Allies. As of October, 1944, less than one third of Rome's schools were functioning. After consulting with other top civil affairs officers, Chief Commissioner Stone decided to allow the subcommission's central office and its field specialists in Allied-controlled territory to "continue as before." But in Italian government territory, the subcommission was to cease to operate "except for specific acts performed at the request of the government."[14]

Curricular Reform

By the time Guido De Ruggiero had restored the educational ministry to its traditional seat in Trastevere in mid-July of 1944, there was little time to reform programs of study for the upcoming school year. The minister had little choice but to utilize the makeshift *programmi* which Washburne and successive teams of Sicilian and Campanian educators had patched together in 1943-1944. At the primary level he adopted without change the AMG base program of studies and the Church-approved variant of the "Advice for the Modernization of the Schools."[15] At the middle school level, however, De Ruggiero reversed several Allied rulings. Despite the unpopularity of the *scuola media unica* in certain quarters (Omodeo had termed it a "monstrosity"), the minister decided to retain it for the coming year. But he chose not to make it the truly comprehensive middle school favored by Washburne and by many leftist anti-Fascists. Instead a selective *scuola media* requiring instruction in Latin would prepare pupils for further secondary schooling. Students not continuing their studies would attend vocationally-oriented *scuole di avviamento*.[16]

As a moderate liberal, De Ruggiero resisted calls by militant anti-Fascists that he impose immediate, sweeping changes in the structure and content of popular schooling. Indeed, he was determined to avoid the pattern of repeated and confusing waves of reform which he felt had tormented Italy's schools under Fascism. There would be time enough following liberation of the entire peninsula to convene a "Constituent Assembly of the School," representing all concerned Italians, which would make definitive changes on a genuinely democratic basis.[17]

As a sober first step toward reform, De Ruggiero appointed ministerial committees to forge new primary and secondary school curricula, to go into effect in 1945-46. In elementary education a beginning had already been made at Salerno by a group of southern educators under the leadership of Adolfo Omodeo. In late July of 1944 a five-man committee headed by Raffaele Pedicini, a central inspector for Secondary Schools, took over this work. The committee president and three of its members (Augusto Lacchè, Luigi Benedetto and Giorgio Gabrielli) were ministerial functionaries. The fifth member, Vittorio Masselli, was one of the editors of the schoolteachers' journal *I diritti della scuola*.[18] Ernesto Codignola, Lombardo Radice's former comrade in arms, and a number of other prominent Italian educators contributed advice. Washburne also remained in constant contact with the group; though not a formal committee member, he exercised the greatest single influence over the new elementary curriculum. The committee completed its labors in November, when it formally submitted a draft to the subcommission for systematic review. In January, the new educational minister Arangio Ruiz made a few modifications of his own. The new curriculm was published on February 9, and officially adopted by Decree Law No. 459 of May 24, 1945.[19]

In his suggestions to Italian educators, Washburne drew both on his experimental work on individualized instruction, dating from the 1920s, and his growing concern with the socialization of the child dating from the 1930s and early 1940s. In a series of workshops, interviews and articles, Washburne sketched a basic, four-point program of pedagogical reconstruction. In the first place, Italy's new democratic schooling should satisfy the basic physical, mental and emotional needs common to all children. Just as importantly, it should discover and develop the unique characteristics, interests and attitudes of each pupil. Thirdly, the schools should offer children the practical skills and experience necessary to become productive members of society. Finally, the schools should teach each child to identify his own well-being with that of the family, the community, the state and the world.[20]

Particularly in its preface, the new elementary curriculum clearly reflected Washburne's thinking. In lieu of Fascist hero-worship and chauvinism, the syllabus promoted a lively sense of fraternity and civic responsibility. It encouraged self-expression, self-direction and even a degree of self-governance by the students. The curriculum also freed individual teachers from over-precise methodological instructions, encouraging them to tailor their lesson plans to the actual interests and capacities of their pupils and the resources offered by the local environment.[21]

However, the new syllabus' presentation of the various subject areas did not reflect this "progressive" perspective in a consistent manner. The framers of the new curriculum intended religious instruction and a new subject entitled "moral and civic education" to play particularly important roles in "refashioning the minds and spirits of the new generations within a free society." American pedagogical influence was most pronounced in the new "civics" which--interestingly enough--also incorporated a tame form of physical education. In addition, Washburne left his mark on the new program of religious instruction. The syllabus' emphasis on the Gospel rather than the catechism clearly suggested the Quaker educator's non-confessional conception of religion. Instruction in "labor," retained from Bottai's School Charter, indirectly embodied Dewey's influence. As expressed in the preface, the new curriculum aimed "to associate the forces of culture and those of work, so as to prevent culture from remaining the sterile accumulation of facts, and work merely the unconscious expression of brute force."[22]

On the other hand, the integration of history and geography promised in the preface was not realized in the detailed instructions for these two subject areas. Geography in fact consisted of a loose taxonomy of the world's surface features, while history remained the episodic celebration of great moments in the growth of civic and national sentiment. This approach to history demonstrated the unbroken spell of pedagogical idealism over a number of areas of the curriculum.[23]

Such inconsistencies may explain why the Education Subcommission reportedly accepted the ministerial draft of the *programmi* in November of 1944 "only with some difficulty."[24] Yet it is also true that Washburne never placed great stock in theoretical consistency, and regarded himself as a philosophical eclectic. Publicly, the Education Director praised the new elementary syllabus warmly. If native teachers followed it, he predicted,

Italy's schools would "soon be among the most modern, practical and advanced in the world."[25]

Washburne had good reason to question the receptivity of some local schoolteachers to Anglo-American educational initiatives. In Rieti province, the local AMG educational officer Francis Gregory reported in August of 1944 that some local teachers and administrators, "probably of left-wing sympathies," denied that any Anglo-Saxon style "education for democracy" could succeed in Italy. Two persons insisted that the Italian people's low standard of literacy dictated "some authoritarian system of government," although "without the corruption and expansionist tendencies of Fascism." In southern Perugia province Gregory encountered reservations of a different kind. A nun there "expressed fears about the religious policy which two officially Protestant countries might folow."[26]

In Rome, the small size and restricted composition of the elementary curriculum committee attracted considerable criticism. A 1944 drew to a close, the *Unione sindacale insegnanti primari* (USIP), a local primary schoolteachers' association spawned by AIDI, protested the ministry's failure to consult more extensively with rank and file teachers or with teachers' associations while drafting the new national elementary school curriculum.[27] A group of USIP teachers and didactic directors, headed by the energetic communist Dina Bertoni Jovine, proceeded to draw up an alternative syllabus. The USIP committee presented its syllabus to Arangio Ruiz in January of 1945. But by this time work was nearly completed in the official ministerial curriculum. Arangio Ruiz therefore had little incentive to give the USIP proposal serious consideration.[28]

This denoument disillusioned many local anti-Fascist educators. As an embittered Dina Bertoni Jovine subsequently put it, although Allied and Italian educational authorities did not reject the "resolutely democratic advice" ("*apporto*") of groups like USIP, they "channeled and contained it according to criteria already established by the liberators."[29]

The ministerial commission charged with the reform of secondary school curricula embraced a wider range of anti-Fascist educators representing a variety of political and pedagogical persuasions. Among its twenty members were Communists Giorgio Candeloro and Pasquale D'Abbiero, the lay moderate Giovanni Ferretti and the Catholic Quinto Tosatti. Although Washburne attended the group's inaugural session, his influence was less pronounced than that exercised over the elementary curriculum committee.[30]

In the new *programma* for the *scuola media*, which was completed in May of 1945, Gentilian and Bottaian elements coexisted uneasily with American progressive imports. The study of "labor" recalled the School Charter of 1940. The introduction of a foreign language harkened back to Gentile's 1923 Reform, as did the history curriculum's emphasis on "transcendent lessons" of the human experience. On the other hand, Washburne's imprint was unmistakable in the *programma's* admonition to instructors to adapt their approach to the psychological and sociological needs of the child. The Education Director had hoped that more of Italy's proud *professori* would emulate her best *maestri* and begin to respond to their pupils' affective as well as intellectual needs.[31]

But conditions were not yet ripe for any meaningful reduction of the the deeply rooted discontinuity between primary and secondary schooling. Giuseppe Bottai's own efforts in this direction had provoked strong opposition. To many teachers, the introduction of "labor" into the primary and middle school curricula and the growing emphasis on Fascist youth group activities had compromised the "seriousness" of the educational process. Given a choice, a great many *maestri* and *professori* preferred to reclaim respected but dissimilar older identities.

More Trouble Over Textbooks

In October 7,1944, the United Nations News Service ran an upbeat story on the resumption of classes by four to five million school children in liberated Italy. The Allies were determined to "exclude political propaganda of any kind" from Italy's schools. The story stressed that "straight, factual teaching" had displaced "Fascist elements" in new *libri dello stato*, which had been "rewritten by Italian educators."[32]

Supported by their ACC superiors, Smith and Rowell had insisted in July on retaining the AMG-modified *libro dello stato* series for the 1944-1945 school year. No privately published elementary texts were to be permitted in classrooms either in AMG-ruled provinces or in Italian-administered territory. The decision rested on several grounds. The Allies opposed any changes in textbook policy which might delay the traditional October reopening of the new school year. The previous spring and summer, with Italy's three traditional textbook publishing centers--Turin, Milan and Florence--still in enemy hands, AMG representatives had signed contracts for the revised state series with Roman, Neapolitan and Palermitan publishers. Allied authorities had dictated modest prices for the books, but had hoped that the large market for the texts would still guarantee the southern publishing firms a profit.[33] Even so, these companies gave priority to other business in drawing up their printing schedules, for fear that many school systems could not pay even modest prices. Continuing shortages of paper and other supplies posed problems as well. Educational officials had hoped that stocks requisitioned in the United States would begin reaching Naples in March; in fact, the first American paper, ink and thread did not arrive until the fall.[34]

As a result, when the new year commenced only one fourth the schoolchildren in liberated Italy used newly published revised textbooks, while a majority depended on the old, clipped-up or inked-over *libri dello stato*. The following chart illustrates the extremely slow progress of production and distribution as late as February of 1945:[35]

City	Quota	Printed	Dist'd
Rome	680,000	440,000	215,000
Naples	900,000	165,000	125,000
Palermo	205,000	61,000	0

The figures might have been even lower had not the Vatican placed a large quantity of high quality stock at the Allies' disposal following the liberation of Rome. The gift appears to have been prompted by clerical unhappiness with sections of the AMG-sponsored series then coming off the presses in Naples. In mid-July, the subcommission received a curt note from Monsignor Luigi Rubino, the Neapolitan representative of the Diocesan Catechistic Office for Religious Assistance and Instruction. Rubino alleged that the revised texts slighted religious instruction and continued to reflect Gino Ferretti's now-suppressed didactic suggestions. Upon receipt of Rubino's note, the subcommission's officer in charge of textbooks, Captain Robin Beard, recommended that the printing of all texts touching on religion be held up until the passages in question could be corrected. Beard also stated that the ACC rather than Italian publishing concerns should bear the costs of ensuing alterations.[36]

Subcommission staff members were also dissatisfied with the revised *libro dello stato*. The initial revision of the state series during the winter of 1943-44 had been a difficult collaborative effort. Forced to work under intense time pressure, neither Carleton Washburne nor the local schoolteachers whom he had recruited as writers had been happy with the result of their labors.[37] After the spring of 1944, Robin Beard had taken over from Washburne the thankless task of coordinating the printing and distribution of the elementary texts. Dismayed at the quality of the books, Beard had nevertheless worked quietly and diligently through the summer. He then prepared a strongly worded memo outlining the inadequacies of the series.

Beard found the presentation of history and geography particularly flawed. Cartographic and textual references to *Mare Nostrum* (In lieu of the "Mediterranean") had escaped earlier Allied censors. Palermitan editions of the 5th grade subsidiary reader retained a map of Germany with the "New Order" frontiers of 1940. The accompanying text explained how among other changes "the state of Czechoslovakia no longer exists and the state of Slovakia has sprung up in its place." This particular anachronism went unrecognized until the Consul General of the Czechoslovak Republic in Rome lodged a formal complaint with the Allied Commission in December, 1944. The general rule, in both elementary and secondary texts, was to delete all references to the Fascist *ventennio*. But this, too, Beard found disturbing: after years of incessant indoctrination, neither teachers nor pupils were offered any alternative explanations of the causes or nature of Mussolini's new Roman Empire, since the state *libri* concluded their historical converge with World War I. The narrative presentation of Italian history ended, as it were, "without a full stop."[38]

The following month Helen Hiett, an American living in Rome, subjected the state series to a detailed examination in a January 18 letter to the editor published in the *New York Herald Tribune*. Aesthetically, the revised works were little better than bad copies of the old. Due to war-time conditions, the new edition had been printed with inferior type on inferior paper. Furthermore, "the attractive colored illustrations of the Fascist text" were replaced by "uninteresting single color pen sketches."

More fundamental was the Allies' failure to offer Italian youth "any new clear-cut political philosophy."   In place of Mussolini's words to the young "you must go forward," and "we must make Italy great!", the new texts substituted Marcus Aurelius' exhortation "In the morning, when you awake unwillingly, think immediately: I awake to attend to my duty!"   But what was that duty?   Who or what deserved the allegiance of Italy's schoolchildren?   In the spring of 1944 T. V. Smith and his colleagues had agreed with Omodeo and other militant republicans to "dim the textbook praise of the eclipsed ruling house." But the subcommission carefully refrained from "propagandizing against the monarchy as an institution." Thus a story was left in the state series in which the king (substituting for the Duce) decorated a child whose father had fallen on the battlefield, consoling him that "to die for the fatherland is to live in glory."[39]

Anti-clerical observers on both sides of the Atlantic criticized the prominent role which the revised texts (in conformity to the 1929 Concordat) accorded to religious instruction.   How could this provision be reconciled with the Allies' insistence that they were simply providing "straight, factual teaching" in the schools?   The New York-based *Legione dell'Italia del Popolo* pointed out that "religious instruction is not the teaching of facts, but of ideas; not objective exposition but the profession of a faith." Beneath the guise of guaranteeing Italian children a politically neutral education, the Allies were in fact conspiring in their "spiritual and political subjugation" by the Church.[40]

As Minister of Public Instruction, the liberal Guido De Ruggiero took issue with the very principal of a state textbook monopoly. In his eyes, the abolition of the *libro dello stato* represented the most important single step in transcending the authoritarian spirit of Italian elementary education.   "Nothing," he wrote to Rowell, "is more repugnant than the Fascist book to the majority of teachers. However expurgated, the *libro dello stato* [retains] indelibly the vices of its origins." Philosophically, De Ruggiero strongly preferred the unregulated circulation and free selection of textbooks characteristic of the decentralized educational systems of Great Britain and the United States. It is not hard to imagine his frustration with the Anglo-Americans who insisted durring the summer of 1944 that he stick with the state series for the ensuing school year.[41]

The liberation of Florence at the end of the summer of 1944 offered the Minister of Public Instruction the pretext to relax restrictions on the use of non-state elementary texts. At the beginning of September, De Ruggiero announced that from the Tuscan capital northward the revised *libro dello stato* would not be required during the 1944-45 academic year. Florence's Le Monnier publishing house, along with several others had taken advantage of Minister Severi's shortlived ban on the *libro dello stato* between July and September, 1943 to ready its own set of elementary books for the market. Sizeable numbers of these alternative works were already in print at the time of liberation. In addition, a newly discovered Sienese warehouse contained paper stock sufficient to print private or state textbooks for all of Tuscany.[42]

De Ruggiero's announcement caught both Allied and Church authorities by surprise. Given their difficulties in securing clerical sanction even of the official AMG elementary series, Allied officials were understandably cautious about reinstituting unbridled freedom of publication. The Vatican would have preferred the exclusive use of suitably reformed *libri dello stato* in state schools. Concerned lest some of the privately published works might misrepresent the catechism, the Vatican immediately sought and obtained the subcommission's promise that the new arrangement would not be implemented until the matter of all religious texts had been settled "to the complete satisfaction of the Church."[43] Nonetheless, non-state elementary textbooks entered the Tuscan market that fall and managed to hold their own in competition with the state series.[44]

Actually such popular non-state series as Le Monnier's *Voci Serene (A Scuola Bimbi!)* were not entirely free of militarist and colonialist sentiments. But they avoided glorification of Fascism and were therefore deemed acceptable under the circumstances. De Ruggiero had no doubt that the quality of textbooks would improve greatly in years to come. For him, the important point was to take a first step toward greater freedom of choice for teachers.[45] In the spring of 1945, Arangio Ruiz and Washburne agreed that the production of elementary textbooks for the 1945-46 school year should be returned to the hands of commercial publishers. The official decree supressing the *libro dello stato* appeared at the end of August.[46] Meanwhile, a ministerial review board was established to screen commercial titles and determine their compatibility with the newly revised elementary curriculum.

This nine-member board included ministerial functionaries, two representatives of the state publishing house (the *Istituto poligrafico dello stato*), a local didactic director and a local *maestra*. The new primary school curriculum was released in February, 1945, and publicized in the *Bollettino ufficiale* in March. Yet new textbook manuscripts had to be submitted to the ministerial review board by the end of May, in order to allow sufficient time for the printing of approved texts by the fall. Authors thus had little time to rethink the pedagogical bases of their works.[47] Not suprisingly, both Italian and Allied observers expressed dissappointment at the quality of many of the new works. Nonetheless, competition among publishing houses was brisk, as textbooks traditionally represented the true "best-sellers" of the Italian book publishing industry.[48]

The restoration of a free market in textbooks overcame the chronic shortages which had plagued Italian schools since 1943. But price continued to be a serious problem. In the south black marketeers had commanded prices of 20 to 40 lire for simple copybooks; textbooks sold for considerably more. In the spring and summer of 1944, the subcommission had responded by mass producing copybooks to be sold at 1.5 to 4 lire each, and by fixing textbook prices at between 18 and 35 lire apiece. Even at these rates, it was nearly impossible for many southern agricultural workers to send their children to school: in Sardinia, for instance the prevailing agricultural wage in 1944 was 30 to 50 lire per day.[49]

In the north, the subcommission struggled to keep textbook prices from climbing much, much higher. The Allied Commission's commerce department refused to impose price controls on any paper besides newsprint: by August of 1945, the price of ordinary paper stock was five times higher than it had been in the south.[50] Large scale shipments of paper from the United States had been expected since the spring of 1945; in September, only a fraction of the anticipated tonnage had left American ports. In lieu of imported American stock, Washburne arranged for "cheap-price paper to be produced in the North with [other] imported materials". He then offered Italian publishing concerns this paper, as well as the American stock as it arrived, at one third the current black market price, on the condition that they hold down new textbook prices. As a result, no commercial textbooks for the 1945-46 school year sold for more than 100 lire and most were priced at less than 70 lire.[51]

In 1945-46 and in subsequent years, commercially produced elementary textbooks realized some features of the new primary school curriculum better than others. The commercially-produced textbooks readily adopted the elementary curriculum's emphasis on human equality and brotherhood. Stories and poems by Hans Christian Andersen, Leo Tolstoy, William Saroyan and other foreign authors found places in primers along side selections from Italian writers. The celebration of nationalism and the glorification of military sacrifice which flourished during the *ventennio* was toned down but did not disappear entirely. In particular, the Risorgimento and World War I continued to be portrayed as edifying demonstrations of Italian martial courage and achievement. Descriptions of World War II were more ambivalent: some focused on the universal human cost of the conflict, others on the intrepid behavior of the Allied troops assisted by Italian freedom fighters. Fascism itself received no mention at all in some immediate post-war texts; authors venturesome enough to touch on the *ventennio* generally judged it benignly until the attack on Ethiopia, when Mussolini began to "overreach himself," and the Pact of Steel, which "sealed" Italy's doom.[52]

If elementary history remained Italocentric in the new books, geography touched on all of the continents, with emphasis on Europe and the Americas. To enliven dry recitations of climactic features and the economic strengths and weaknesses of individual states, elementary and even secondary schools texts served up simplistic portraits of different "national characters." A 1946 primary text praised the Dutch for their "solidity, reliability, cleanliness and loyalty," while a middle school geography book from the early 1950s presumed to dissect the English personality in terms of its "Norman," "Celtic" and "Anglo-Saxon " components.[53] It is an open question whether such instruction promoted or impeded international understanding.

The new "civics" and "labor" proved more difficult to incorporate into textbooks. Elementary texts did not contain separate sections devoted to civic training. Instead, primers offered stories on social activities such as setting up a class library or forming a section of the "Young Explorers," Italy's new Anglo-American style scouting organization.[54] After the adoption of the republican constitution, a growing emphasis on the responsibitlities of citizens tended to supplant descriptions of classroom self-governance. Coverage of the United Nations and its affiliated organizations began only after Italy was admitted to that international body in 1955.

"Labor" was perhaps even less popular, at least among instructors. Particularly in 1945 and 1946, elementary texts offered numerous poems and stories extolling the "dignity of labor." Such selections frequently sentimentalized the "poor but virtuous" manual laborer in particular. Yet most teachers felt completely unprepared to initiate or to evaluate work projects within the classroom. It is not surprising that the texts themselves often suggested that "the child's work was to study," rather than depicting children engaging in constructive activities.[55]

Reform of the Teacher Training Institutes

In a letter accompanying its proposed *programmi*, the elementary curriculum committee had urged the Minister of Public Instruction to pursue a series of collateral reforms which would enhance the effectiveness of the new syllabus. The committee assigned top priority to the rehabilitation of the Italian teaching profession. Teachers who had entered the classroom "in recent years" should be required to attend special in-service training programs. Other reforms suggested by the committee included the establishment of five years of primary schooling in every commune, the closer coordination of middle school entrance examinations with the elementary curriculum and the reduction of overcrowding in classrooms (with a maximum of 40 pupils to be permitted in any one class).[56] But an impoverished Ministry of Public Instruction was not yet in a position to implement all of these proposals. The earliest and most tangible changes came to the *istituti magistriali*.

The initial steps at revising teacher training in Allied-liberated territory had been taken in Naples during the first four months of 1944. The Allied subcommission developed a preliminary reform proposal and submitted it to a four-member committee of local educators, headed by Guido della Valle, Professor of Pedagogy at the University of Naples. Washburne and his colleagues envisioned philosophy, pedagogy and psychology as forming the professional core of the *istituto magistrale* curriculum. In these fields an "overly academic, theoretical and historical" approach was to give way to a pragmatic concern for concrete educational problems. During their first two years, *istituto magistrale* students would also "observe the best possible teaching in actual elementary schools;" during their third and fourth years, observation would give way to practice teaching.[57]

Chastened by his earlier experiences in Sicily, Washburne assured Della Valle that these proposals "should not be considered a mandate," but only "very tentative suggestions" designed to "stimulate the thinking" of his committee. Della Valle's group endorsed the subcommission's proposals with minor revisions. But they insisted that the revised program remain optional. Della Valle pointed out that many *istituto magistrale* teachers had neither the time, preparation or the energy to overhaul their lesson plans, particularly while wartime hardships prevailed.[58]

Further progress in the reform of the *istituto magistrale* curriculum awaited completion of the definitive elementary school *programmi* in the spring of 1945. A new teacher training curriculum was finally prepared between April and September by a ministerial commission of university professors, central inspectors and secondary and primary schoolteachers. The commission embraced a variety of ideological perspectives. Gesualdo Nosengo, a prominent

Catholic pedagogue, represented the Italian secondary schoolteachers' syndicate (the *Sindacato nazionale insegnanti medie*), while Dina Bertoni Jovine, the communist didactic director, represented the elementary schoolteachers' union (the *Sindacato nazionale scuole elementari*). Carleton Washburne supervised the work of the commission: in its final form, the teacher training curriculum reflected not only a range of Italian viewpoints, but a number of Washburne's recommendations as well.[59]

The reformed *istituto magistrale* was to become "professional" without ceasing to be "humanistic." In its preface the new curriculum continued to suggest that aspiring *maestri* would naturally acquire the "art of teaching" (*l'arte magistrale*) as they absorbed and reflected upon the classics of literary and scientific culture. But the program also called for the explicit discussion of the didactic problems and challenges of each elementary subject, particularly during the fourth and final year of the *istituto magistrale*. The addition of psychology to the core program in philosophy and pedagogy emphasized the new commitment to professionalization, as did the provision for two years of "didactic exercises" (*esercitazioni didattiche*).[60]

The philosophy and pedagogy component of the curriculum offered instructors a choice between a traditional historically-organized approach and a new, problem-oriented program based on the Education Subcommission's proposals of 1944. Regardless of the program which they followed, however, students were required to master a demanding range of philosophical and pedagogical classics, ranging from St. Augustine's *Confessions* and his *De Magistro* to Kant's *Critique of Pure Reason* (extracts) and his *Pedagogy*. This requirement undoubtedly encouraged a great many instructors to retain the more traditional approach to these key subjects. Though Giovanni Gentile's name was omitted from the list of required authors, the Gentilian equation of pedagogy with general philosophy remained very strong.[61]

On the other hand, the linkage of pedagogy and psychology proved ephemeral. True, with the introduction of psychology in the new curriculum, Italy ceased to be the one European nation which deliberately neglected that subject in its teacher training programs. But the *istituto magistrale* curriculum allotted psychology but a single hour per week in the middle two years of the program. Allied educators expressed disappointment at this "curious half-measure." Not until 1952 was the new subject even incorporated into the certification examination (*esame di abilitazione*) which aspiring teachers took following the completion of their course work.[62]

Professors of philosophy and pedagogy were assigned to teach psychology as well. Given their own lack of formal psychological training, these *professori* were ill-equipped to interpret the curriculum's coverage of recent international discoveries in developmental psychology. The scientific study of psychology would only make an effective contribution to teacher training when it had established a firm position within the Italian university system. This only happened during the 1960s.[63]

The reintroduction of the *esercitazioni didattiche* was also less effective than the new curriculum's authors had hoped. According to one contemporary source, the new requirement was greeted with scant enthusiasm by instructors and *istituto magistrale* students alike. The student teacher's pedagogy professor and the regular elementary classroom teacher were both expected to provide the young teacher some measure of supervision and direction, yet neither was granted extra pay or other compensation for these added responsibilities. In many cases, "student teachers" never exercised effective teaching responsibility in the classroom, remaining instead marginal "teachers' helpers."[64]

Latin occupied a slightly less conspicuous place in the new syllabus than it had in Gentile's 1923 curriculum. At the instigation of Washburne and De Ruggiero, among others, the number of hours allotted to that tongue was trimmed in order to permit two years of instruction in a modern foreign language. Still, some Latin continued to be studied in all four years of the *istituto*. In fact, the new syllabus required that students devote as much time to the study of the *lingua madre* as to the study of philosophy, pedagogy and psychology combined.

What accounted for Latin's impressive staying power? Despite its perversion at the hands of the "empire builder," Mussolini, the Roman legacy retained tremendous symbolic value to many Italians. In an interview published in the schoolteachers' journal *I diritti della scuola* in December of 1944, De Ruggiero had gone so far as to suggest that Latin be dropped completely from the new *istituto magistrale* curriculum, on the grounds that it was of little utility to elementary schoolteachers, and was poorly taught in the *istituti magistrali*. De Ruggiero's proposal elicited vigorous protests from schoolteachers who feared a loss of social status in the towns and villages of the peninsula. Heretofore, they argued, an exposure to Latin had demonstrated the "seriousness" of the schoolteacher's cultural preparation. It enabled him to hold his head high in the company of the local doctor or priest. But ignorance of the *lingua madre* would humiliate and embarrass him: how would he answer "if a pupil were to ask him the meaning of a sacred epigraph, or a verse of Virgil?"[65]

This glorification of Roman culture and the Roman tongue extended far beyond the *classe magistrale*. In the winter of 1944–45, Roman city officials restored the Pyramid of Cestus and portions of the city's ancient walls before even beginning to overhaul damaged school buildings--much to the dismay of the Regional Education Officer.[66] Outside of the anti-Fascist left, the great majority of educators and middle class Italians insisted that

Latin retain a central place in both the *scuola media* and the *istituto magistrale*.

A program of religious instruction "as established by ecclesiastical authorities" retained a modest place (one to two hours per week) in the new curriculum, in accordance with the terms of the 1929 Concordat. In addition, Catholic perspectives expanded their place within the philosophy/pedagogy program. The "Pedagogy of the Gospel" was incorporated into the historical variant of that program, while the problem-oriented option now included "the educational role of Family, State and Church"--phraseology strikingly reminiscent of Pope Pius XI's encyclical *Divini ilius magistri.*[67]

Despite the efforts of Anglo-American and Italian reformers to reorient and professionalize the *istituto magistrale*, it remained little more than a second class version of the *liceo classico* or *liceo scientifico*. Attempts to expand its curriculm from four to five years (as was done for the *liceo scientifico* in 1945) proved unsuccessful, despite widespread recognition that four years was too short a span for the syllabus' demanding range of technical and humanistic subjects. In fact, the institution's four-year curriculum, with its smorgasboard of general culture, attracted middle and lower middle class parents who wanted an inexpensive but respectable secondary education, particularly for their daughters. As a rule, the male minority enrolled in the *istituti magistrali* attended that institution only because it had failed to gain entry into the more prestigious *licei*. Ultimately, this wider configuration of societal expectations prevented Washburne, De Ruggiero and others from realizing their vision of a streamlined institution dedicated solely to the training of future elementary school teachers.[68]

Conclusion

During the 1944-45 school year, the Education Subcommission and the Ministry of Public Instruction labored on three phases of pedagogical reconstruction: textbook revision, curricular change and the reform of teacher training. Henry Rowell's decision in September, 1944 to retain the expurgated, purely "factual" variant of the old *libro dello stato* for the coming school year demonstrated an undiminished confidence in a scrupulously "apolitical" approach to educational reconstruction. In Rowell's eyes, the state series possessed the additional merit of having finally garnered Vatican approval. Rowell's successor Carleton Washburne regarded the *libro dello stato* more critically, considering it a wartime expedient to be set aside as soon as liberated publishing houses and paper stocks permitted.

The Winnetka pedagogue focused his own energies on the reform of the nation's elementary, middle school and teacher training

institute curricula. Washburne exercised great influence upon each
of the ministerial committees of Italian educators charged with
each of these tasks. His contributions reflected his deepseated
belief in the liberating potential of modern psychology. The new
elementary curriculum's emphasis on social awareness and civic
responsibility mirrored the new American confidence in the
meliorative application of social psychology.[69] At Washburne's
insistence, the primary and *scuola' media* curricula also urged
teachers to develop a systematic instructional methodology, by
applying and adapting the scientific principles of child psychology
to the particular needs of their students. Toward the same end,
he introduced the study of psychology and practice teaching into
the new *istituto magistrale* curriculum of 1945.

Of the three, the new primary school *programma* was clearly the
most innovative. It met with varying responses within the *classe
magistrale*. Particularly in the north, many schoolteachers were
determined to break cleanly with Italy's past, and welcomed the
1945 curriculm as a breath of fresh air. A number of
schoolteachers from Tuscany and Lombardy have testified that the
new *programmi* were "well-received" by their colleagues.[70] The
testimony of teachers from further south yields a wider range of
responses. Martellotta Martino, a veteran Neapolitan instructor,
recalls that the new *programmi* were greeted with "considerable
enthusiasm," particularly by younger *maestri*. Yet according to
Mario de Guzzis, another Neapolitan, the Allied-influenced reform
was merely "tolerated." It is likely that many of the more
reticent *maestri* remained, like De Guzzis, committed to the
idealistic (and in their view, clearly non-Fascist) pedagogy of
Lombardo Radice.[71] For supporters and skeptics alike, the full
significance of the "new progressivism" only became evident several
years after the war's end as the *classe magistrale* freed itself
from the immediate concerns of physical reconstruction, and as the
writings of American, French and other foreign educational
innovators were translated and published in Italy.[72]

ENDNOTES

[1]Kogan, *Italy and the Allies*, pp. 96-98; Gabriel Kolko, *The
Politics of War* (New York: Randon House, 1968), p. 63.
[2]Kogan, *A Political History of Post-War Italy*, p. 8.
[3]Gayre, *Italy in Transition*, p. 191.
[4]Aldo Agazzi, *Panorama della pedagogia d'oggi* (Brescia: La
Scuola, 1950), p. 183; Harris, *Allied Military Administration*, pp.
137, 149. See also the obituary of Arangio Ruiz in the Neapolitan
newspaper *Il Giornale*, 20 Jan., 1953.
[5]De Ruggiero, "Esperienze," in Spadolini, *L'Italia dei laici*,
p. 111.
[6]Washburne, "La riorganizzazione dell'istruzione in Italia,"

273-275.   See also Vittorio Masselli's flattering portrait of the Education Director in *I diritti della scuola*, XLV, 7 (March, 1945), 66.

[7]"Summary of Functions of the Education Subcommission," 17 Nov 1944, NARA, RG 331, 10000/14/106.   See also Ellwood's comments in *l'alleato nemico*, pp. 261-262.

[8]*Ibid.*

[9]"Outline of Basic Improvements Needed in the Italian Educational System," n.d., NARA, RG 331, 10000/144/62; Smith, *A Non-Existent Man*, p. 191.

[10]Letter, Washburne to VP, CA Section, ACC, 10 Oct 1944, NARA, RG 331, 10000/144/107.

[11]Newspaper clipping, E. A. Mowrer, "Return to Diplomatic Sanity," *New York Post*, 31 Oct 1944, CP Papers, File S47.

[12]Harris, *Allied Military Administration*, p. 233.

[13]Memo, Washburne to VP, CA Section, 18 Nov 1944, NARA, RG 331, 10000/144/107.

[14]"Summary of Functions of the Education Subcommission," 17 Nov 1944, NARA, RG 331, 10000/144/106; Memo, Washburne to VP, CA Section, 31 Oct 1944, NARA, RG 331, 10000/144/277; Handwritten comment at bottom of memo, Washburne to VP, CA Section, 18 Oct 1944, NARA, RG 331, 10000/144/107.   Stone's decision was implemented in January, 1945, in response to Mss FAN-487, CCS to AFHQ, 30 Jan 1945, NARA, RG 331, 10000/105/470.

[15]"Programmi di studio e indicazioni didattiche per le scuole elementari. Anno scolastico 1944-45," *I diritti della scuola*, XLV, 1-2 (Sept-Oct, 1944), 11.

[16]*Ibid.*, 5-6; Memo, Washburne to Minister of Public Instruction, 31 July 1944 and "Appunto: Programmi di studio per l'anno scolastico 1944-1945," De Ruggiero to Washburne, 6 Sept 1944, both in NARA, RG 331, 10000/144/494.

[17]De Ruggiero, "Esperienze," in Spadolini, *L'Italia dei laici*, pp. 111-112; Bertoni Jovine, *Scuola italiana dal 1870*, pp. 400-401.

[18]Dante Grossi, *Giorgio Gabrielli e il metodo globale naturale* (Rome: Selenia, 1979), p. 159n, 160.

[19]Tomasi, *Scuola italiana dalla dittatura alla repubblica*, p. 217.

[20]Orlando, *Carleton Washburne*, p. 74; Carleton Washburne, "La libertà attraverso la padronanza di se," in Remo Fornaca, ed., *La liberta nell'educazione* (Turin: Paravia, 1975), pp. 83-87; Bertoni Jovine, *Scuola italiana dal 1870*, pp. 399, 403-404; v.m., "Il Prof. Washburne," *I diritti della scuola*, XLV, 7 (March, 1945), 66.

[21]Vessolo, "Italy: Education," pp. 585-586.

[22]Fornaca, *Problemi della scuola italiana*, pp. 69-71; Tomasi, *Massoneria e scuola dall'unità ai nostri giorni*, p. 173.

[23]Tomasi, *Scuola italiana dall dittatura alla repubblica*, p. 218.

[24]Giorgio Gabrielli, "Se e perchè e necessaria una riforma dei programmi," *Scuola di base*, I,4 (October-December 1954), 10.

[25]Washburne, *A Living Philosophy of Education*, pp. xv-xvi; Tomasi, *Scuola italiana dalla dittatura alla repubblica*, p. 217n.

[26]Memos, Gregory to REO, Region IV, 28 Aug 1944 and 11 Sept 1944, in NARA, RG 331, 10000/144/279 and 281.

[27]The Catholic journal *Scuola italiana moderna* later echoed this charge. "Scuola e programmi," *Scuola italiana moderna*, LV,1 (Oct 1945), 1.

[28]*I diritti della scuola*, XLV, 5 (Jan 1945), 55.

[29]Bertoni Jovine, *Scuola italiana dal 1870*, p. 398. The author was unsuccessful in his efforts to locate a copy of the USIP curriculum during his stay in Rome in 1981-82.

[30]De Ruggiero, "Esperienze," in Spadolini, *L'Italia dei laici*, p. 120; Fornaca, *Problemi della scuola italiana*, pp. 72-74; Letter, De Ruggiero to Washburne, Oct 1944, NARA, RG 331, 10000/144/497.

[31]Giovanni Gozzer, "Cenni storici sull'evoluzione dei programmi scolastici della scuola primaria e secondaria di primo grado" in Giovanni Gozzer et. al., *Programmi della scuola media. Strutture e valutazioni* (Rome: Armando, 1981), pp. 41-42.

[32]Press Release, United Nations News Service, 7 Oct 1944, NARA, RG 331, 10000/144/607.

[33]Letter, ACC Education Subcommission to RCAO, Region III (Attn.: Chief, Education Division), 5 Feb 1944, cited in Robert Hearst, "The Evolution of Allied Military Government Policy in Italy" (unpublished Ph.D. Dissertation, Columbia University, 1959), pp. 254-255.

[34]Washburne, "Education under Allied Military Government," pp. 266-267; Monthly Report, Education Subcommission, July 1944, NARA, RG 331, 10000/144/165.

[35]Helen Hiett, Letter to the Editor, *New York Herald Tribune*, 27 Jan. 1945, NARA, RG 331, 10000/144/607; Memo, Beard to Education Subcommission, AC, 7 Dec 1944 and Concluding Report, Beard to Education Advisor, AC, 5 Feb 1945, both in NARA, RG 331, 10000/144/429.

[36]Letter, Monsignor Rubino to Education Subcommission, ACC, 10 July 1944 and Memo, Beard to Education Subcommission Advisor, 12 July 1944, both in NARA, RG 331, 10000/144/158.

[37]Washburne, "Education under Allied Military Government," 266-267.

[38]Memo "On the Minister's letter," Beard to Education Subcommission Director, 15 Sept 1944 and "Appendix B," p. 2, n.d., both in NARA, RG 331, 10000/144/429; Complaint (document number 704/44), Consul General, Czechoslovak Republic to Political Section, AC, Rome, 18 Dec 1944, NARA, RG 331, 10000/144/429.

[39]Hiett, Letter to the Editor, New York Herald Tribune, Jan 18, 1945, NARA, RG 331, 10000/144/607; Smith, "Swan Song," pp. 11-12.

[40]*Ibid.*; Press release, "La riapertura delle scuole in Italia," *L'Italia Libera*, Nov 1 1944, NARA, RG 331, 10000/144/607.

[41]Letter, De Ruggiero to Rowell, 17 Sept 1944, as cited in Report, Beard to Education Advisor, 5 Feb 1945, NARA, RG 331,

10000/144/429; De Ruggiero, "Esperienze," 19.

⁴²De Ruggiero, "Esperienze," 19; Monthly Report, Education Subcommission, July, 1944, NARA, RG 331, 10000/144/165; Memo "Elementary Textbooks in Florence," Beard to Education Advisor, n.d. (Oct 1944), NARA, RG 331, 10000/144/429.

⁴³Letter, Rowell to Cardinal Giuseppe Pizzardo, 23 Sept 1944, NARA, RG 331, 10000/144/157.

⁴⁴Report, Beard to Education Advisor, AC, 5 Feb 1945, NARA, RG 331, 10000/144/429.

⁴⁵De Ruggiero, "Esperienze," 19.

⁴⁶Canestri, *La scuola in Italia*, p. 216.

⁴⁷La voce repubblicana, May 8, 1945, as cited in *I diritti della scuola*, XLV, 10 (June, 1945), 93-94.

⁴⁸Monthly Report, Education Subcommission, August 1945, NARA, RG 331, 1000/144/173; Vittorio Masselli, *La scuola di tutti* (Sesto San Giovanni: Bietti, 1965), p. 248.

⁴⁹Vessolo, "Italy: Education," 585; Monthly Report, REO, Region III, March 1944, and Memo, G. T. F. Wagstaff, REO, Sardinia to Education Subcommission HQ, 17 July, 1944, NARA, RG 331, 10000/144/279 and 271.

⁵⁰Memo, Vessolo to Education Subcommission, 28 July 1945 and Letter, Presidente Associazione Editoriale Libreria Italiana to AMG, Lombardy, 6 Aug 1945, both in NARA, RG 331, 10000/144/364.

⁵¹*I diritti della scuola*, XLV, 8 (April, 1945), 77 and XLV, 9 (May 1945), xlii; Monthly Report, REO, Lombardy, September, 1945, NARA, RG 331, 10000/144/366; Closing Report, Education Subcommission, 26 April 1946, p. 18, R. T. Alexander Papers (Collection No. 9796), Box 13, University of Virginia Manuscripts Department.

⁵²A cross-section of elementary texts consulted by the author from the immediate post-war period appears in the bibliography. The portrayal of Fascism cited is from Angelo Colombo, "Dalla scoperta dell'America ai giorni nostri," pp. 70-100 in *La buona raccolta. Testo unico per la scuola elementare. Classe quarta.* (Milan: Signorelli, 1947).

⁵³Alberto Albertoni, *Voci serene (A scuola bimbi!). Testo sussidiario unico per la classe quinta* (Florence: Le Monnier, 1946). pp. 205-207; Piero and Dino Gribaudi, *L'uomo e il suo regno. Testo di geografia e letture geografiche per la scuola media. Vol. III, L'Europa.* (Turin: SEI, 1951), pp. 216-217.

⁵⁴Francesco Jovine, *Sole sul cammino (terza classe)* (Milan: Mondadori, 1946), pp. 27-30, 65-87.

⁵⁵Dina Bertoni Jovine, *Sole sul cammino (prima classe)*, p. 75; Albertoni, *Voci serene (a scuola bimbi)*, p. 152.

⁵⁶Fornaca, *Problemi della scuola italiana*, pp. 69-70.

⁵⁷ "Suggestions for Professional Education of Teachers," n.d. NARA, RG 331, 10000/144/491.

⁵⁸Letter, Washburne to Guido Della Valle, 3 Feb 1944, and

"Programma per la Scuola Magistrale," n.d., both in NARA, RG 331, 10000/144/492.

[59]Claudio Varese, "Appunti sui programmi dell'Istituto Magistrale," *Società* (April-June, 1946), 407 n.; *I diritti della scuola*, XLV, 10 (June, 1945), 95.

[60]Italy. Ministero della Pubblica Istruzione. *Programmi e orari d'insegnamento per gli istituti magistrali* (Rome, Libreria dello Stato, 1945), pp. 2-7.

[61]Tomasi, *Scuola italiana dalla dittatura alla repubblica*, p. 80n; Fornaca, *Problemi della scuola italiana*, pp. 75-76; F. M. Sciacca, A. Ciribini-Spruzzola, and G. Castiglioni, *Commento ai programmi di filosofia-pedagogia-psicologia* (Milan: Marzorati, 1947), p. 114.

[62]Allied Commission. Education Subcommission. *La politica e la legislazione scolastica*, pp. 391-394; Luciano Zanobini, ed., *Raccolto delle circolari sulla pubblica istruzione*, Vol. 2, 2nd ed. (Milan: Giuffre, 1966), pp. 1935-1936.

[63]Sciacca, *Commento ai programmi di filosofia-pedagogia-psicologia*, p. 117; Interview with Rafaele Laporta, 4 Feb 1982; Steven F. White, "The Politics of Psychology in Post-Fascist Italy," Paper delivered to American Historical Association Annual Meeting, December 29, 1990.

[64]Zanobini, *Raccolta delle circolari sulla pubblica istruzione*, p. 1931; Ernestina Brenna, *Il primo passo sulla via del magistero* (Bergamo: Istituto italiano d'arti grafiche, 1947), p. 1; Mariano Maresca, "Il tirocinio," *I diritti della scuola*, XLVI, 14 (April 30, 1946), 167.

[65]"La Riforma degli studi magistrali," *I diritti della scuola*, XLV, 4 (December, 1944), 41 and 6 (February, 1945), 58.

[66]Monthly Report, REO, Lazio-Umbria Region, Jan 1945, NARA, RG 331, 10000/144/279.

[67]Fornaca, *Problemi della scuola italiana*, pp. 75-76; Gesualdo Nosengo, "Per una scuola secondo la pedagogia di Gesù," *Il Maestro*, single issue published in 1945 by the *sezione maestri* of Catholic Action and shown to the author by Dr. Maria Badaloni.

[68]De Ruggiero, "Appunto: Programmi di studio per l'anno scolastico 1944-45" 6 Sept 1944, NARA, RG 331, 10000/144/494; Varese, "Appunti sui programmi dell'Istituto Magistrale," pp. 412-413; see also Adele Bianchi, "il decadimento dell'Istituto Magistrale," *La scuola e l'uomo*, III, 6 (June, 1947), 4.

[69]A free post-war United States Information Service American history textbook prepared for Italian secondary school students compared the long-term promise of the "new American science" of psychology with that of atomic energy. By "applying experimental psychology to the dynamics of social groups, psychology offered the promise that, in time, all social problems could be studied" and, by implication, prevented. United States Information Service and Missione Americana per l'European Reconstruction Program in Italia:

Ufficio Informazioni, *Breve storia degli Stati Uniti* (Rome: Missione Americana per l'ERP, 1951), p. 221.

[70]Questionnaire responses, Arminda Carla Capelli (4/1/82), Liliana Salvadori (4/15/82), Alfredo Meneghetti (6/1/82), Franco Peroni (6/3/82), Gastone Tassinari (7/27/82).

[71]Questionnaire responses, Maria Elizabette Zucco (11/19/81), Lara Lei (3/7/82), Giuseppe Acone (4/16/82), Mario de Guzzis(4/27/82), Martino Martellotta ($/30/82).

[72]Interview, Giovacchino Petracchi (12/18/81); Questionnaire response, Gastone Tassinari (7/27/82).

CHAPTER 6

FROM HOT WAR TO COLD:

THE LIBERATION OF THE NORTH

Introduction

On April 9, 1945, the Anglo-American armies opened their final offensive to liberate Italian territory north of the Appenines. By April 21, Bologna had fallen; ten days later, Allied troops reached the foothills of the Alps. The German armies in Italy surrendered on May 2--some 20 months after the Allies had first landed on the peninsula's heel.

During the preceding fall, winter and early spring, the subcommission had operated at maximum strength and "peak efficiency." The Education Director had been able to assign three or four Regional Educational Officers to each region. Thanks to the Allies' slow northward progress, Washburne's jurisdiction expanded at a slow pace. In the spring of 1945, however, the subcommission suddenly confronted a large expanse of newly liberated territory. In the north, Regional Educational Officers, sometimes assisted by a single deputy, had to organize several provinces simultaneously.[1]

The Education Subcommission also faced a new range of challenges in the newly liberated northern regions. Local Committees of National Liberation had seized the initiative in freeing Milan, Turin, Genoa and other cities ahead of the advancing Allied armies. The radical "Wind from the North" which would bring the Milanese Action Party hero Ferruccio Parri to the prime ministership in June now swept through the educational institutions of the Po Valley. Well-organized and determined partisan educational organizations launched thorough purges of school personnel. In Piedmont, a regional "CLN of the School" also initiated a comprehensive program of administrative decentralization designed to remove primary and secondary schooling from the supervision of the national government. In the Val D'Aosta, Trento and Bolzano provinces and in Venezia Giulia, French, German, Slovene and Croat communities agitated for greater autonomy and for elementary schooling in their native tongues. Each of these grass roots movements called into question the short term jurisdiction of AMG and the long term authority of the central Italian educational bureaucracy.[2]

Little of this ferment penetrated the corridors of the Ministry of Public Instruction. Vincenzo Arangio Ruiz, educational minister during the second Bonomi government (December 1944 to June 1945), stayed on under Parri (June 1945 to December 1945). However the fall of the Parri government in December, 1945

brought Arangio Ruiz' ministry to an end. The Labor Democrat
Enrico Mole took his place in the first De Gasperi cabinet. A
journalist, Mole had launched his career in the pages of Filippo
Turati's journal *Critica Sociale*. By the 1940's his political
views had shifted to the right. After liberation he joined Ivanoe
Bonomi's moderate Democracy of Labor party, which shared the
general cultural and political outlook of the Liberals. But
compared to his Liberal predecessor, Mole demonstrated little
interest in the Education Subcommission or its director. Indeed,
Washburne found it "almost impossible to get appointments" with the
new minister. When the two men did meet, Mole made it "abundantly
clear" to Washburne that he did "not intend to do anything in
regard to educational reconstruction, new plans or policies." He
considered himself merely a "bird of passage" and did not think
anything new could or should be undertaken before the June 1946
general elections. His colorless seven month hitch as educational
minister was marked chiefly by the central Roman bureaucracy's
complete reconsolidation of control over Italian schooling.[3]

Meanwhile the Education Subcommission's field staff began to
disperse within two months of the final defeat of German and
Fascist republican forces on the peninsula. At the beginning of
the summer, Dexter Tilroe and Joseph Murphy were called across the
Dolomites to begin educational reconstruction in Austria. George
Geyer went to newly-occupied Germany. Two of Washburne's most able
REOs, Arthur Vessolo and Willis Pratt, contracted serious illnesses
which forced their early departure from the Italian theater. By
August, most northern REOs had launched the physical restoration
of schools and turned over their preliminary vetting findings to
Italian provincial review boards. The Educational Subcommission
proceeded to relinquish control over northern Italy in stages. In
September and early October, Liguria, Piedmont and then Lombardy
reverted to Italian ministerial supervision, and Allied field
specialists withdrew. By the end of December, all of Italy save
Venezia Giulia and the adjacent province of Udine had been returned
to Italian jurisdiction.[4]

The demobilization of all Allied forces would have proceeded
more quickly had it not been for doubts as to the peaceful
intentions of left-wing former Italian partisans and of the
Yugoslavs in Venezia Giulia. As it was, Italians of various
political persuasions grew restive at the peacetime persistence of
AMG and the Allied Commission itself.[5]

In the fall of 1945, the Allied Commission leadership proposed
the immediate discontinuation of the subcommission. Washburne
reacted vigorously. As he wrote to his immediate superior in early
October, 1945,

> those higher authorities which oppose the continuation of the
> Educational Subcommission. . . apparently are thinking of
> its emergency functions, and are not considering the basic

work of helping the Italians to establish a democratic, practical and modern system of education.[6]

The Education Director granted that AMG's initial mission had not envisioned the substitution of a positive program for the eliminated Fascist aspects of Italian schooling. But he maintained that under Roosevelt's "New Deal for Italy" (the Hyde Park Declaration), the subcommission had in fact been "instructed to foster cultural rehabilitation instead of being in danger of military criticism for doing so."[7]   In his two years in Italy, Washburne claimed to have met "only two or three" natives who "had any concept of what has been going on in education in Britain and America."   Even they "lacked the knowledge or ability to bring about the educational reconstruction toward which the   Italian government is groping."   The Educational Director concluded his appeal by noting that both "past and present Ministers of Public Instruction have expressed a strong desire to have me remain and help."[8]

The Allied Commission leadership acquiesced, and Washburne stayed until the spring of 1946, chiefly to advise the educational ministry in implementing the new elementary and *instituto magistrale* curricula.   Confonted by the indifferent Mole and an unsupportive Allied Commission leadership, however, he despaired of contributing further to the larger reconstruction of Italian schooling.   Finally on April 26, he closed up the subcommission's headquarters on the Via Veneto and left for the United States.

But he did not stay away long.   Once it was clear that the Education Subcommission's mandate would soon be terminated, Arangio Ruiz had intervened with the American ambassador and urged him to find a new post for Washburne.   In September, the American educator returned to the peninsula as the new director of the United States Information Service's northern Italian office.[9]

The Last Round of the Purge

Allied vetting policy over the course of the two-year campaign reflected the principle of "striking hard at the big shots and letting the small fry go."   Overall, the Anglo-Americans found it necessary to remove some 90% of Italy's incumbent *provveditori* and university rectors.   Vetting rates for school inspectors ranged as high as 40% in some provinces.   The average dipped to 25% for elementary and secondary heads.   Ordinary professors and teachers fared better: only ten percent or lower of permanent university lecturers had to be replaced, while, on the average, a mere four percent of classroom instructors lost their posts for political reasons.[10]

Still, Italian educators suffered more severely than the average civil servant.   By March of 1945, Allied officials had investigated some 38,000 school employees and dismissed 1,889 (approximately five percent), mostly in "the higher administrative brackets."[21] Out of 165,254 state and non-state employees investigated as of April 1, 2,330 (1.4 percent) were dismissed and 4,831 (three percent) received lesser punishments.[12]

Subcommssion field officers anticipated that preliminary purge rates would be higher in the Po Valley than they had been further south. The lengthly struggle between partisans and Fascist republicans had forced sizeable numbers of teachers to get off the fence. In determining the political temper of local school personnel, Anglo-American REOs availed themselves of the vetting initiatives already undertaken by local and regional anti-Fascist organizations. For the most part, REOs confirmed the partisans' suspensions and appointments of *provveditori* and lesser officials. In some cases, however, CLN appointees had to be removed on the grounds that they lacked "professional qualifications," or that they had been put in office simply for "political reasons." In Piedmont, for example, REO Sam Noe concluded that local anti-Fascists' "speedy" and sometimes "categorical" suspensions had produced considerable injustice. In Turin, he agreed to reinstate 68 of 109 previously vetted didactic directors, *presidi* and inspectors. Still, Wasburne felt that, on the whole, the northern CLNs proved "far more an asset than liability" to the subcommission in the preliminary work of purification.[13]

The Allies expected to find the largest percentage of "relics of Fascism" in Lombardy--the seedbed of Mussolini's movement and a stronghold of the late Italian Social Republic. For this reason, the region deserves detailed discussion. Unlike his Piedmontese equivalent, the REO for Lombardy, Arthur Vessolo, established a harmonious rapport with local anti-Fascist educators. In his final report from the region, Vessolo affirmed that contact between AMG and the regional CLN had "been closer and more fruitful in the field of education than in any other."[14]

In Milan, a regional "Committee of Liberation of the School," had emerged clandestinely in 1944. Like the Rome-based AIDI, the Milanese CLN of the School contested the Republic of Salò's efforts to impose oaths of allegiance on schoolteachers, and challenged other Fascist initiatives at every level of the school system. On April 28, 1945 representatives of this group occupied the offices of Milan's *provveditore*, and replaced the incumbent with one of their number: Antonio Basso, of the *Istituto magistrale Virgilio*. Basso immediately launched a stiff purge. All local secondary school *presidi* were removed from office pending investigation by teachers' councils. At the elementary level, some 30 didactic directors were dismissed. Events followed a similiar course elsewhere in Lombardy. By May 1, all nine of the region's *provveditori* were supplanted by committed anti-Fascists--usually secondary school *professori*.[15]

Both Vessolo and Lombardy's regional commissioner, Charles

Poletti, sympathized with local anti-Fascists' desire to settle scores with backers of the Republic of Salò. The REO thus chose to retain the partisans' *provveditori* and other top appointees despite their "inexperience" and occasional "inconsistency."[16]

The purge of the Catholic Sacred Heart University of Milan presented the Education Subcommission with a particularly delicate challenge. The founder and incumbent rector of that institution, the psychologist Father Agostino Gemelli, had made a number of widely publicized statements prior to the war aimed at rallying Italy's Catholic faithful to the Fascist regime. In 1937 he praised Fascism as Catholicism's partner in the international crusade against Communism. Specifically, he then claimed, Fascism and Catholicism shared the lofty principles of "hierarchy, order, discipline and sacrifice."[17]

Despite ample evidence of his pro-Fascist sympathies, Gemelli's influential connections within the Vatican prevented Vessolo from suspending him according to the usual criteria and procedures. The Lombard REO hoped that Gemelli could be persuaded to "voluntarily retire" as rector of the Catholic University. Instead, Vessolo was compelled to place all vetting at Catholic University in the hands of a special vetting committee, to be appointed by him from a list drawn up by the Vatican. Washburne himself served on this committee. According to Vessolo, during one stormy session the Catholic University's Pro-Rector Monsignor Ogiati "was extremely and gratuitously rude" to the Education Director, "who however replied by turning the other cheek, thus showing that Christian precepts are not the prerogative of priests." By early fall the committee had suspended 11 members of the Catholic University's faculty. But it recommended that Gemelli remain rector, on the grounds that he had defended Jews and offered asylum to certain partisans. In these and other ways, the rector had purportedly demonstrated that "despite his earlier statements, he was not a true Fascist."[18]

The Subcommission's procedural concessions to the Church and the final verdict on Gemelli outraged Italian lay opinion. In late September the Allied Commission leadership reopened the case. Chastened perhaps by his earlier conflicts with the Church over the elementary school *programmi*, Washburne now defended the Catholic University Committee and its decision. As he observed at the time,

> The press opposition from the left to our action is nothing to the opposition both here and in Britain and America that would follow our violation of our agreement with the Vatican and refusal to allow Gemelli to continue his functions.[19]

In the end, the Allied Commission leadership concurred, and Gemelli was confirmed as rector.

Elsewhere on the peninsula, the results of Allied-sponsored purging were coming under attack from a different quarter. Even before the Po Valley had been liberated, a growing number of Allied-appointed officials, particularly *provveditori*, found themselves being eased out of their posts by the central ministry. In the summer of 1944, De Ruggiero and the subcommission had agreed that all Allied appointees should be considered provisional until confirmed by the Italian government. The minister promised, however, that no dismissals of Allied appointees would be made during the 1944-45 academic year without the concurrence of the subcommission. Yet by February of 1945, Arangio Ruiz had unilaterally removed a number of Allied-appointed *provveditori*.[20] Despite Washburne's objections, the practice continued through the spring.

Finally the Education Director and the Italian minister forged a compromise. It was agreed that once jurisdiction for the entire peninsula returned to the Italian state, open examinations would be held to fill the posts of provincial superintendent on a permanent basis. All incumbents would be permitted to take this examination, regardless of their civil service ranking, and all would receive extra credit on the basis of their experience. All other candidates would have to have attained a civil service level of seven--the traditional minimum necessary to be considered for such a post. This decision to include provincial superintendencies among the offices to be filled through open competition rather than ministerial fiat marked an important liberalization of Italian administrative practice. Until these *concorsi* were held, however, well-connected functionaries from the central bureaucracy continued to replace energetic anti-Fascists from the periphery.[21]

Leftist educators found it particularly difficult to hold on to administrative posts. As long as they remained, Allied field-officers did what they could to protect their appointees, regardless of their partisan affiliation. According to Paul Heilman, the assistant REO in Piedmont, he and his colleagues "were not concerned as to the politics of educational officials," but only their professional competence. Thus in the Piedmontese province of Alessandria, Heilman vigorously defended the Communist *provveditore* Stelio Lozza against a Christian Democratic campaign to replace him with one of their own men. In a lengthy memo to the Educational Director, Heilman described Lozza as "popular, hardworking and serious." Since he was "one of our very best *Provveditori agli studi*," Heilman concluded, "it would seem absurd to consider a change at this time." The Allies' Piedmontese educational office closed at the end of September. Lozza kept his office until Piedmont returned to Italian governmental jurisdiction later that fall.[22] After being forced out by his Catholic opponents, Lozza won a seat in the Chamber of Deputies, where he played a conspicuous role in debating and drafting educational legislation.

The Allies' withdrawal also exposed their Italian assistants in the various regional educational offices to political retaliation. Perhaps inevitably, these assistants attracted the resentments of the many educators whose careers had been interrupted or terminated by Allied fiat. Arthur Vessolo was quite concerned over the "slander and rumor campaigns" which vetted teachers would spread about his staff, "especially in a distant, large, variegated organization like the Ministry of Public Instruction." In late November, some two months after closing down his office in Milan, Vessolo asked Washburne to intervene directly with the educational minister in order to stymie just such a vendetta aimed at removing his ex-assistants from the ministry.[23]

In late 1945 and 1946 sharpening political competition between Italy's major political parties permitted the rehabilitation of many purged civil servants. By August of 1945, conservatives within Parri's governing coalition engineered the termination of the purge in southern Italy, despite widespread feeling that it had failed there. The following March, De Gasperi dissolved the High Commission for the Purge. Then on June 2, Communist party leader Palmiro Togliatti, acting in the capacity of Minister of Justice, decreed an amnesty for all political prisoners to coincide with the inauguration of the Italian Republic. By the end of 1946, almost all purged civil servants had won reinstatement.[24]

It is not possible to quantify this process of rehabilitation as it affected teachers and educational administrators, as the pertinent ministerial records are not yet open to researchers. The large surplus of instructors for available posts in the immediate post-war years probably forestalled the return to the classroom of some "compromised" educators. Nonetheless many ex-Fascists clearly managed to retain or regain their jobs. In his autobiographical narrative *Immigrant's Return*, published in 1951, the Italo-American author Angelo Pellegrini describes meeting an embittered former state accountant who had been prevented from resuming his career "while the man who taught him to believe, to obey and to fight was high in the service of the new regime."[25] For all of the anxiety and resentment which the purge had generated, both during the war and afterward, it had failed to free the schools from the legacy of Fascism.

Experiments with Decentralization

Among the most deepseated preferences which Allied educators brought with them to Italy was their bias in favor of decentralized educational policy-making and administration. The Anglo-American doctrine of regional and institutional pedagogical self-determination had two basic components. To serve as effective catalysts of democracy, schoolteachers should themselves enjoy broad influence over both the form and content of popular schooling. It was equally important that the parents and neighbors of schoolchildren help determine the direction taken by local schools. Leading Italian pedagogues, including De Ruggiero and Giovanni Ferreti, shared these values. So, too, did a great many moderate and leftist anti-Fascists teachers--most notably in Sicily and in Piedmont.

Robert Gayre was convinced that the extreme centralization of the Italian government, in education as in other fields, had "contributed in no small measure to dictatorship there." One of his first orders as AMG Educational Advisor had been to create provincial education committees, first in Sicily and then on the mainland. Initially, these committees helped local civil affairs officers determine the condition of local school buildings and textbooks and compile rosters of available teachers. Gayre also expected the committees to provide his office with local communities' views on the kind of schooling which they required. In addition, the committees would set up small groups of teachers to consider lasting changes in curricula and textbooks. Through such activities, both teachers and citizens as a whole would "begin to learn how to take responsibility in local education."[26]

Gayre regarded his committees as valuable counterpoises to the *provveditori*, who had in the past been "completely" under centralized control." The provincial superintendents were permitted to designate half of the committees' members. But "in order...to begin developing a democratic tradition," the education advisor insisted that the remaining members come directly from the ranks of the "more important schools and colleges" and other provincial "societies and organizations concerned with cultural problems."[27]

This scheme soon withered for lack of outside support. Already in September, Sicilian *provveditori* questioned the need for the provincial committees to involve themselves in textbook and curricular reform. T. V. Smith, who served as Gayre's liason in Brindisi, felt that such committees "accomplished little of positive value in bringing education up to more modern standards."[28]

In November, Gayre and Washburne called Sicily's *provveditori* together to discuss administrative and legal changes which would enable them to reopen and administer schools in the absence of a functioning central ministry. Instructed by top ACC leaders to keep legal innovations ata minimum, the conferees placed responsibility for local schooling squarely on the shoulders of the *provveditori* themselves. On November 19, the provincial education committees were placed under the care of the *provveditori* and they soon atrophied.[29]

With only modest modifications, these decrees formed the effective basis for school administration in newly-occupied AMG territory for the remainder of the campaign. By bolstering the province as the traditional fulcrum of local administration, the Allies left Italians little subsequent opportunity to initiate novel communal or regional forms of governance.

The conservative administrative guidelines of November, 1943 did not prevent the subcommission from establishing a particularly fruitful rapport with local schoolteachers in the province of Avellino. In March of 1944, Willis Pratt, an ex-college president and superintendent of schools from Pennsylvania, arrived in the province in order to conduct a thorough study of its schools and educational needs. On the basis of a questionnaire drawn up with the help of a local secondary school English teacher, Pratt composed a far more detailed and nuanced portrait of a provincial Italian school system than the Allies had possessed to date.

While in Avellino, Pratt also convened primary and secondary teachers' advisory committees. The elementary committee worked with the *provveditore* in drawing up a curriculum to be followed in this war-torn province for the remainder of the school year. Pratt was disappointed that the *provveditore*, "although conscientious, accepts as inevitable the restricted educational opportunities which many rural youth have or at least of which they avail themselves." On the other hand, the elementary school committee proved quite resourceful in finding ways to increase the number of functioning rural fourth and fifth-grade classes. The elementary and secondary advisory committees also discussed the traditional lack of coordination between the two levels of schooling, and expressed the "desire for joint meetings, to inform each other of their respective reform proposals."[30]

In Rome it proved harder for the subcommission to establish and maintain collaborative efforts with local teachers. Once the capital was liberated, the subcommission did make contact with AIDI, and worked closely with that group in prosecuting a vigorous joint vetting campaign early in the summer. The Allies also encouraged the resistance organization's transformation into the *Federazione Italiana della scuola* (FIDS). But such cooperation did not carry over into other areas of policy-making.

Yet the fall of 1944 marked a high point in the efforts of the FIDS to win for its members an effective voice in the governance of Roman schools. Working closely with the newly reconstituted General Confederation of Labor (*Confederazione generale del lavoro*), secondary school teachers demanded that "internal commissions" composed of their collegues be consulted in vetting school personnel, in selecting new staff (including new principals, who were to be elected by teachers to serve 2 or 3 year terms) and in conducting the general administration of their institutions. On November 2, 1944, educational minister De Ruggiero suppressed the councils on the grounds that these organizations had originated in factories and businesses, and were inappropriate for schools. This decision alienated energetic schoolteachers who might have helped De Ruggiero implement his own ultimately unsuccessful plan to return primary schooling to the regional rather than national administration.[31]

Under Arangio Ruiz the educational ministry proved even less receptive to FIDS iniatives. In January the new minister gave only the most cursory attention to an elementary syllabus drawn up by Dina Bertoni Jovine and a group of FIDS educators who were dissatisfied with the official ministerial curriculum then nearing completion.[32] Roman authorities obstructed the creation of parents' councils and school teachers' associations promoted by local anti-Fascists. By March, 1945, local teachers were appealing to the Education Director, urging him to intervene on their behalf with ministerial authorities.[33]

But there is no evidence in the records of the Education Subcommission that Washburne ever defended the Roman schoolteachers' initiatives in his meetings with either De Ruggiero or Arangio Ruiz.

It is unlikely that he would have done so without the backing of senior civil affairs officers. Yet those officers remained wary of structural meddling in Italian government territory. Allied Commission leaders seem to have ignored a State Department proposal, released in October, 1944, to decentralize the Italian government along regional lines and to broaden communal autonomy within the regions. Instead Chief Commissioner Stone stressed to Allied army commanders in the north that "it should be our endeavor to help the Italians make of Italy one administrative entity."[34]

To further this objective, Stone insisted that all civil affairs directives for the key regions of Lombardy, Piedmont and Liguria had to be identical. On May 1, northern Regional Commanders issued a uniform set of "Special Orders and Authorizations for Opening and Functioning of Schools." The first paragraph of these instructions read as follows:

> All existing laws and regulations relative to the educational system and the functioning of the schools shall continue in full force except where the present orders and authorizations negate, replace or supplement them. In general it is the policy of the Allied Military Government to avoid any change in the legal situation, the administrative organization, or the school program, except where changes are necessary to eliminate Fascism or to make schools function effectively.[35]

In Piedmont the Allies encountered a vigorous and original program of educational reconstruction already underway. On April 28, the Turinese *liceo* professor Augusto Monti had been appointed head of a new Regional Instructional Bureau (or *Sovraintendenza generale scolastica*) by the Piedmontese CLN. In cooperation with over 120 local partisan committees, Monti's office initiated a thorough purge of the schools' "most dangerous and compromised Fascists," and brought back into the classroom many instructors who had suffered discrimination and persecution under the former regime. The local CLN committees also offered advice on textbook reform, assisted ex-partisans, sponsored political debates on educational matters and worked on a variety of practical problems, from heating to school lunches.[16]

Monti was convinced that the democratic renewal of the school required the removal of primary and secondary schooling from the jurisdiction of the centralized bureaucracy in Rome. In place of the sterile, regimented schools of Italy's pre-Fascist and Fascist past, Monti intended for Piedmont's schools to reflect the dynamics of local social and cultural life. A naturally effective and disciplined form of education would emerge only as Piedmont's students, teachers and citizens felt the school system to be their own. Elementary schools would be returned to control of the communes, where they had originated. Only after primary schools were torn away from their communal roots, Monti argued, had they become such "malleable instruments of miseducation."[37]

Monti hoped to establish a fruitful working relationship with Anglo-American authorities as they moved into Turin at the beginning of May, 1945. In his initial contact with the Piedmontese partisans, the Allied REO Sam Noe indicated reassuringly that the Allies had "not come to destroy, but to help." Yet on May 20, the REO announced that the AMG would not recognize the Piedmontese CLN's Regional Instructional Bureau "since no such organization exists under AMG or under the Italian government." Monti replied that a number of earlier school reforms, including the Daneo Law of 1911, had specifically strengthened regional control over aspects of education. Monti also pointed out in Lombardy, a similiar CLN regional authority, the *Alto Commissariato per la Scuola della Lombardia*, had been allowed to continue its activity. But Noe remained adamant.[38]

For the next several weeks, Monti stayed on as a "professional consultant" at the AMG regional educational office. But the trust necessary for a fruitful collaborative effort was lacking. The former CLN official was hired only on the condition that he "would not profit from his relations with the High Command either to pursue political aims or to derive personal advantage of any kind." After a series of clashes over examination schedules and several vetting decisions, Monti submitted his resignation on June 6.[39]

Soon thereafter, a Central Inspector from the ministry in Rome took Monti's place. In view of their scheduled departure from Piedmont on September 29, Noe and his associates used this official "to the fullest possible extent," making him familiar with all operations so as to hand over the functions of their office "with the least possible interruptions."[40] Watching from the wings, Monti was profoundly saddened to see Piedmont again fall

> under the shadow of the Roman bureaucracy, of *Minerva*...blind and deaf, not only to everything that had happened...since September 9, 1943, but even ...since October 28, 1922, eager once again to reduce the school to the docile instrument of dictatorship.[41]

Monti's own successor was one of many ministerial functionaries whom Giovanni Gentile had originally promoted from lesser posts, and who now proceeded to consolidate their control by means of the "all too familiar bulletins and circulars."[42]

What was Washburne's attitude towards events in Piedmont? Preoccupied with other concerns in Rome, the subcommission director was apparently content to leave initiative in the hands of his REO. In one brief memo to Noe dated July, 26, Washburne confessed that the Monti affair "is not clear to me, but is clearly in your jurisdiction."[43] One prominent Italian scholar has tentatively attributed Washburne's reluctance to interevene to political suspicions of the northern partisans. In the summer of 1945, however, there was little evidence of such suspicions within the subcommission. Washburne simply felt that his hands were tied. On the eve of the Allies' liberation of Turin, Paul Heilman had asked the Education Director whether standard AMG procedures might be modified in Piedmont. Washburne carefully responded that, at least in the three northwestern AMG regions, top military and civil affairs leaders were determined to maintain maximum adminstrative uniformity.[44]

In the meantime, Washburne had enlisted the central ministry's assistance in launching his own program to "help stimulate teachers to reflect on pedagogical problems and make their own views known to the ministry." At the inaugural meeting of the ministry's elementary reform commission on August 4, 1944, the Education Director had outlined the creation of a "democratic system of representative commissions, each one composed of not more than ten teachers." Each group would discuss policies and problems confronting Italian education, formulate recommendations and select a delegate to a similiar, higher level commission, where the process would be repeated. By the fall of 1945, Washburne reported that groups of teachers in and around Rome were enthusiastically engaged in developing improvements in the curriculum and in the organization of the schools. In Naples, educators were systematically canvassed on optional ways to structure the schooling of 10 to 14-year olds. However, the Educational Subcommission was curtailed and then disbanded before this initiative could be applied on a nationwide scale.[45]

Throughout the campaign, the Education Subcommission had sought ways to involve teachers and ordinary citizens in educational decision-making. From the outset, however, these consultations were shaped by internal and external limitations operating on the subcommission. Top Allied Commission officials were determined to safeguard the authority of the fledgling Italian state, including its educational ministry. For their part, Washburne and his colleagues preferred to initiate and conduct the dialogue with local Italians. In Rome in the fall of 1944, and in Turin in the late spring and summer of 1945, the subcommission was unprepared to support autonomous drives for pedagogical and administrative self-determination by local anti-Fascist educators. As a result, by the end of 1945 the central minsterial bureaucracy had reestablished its traditional grip over all important aspects of Italian school life.

A Test of Wills in Venezia Giulia

The Education Subcommission faced its most explosive and difficult challenge in rehabilitating and reopening schools in Venezia Giulia. Allied military officials, including educational specialists, remained stationed in the Free Territory of Trieste from its liberation in May, 1945 until its formal division between Italy and Yugoslavia in October, 1954.

Ever since the flamboyant Gabriele D'Annunzio's seizure of Fiume in 1919, Italian domination over the northern Adriatic had been a fundamental symbol of Fascist potency and national greatness. Mussolini's regime zealously suppressed all manifestations of Slovene and Croatian culture. Yugoslav children were offered Fascist prizes to learn Italian, and in 1925, all Slavic language schools were closed. These changes in popular schooling formed part of a wider program of ethnic repression; in the course of the *ventennio*, some 100,000 Slavic family names were forcibly Italianized.[46]

Slovene and Croatian cultural fortunes began to revive after September 8, 1943, when the Julian region passed under German military and civil adminstration. In a conscious revival of pre-World War I Austrian practice, German authorities permitted the opening of local Slovene and Croat language schools. In spring of 1945, Yugoslav partisans liberated the peninsula and took over these schools. The Communist-dominated Slovene Partisans' National Liberation Committee (*Slovenski narodno-osvobodilni odbor*, or SNOO) was particularly effective in portraying itself as the champion of Slovene cultural self-determination. The SNOO quickly dismantled the pre-existing Italian framework of local administration, including the *provveditorati*, and set up its own systems of governance and its own highly political program of popular instruction.[47]

Anglo-American forces reached Trieste in the first week of May. After a month of delicate negotiations, culminating in the Belgrade Agreement of June 9, an Anglo-American military government was established throughout western Venezia Giulia ("Zone A"), while the Yugoslavs retained control east of the Morgan Line. Elsewhere in northern Italy, AMG officers' initial relations with local partisan forces had been marked by at least a degree of fruitful collaboration. In Venezia Giulia, enmity eclipsed such cooperation from the outset. Field Marshal Alexander quickly removed responsibility for the preliminary vetting of Fascists from partisan committees and placed it in the hands of Allied military commissions and a military court of assize. He also ruled that all laws of the territory in effect on September 8, 1943 would remain in effect, unless specifically countermanded by his office. Finally, on August 11, Allied leaders officially replaced partisan organs of local government with their own administrative network. Western Venezia Giulia was now divided into the "areas" of Gorizia and Trieste (modelled on the former Italian provinces of those names) and the commune of Pula. Traditional provincial offices, including that of *provveditore*, were reinstituted.[48]

Carleton Washburne travelled to Venezia Giulia in July of 1945 to formulate a basic policy of educational reconstruction in the region. Washburne named John Simoni, a hardworking but rather brusque American, Chief Education Officer for the region. Italian and Slovene advisers of equal status assisted Simoni on his central staff. At the "area" or provincial level, however, Slovenes were disappointed in their aspiration for separate superintendents to supervise Slavic language schools.   Instead, Slovene school inspectors in Gorizia and Trieste were made responsible to area *provvoditori*, both of whom were Italian.[49]

With characteristic optimism, Washburne expressed the hope that reformed schools would play a fundamental role in promoting mutual understanding and cooperation between nationalities in this troubled territory.   He proposed that all elementary school children be able to attend schools taught in their mother tongue. Regardless of their own nationality, however, all pupils were to study the history and language of both Italy and Yugoslavia. The remainder of the elementary school curriculum would be based on the Allied *programmi* of 1944-45.[50]

This seemingly fair-minded proposal encountered immediate resistance. The Allied Commission leadership in Rome tended to share Italian perceptions of the Julian region and its needs. Washburne's immediate superior, Civil Affairs chief Brigadier Upjohn, asserted in a memo of July, 1945 that

> The country is Italian and Italian history must be the basic history; moreover, Italian history has a long and until recently, glorious record, whereas that of the Slav people is short and barbarous.[51]

AMG proceeded to implement a plan which obliged Croat and Slovene children to study Italian (subsequently this "obligation" was changed to an "opportunity"), but did not impose the reciprocal requirement on the Italian majority. According to Alfred Bowman, the Senior Civil Affairs Officer in Trieste, even AMG's decision to offer the Slovene language and Yugoslav history on an elective basis caused a "tide of Italian resentment."[52]

The dearth of "acceptable" Slovene and Croat-speaking teachers in Zone A posed another obstacle to the implementation of a completely even-handed educational program. Washburne's suggestion that Slovene and Croat teachers be imported from east of the Morgan lined was vetoed by the AMG regional leadership. Nor would AMG accept partisan teachers or members of the partisan-backed unified labor union, the *Sindacati unici*. The Anglo-Americans did hire a number of anti-Communist refugee teachers. Still, the supply of qualified instructors fell short of the demand, and in 1945-46 AMG wound up employing a heterogeneous group of individuals, many of whom lacked professional preparation as teachers. Even then, the pupil:teacher ratio in December of 1945 was 58.1 pupils per teacher in Slovene schools, but only 10.4 in Italian elementary institutions. The following April, a new Slovene-language *instituto magistrale* in Gorizia launched an intensive six-month course to train teachers for Slovene primary schools. Additional teacher training courses were established for Slovenes in Trieste and for Croats in Pula.[53]

The most controversial issue of all proved to be the selection of a suitable elementary primer for the Slavic schools in AMG territory. Initially, AMG authorities invited the SNOO to help choose a primary text to replace the *libro dello stato*. The Yugoslavs immediately vetoed as "Fascist" the AMG education office's own first recommendation. The volume in question was a Slovene primer written prior to the war. According to Washburne it contained nothing more objectionable than a couple of fairy tales which portrayed monarchism in a favorable light: only "by an extreme stretch of the imagination" could these be considered "Fascist."[54]

As an alternative, the partisans urged the retention of their own set of textbooks. In the partisan materials first grade children learned how to read and write by using phrases such as the following:

> The war is over; Tito's partisans have won the war. My father is a partisan. The great Stalin calls us from the plains of Russia, and from these mountains our friend Tito answers.[55]

Allied authorities in turn found such materials unacceptable. Washburne went so far as to assert in an October interview with D. Pitkin of the Associated Press that "Fascist propaganda" had been "child's play compared to the propaganda put out by the Yugoslav partisans." The latter "glorified Tito much more than Fascist books used to glorify Mussolini." In addition, Washburne deplored the partisan primer's communism, militarism and nationalism. Indeed, the book's "most innocent picture was a blacksmith raising a hammer to forge a sickle."[56]

The Education Director's remarks provoked caustic responses in the Italian left-wing press, and landed him once again in hot water with his superiors. After seeing Italian accounts of his interview, Washburne conceded that he had erred in expressing himself so forthrightly. One unanticipated result of the flap was that the Soviet embassy requested that its name be added to the distribution list of the subcommission's monthly reports.[57]

At the subcommission's request, a group of Slovene teachers now "buckled down with typewriters and mimeograph machines" to produce a sufficently non-political elementary textbook. But in many rural areas in Zone A the SNOO intimidated teachers into using partisan materials instead. By March of 1946 Allied authorities were forced to issue their own Order No. 89: henceforth, any teachers who used partisan materials would be dismissed. The SNOO retaliated by organizing a massive boycott of AMG schools by Slovene parents. Large numbers of Slovene children attended clandestine partisan classes for the balance of the 1945-46 school year.[58] This partisan-orchestrated resistance only abated in February, 1947, when the Italian and Yugoslav governments signed a peace treaty creating the Free Territory of Trieste, and establishing a boundary commission to divide the remainder of Venezia Giulia between the two Adriatic neighbors.

In the western zone of the new Free Territory, Italians played an increasingly dominant role under the umbrella of a reorganized Allied Military Government. The rector of the University of Trieste, Angelo Cammerata, began to advocate such "super-irredentist" political and ethnic policies that Simoni felt compelled to recomend his dismissal. When Senior Civil Affairs Officer Alfred Bowman carried out this recommendation, he was engulfed by accusations of repression in the Italian and western press. Bowman left his post shortly thereafter; by 1949, Cammarata had regained his rectorship. In the meantime Simoni too had been succeeded, first by a British officer and then by Giuseppe Fadda, who had served as Italian advisor under his predecessors. As AMG education chief in the western zone, Fadda wasted little time in abolishing the position of Slovenian advisor and subjecting all schools to directions received from the Italian educational ministry in Rome. The Slovene schools were never formally recognized under Italian law; enrollments dropped from a 1946-47 high of 6,317 pupils to 3,733 students in 1954-55.[59]

On October 5, 1954 Italy gained formal authorization from the U.N. Security Council to administer the western zone of the Free Territory of Trieste, while Yugoslavia obtained parallel permission in the east. All remaining American and British civil affairs officials now withdrew, thus bringing the last chapter of Allied military governance in Italy to a close.[60]

The course of events in Venezia Giulia demonstrated with particular sharpness the difficulties of trying to supplant authoritarian schooling with a more democratic alternative in a context of escalating domestic and international ideological polarization. Initially, Washburne hoped that fairminded school reform could lead the way in dampening the virulent nationalism existing on both sides of the Morgan Line. Instead, as Washburne himself eventually conceded, the U.S. occupation forces in the Triestrian hinterland wound up imposing a traditional Italian administrative arrangement on the local Slavic population.[61] By the height of the Cold War, AMG's Regional Education office in Trieste had been reduced to a reluctant accomplice in a new round of Italian cultural irredentism.

Conclusion

Liberation of northern Italy dramatized the Education Subcommission's limitations as an agency of cultural reconstruction. To Washburne, the reunification of the peninsula signalled that the most exciting and promising period of positive reconstruction was about to begin. In his eyes, the publication of the Allied-inspired elementary curriculum in May symbolized the ongoing contribution which the subcommission would make to Italian national renewal. Yet the final defeat of the Germans and the neo-Fascists that same month also heralded the imminent reduction of all phases of Anglo-American military adminstration. As he witnessed the steady emasculation of his staff, Washburne finally had to relinquish the chimera that military government would sponsor the broad liberal reconstruction to which he was so deeply committed.

From the outset of the campaign, the multinational composition of the subcommission had reassured its staff of the agency's suitability as a healer of excessive chauvinism. As Education Director, Washburne countered accusations that he aimed to "Americanize" Italy's schools by emphasizing the subcommission's international contacts. He promoted exchanges of both educators and didactic materials between Italy and a range of countries, including Switzerland, Holland, China and Russia, as well as the United States and the United Kingdom. As late as the fall of 1945 Washburne continued to hold the door open to Soviet participation in the subcommission's projected monograph series on contemporary education in Allied lands, even though no Russian publications were submitted. The Education Director felt quite confident in insisting that the subcommission's activities were "free from the possible suspicion of serving the interests of any one nation."[62]

As it turned out, the Education Subcommission found it impossible to insulate its initiatives from the budding domestic and international Cold War. Between May and December of 1945 it was forced to take sides in a series of controversies pitting conservative against radical political forces on the peninsula. The outcome of the Gemelli affair in Lombardy demonstrated that the special consideration already accorded to the Church in textbook and curricular matters might, in special circumstances, extend to the realm of the purge as well. The mild treatment accorded Gemelli, coupled with the subcommission's suspension of recently appointed partisan educators in Piedmont and elsewhere, seemed to align the subcommission with the defenders of the status quo. This impression was reinforced by the Allies' suppression of Augusto Monti's *Sovvraintendenza Generale Scolastica*, despite its similarities with Gayre's and Washburne's own earlier decentralization proposals.

These decisions did not reflect deliberate ideological choices on the part of the subcommission director or his staff. Rather, they reflected the policy preferences of the Allied Commission leadership as a whole. The Allied Commission's committment to honor Vatican privileges sanctioned in the 1929 Concordat played a large role in the Gemelli affair. AMG's preference for administrative uniformity exercised an equivalent influence on the decision to suppress Piedmont's experiment in regional autonomy. After the beginning of 1945, Chief Commissioner Ellery Stone was also determined to bolster the Catholic Church and the central Italian government in order to contain the revolutionary threat posed by the northern partisans. Within a number of individual subcommissions, however, including the Education Subcommission, Anglo-American specialists strove to maintain a conscientiously apolitical stance through the end of their tours of duty. Paul Heilman's defence of the communist *provveditore* Stelio Lozza in Alessandria was only one of several similiar incidents in the north.[63]

Only in Venezia-Giulia did anti-communism become a deliberate and explicit component of subcommission policy. Washburne's controversial denunciation of Titoism of October, 1945 is the first such polemical statement to appear in the subcommission's documentary record. Near the end of his tenure as Educational Director, he penned a broad-ranging essay on "Education in the Post-war World." In it he noted that the Russians, the Nazi and, less efficently, the Fascists had all demonstrated the potential of popular education to transform an entire society. It was now up to the western democracies to match the reformist commitment of those European dictatorships, but in a liberal and humane direction.[64] In this spirit Washburne welcomed his appointment between 1946 and 1948 as head of the USIS office in Milan. He was now ready--as he himself put it--to assume an "active part in the international contest with communism."[65]

ENDNOTES

[1]Memo, Washburne to Public Relations Branch, ACHQ, 10 Sept 1945, NARA, RG 331, 10000/144/605.

[2]Harris, *Allied Military Administration*, p. 295; Coles and Weinberg, *Civil Affairs*, pp. 550-551.

[3]Letter, Washburne to Ernesto Codignola, 26 March 1946, Archivio Ernesto Codignola (hereafter "Archivio EC"), Raccoglitore

44. See also the letter sent by Washburne's secretary Gabriela Rombo to Codignola, dated 29 April 1946, in the same file; Tomasi, *Scuola italiana dalla dittatura alla repubblica*, pp. 78-79.

⁵Msg, CSS to AFHQ, 8 Dec 1945, cited in Coles and Weinberg, *Civil Affairs*, p. 638; Monthly Report, REO, Piedmont Region, Sept 1945, NARA, RG 331, 10000/144/354.

⁵Interview, Angelina Cristoferi, 14 March 1982.

⁶Memo, Washburne to VP, CA Section, 3 Oct 1945, NARA, RG 331, 10000/144/106.

⁷Washburne, "Education under Allied Military Government," 261. To help overcome the effects of "twenty years of Fascist segregration," the New Deal did encourage scientific, political, philosophical and artistic exchanges between Italy and the United Nations. Harris, *Allied Military Government*, p. 239.

⁸Memo, 3 Oct 1945, NARA, RG 331, 10000/144/106.

⁹Washburne, "Cultural Relations and the Education Subcommission," n.d. NARA, RG 331, 10000/144/605; Letter, Washburne to Ernesto Codignola, 26 March, 1946, Archivio EC, Raccogl. 44; Washburne, "La riorganizzazione dell'istruzione in Italia," 275.

¹⁰Washburne, "Education under Allied Military Government," 262; Vessolo, "Italy: Education," 580.

¹¹Allied Commission. *A Review of Allied Military Government and of the Allied Commission in Italy* (Rome: Public Relations, Allied Commission, U.S. Army, 1945), p. 87.

¹²Benson and Neufeld, "American Military Government in Italy," 126.

¹³R. T. Alexander Papers, Box 13; Monthly Report, REO, Piedmont Region, May, 1945 and Memo, REO, Piedmont to Dir, Ed Sub, 17 July 1945, NARA, RG 331, 10000/144/354 and 358.

¹⁴Monthly Reports, REO, Lombardy Region, June 1945 and September 1945, NARA, RG 331, 10000/144/366. In his September report, Vessolo cited a warm letter of acknowledgement from the Communist president of the Lombard CLN as confirmation of the "friendly relations" existing between partisans and Allies.

¹⁵Tomasi, *Scuola italiana dalla dittatura alla repubblica*, pp. 54-56; *I diritti della scuola*, XLV, 11(July, 1945), 1. For a bitter account of school vetting under Milanese CLN auspices see Cremaschi, *Cinquant'anni di battaglie magistrali*, p. 207.

¹⁶Lombardy Regional Monthly Report, May 1944, CP Papers, file S35; Monthly Report, REO, Lombardy REgion, June 1945, NARA, RG 331, 10000/144/366; *La politica e legislazione scolastica*, pp. 347-348.

¹⁷Tannenbaum, *The Fascist Experience*, p. 199. See also Carlo Falconi, *La Chiesa e le organizzazioni cattoliche in Italia (1945-1955)* (Turin: Einaudi, 1956), pp. 140-147.

¹⁸Monthly Reports, REO, Lombardy Regiom, August and Sept 1945, p. 20, 26 April 1946, R. T. Alexander Papers, Box 13.

¹⁹Memo, Washburne to VP, CA Section, AC, 28 Sept 1945, NARA, RG 331, 10000/144/376.

[20]Letter, Washburne to Minister of Public Instruction, 15 Feb 1945, NARA, RG 331, 10000/144/125.

[21]Allied Commission, Education Subcommission. *La politica e la legislazione scolastica*, pp. 398-399.

[22]AMG Piedmont Region Headquarters, "Contacts of Scholastic Officials in the Field," N.D. (stamped document numbers 4440-4441), NARA, RG 331, 10000/144/354; Memo, J. V. Vella to Minister of Public Instruction, 20 Nov 1945, NARA, RG 331, 10000/144/359.

[23]Letter, Vessolo to Washburne, 24 Nov 1945, NARA, RG 331, 10000/144/371.

[24]Miller, "Epurazione Mancata," 11-13; Kogan, *Political History of Post-War Italy*, pp. 35-36; Grindrod, *The New Italy*, p. 57.

[25]Angelo Pellegrini, *Immigrant's Return* (New York: Macmillan, 1951), pp. 223-224.

[26]"Review of Educational Activities," 4 Nov 1943, NARA, RG 331, 10000/144/17.

[27]*Ibid.*

[28]Monthly Report, SCAO, Palermo Province, Sept 1943, p. 31, CP Papers, File S-27; Smith, General Report on Educational Activities, date unknown, NARA, RG 331, 10000/109/586, as cited in Hearst, "Evolution of Allied Military Government," pp. 256-257.

[29]Washburne, "Education under Allied Military Government in Italy," 286; Monthly Report, AMG Region I, Nov 1943, pp. 26-27, CP Papers, File S-28; AMG, Education Division, Directive to Specialist Personnel, 19 Nov 1943, NARA, RG 331, 10000/144/23.

[30]Pratt, Educational Survey, Avellino Province, 23 March 1944, pp. 1, 6, 29-30, NARA, RG 331, 10000/144/216.

[31]Colombo, "Gli insegnanti tra impegno antifascista e sindicalizzazione della categoria," pp. 99-106; Bertoni Jovine, *Scuola italiana dal 1870*, pp. 402-403; De Ruggiero, "Problemi della scuola," 5-6 and "Esperienze," 113-115.

[32]*I diritti della scuola*, XLV, 5 (Jan 1945), 55.

[33]Bertoni Jovine, *Scuola italiana dal 1870*, p. 403; Monthly Report, REO, Rome Region, March 1945, NARA, RG 331, 10000/144/279.

[34]Ellwood, *L'alleato nemico*, pp. 263-264; Letter, Stone to Northern Army Commanders, ACC, n.d., NARA, RG 331, 10000/136/574; Steven White, "An Experiment in Italian Regionalism: Piedmont Under Partisan and Allied Rule, 1945," Paper delivered to American Historical Association Annual Meeting, December 30, 1987.

[35]Administrative Instruction No. 4, HQ AMG Lombardia Region to Provveditori agli Studi, 1 May 1945, NARA, RG 331/144/364.

[36]Augusto Monti, "Regione e Scuola. Un esperimento di governo regionale della scuola." *Belfagor* XXI, 2 (March 1966), 206-207.

[37]Fornaca, *Problemi della scuola italiana*, p. 53; Monti, "Regione e Scuola," 206-207.

[38]Monti, "Regione e Scuola," 196-211.

[39]Monthly Reports, REO, Piedmont Region, May and June 1945, NARA, RG 331, 10000/144/354; Monti, "Regione e Scuola," 201, 211;

Fornaca, *Problemi della scuola italiana*, p. 54.
⁴⁰Monthly Report, REO, Piedmont Region, September 1945, NARA, RG 331, 10000/144/354.
⁴¹Monti, "Regione e Scuola," 205.
⁴²*Ibid.*
⁴³Memo, Washburne to Noe, 26 July 1945, NARA, RG 331, 10000/144/353.
⁴⁴Fornaca, "La politica scolastica degli Alleati in Piemonte," 276-277; Memo, Washburne to Heilman, 25 April 1945, NARA, RG 331, 10000/144/364.
⁴⁵*I diritti della scuola*, XLV,1-2 (Sept-Oct 1944), 25-26: Prot. 2186, Francesco Scaglione, Provveditore agli Studi, Naples, to Minister of Public Instruction, 24 Oct 1945, NARA, RG 331, 10000/144/Box 5.
⁴⁶Bogdan C. Novak, *Trieste, 1941-1954. The Ethnic, Political and Ideological Struggle* (Chicago: University of Chicago Press, 1970), p. 238n; Alfred C. Bowman, *Zones of Strain. A Memoir of the Early Cold War* (Stanford: Hoover Institution Press, 1982), p. 35.
⁴⁷Novak, *Trieste, 1941-1954*, pp. 73-74.
⁴⁸*Ibid.*, p. 206-211; Harris, *Allied Military Administration*, pp. 346-347.
⁴⁹Novak, *Trieste, 1941-1954*, p. 298; Tomasi, *Scuola italiana dalla dittatura alla repubblica*, p. 82.
⁵⁰Alfredo Vernier, "La politica scolastica dell'amministrazione militare alleata a Trieste dal 1943 al 1954," in Federazione Nazionale Insegnanti Scuole Medie, *Contributo per una storia delle istituzioni scolastiche a Trieste* (Trieste: Libreria internazionale Italo Svevo, 1969), p. 213.
⁵¹Memo, Upjohn to Executive Commissioner, AC, 17 July 1945, NARA, RG 331, 10000/144/606; Harris, *Allied Military Administration*, p. 255.
⁵²Bowman, *Zones of Strain*, p. 97.
⁵³Closing Report, Education Subcommission, 26 April 1946, R. T. Alexander Papers, Box 13; Memo, Upjohn to Executive Commissioner, AC, 17 July 1945, NARA, RG 331, 10000/144/606; Novak, *Trieste, 1941-1954*, pp. 215n, 216n, 217, 230.
⁵⁴Bowman, *Zones of Strain*, p. 98; Memo, Washburne to VP, CA Section, 22 Oct 1945, NARA, RG 331, 10000/144/606.
⁵⁵English translation of newspaper article from *Il Momento*, 25 Oct 1945, NARA, RG 331, 10000/144/606.
⁵⁶*Ibid.*; Memo, Washburne to VP, CA Section, 22 Oct 1945, NARA, RG 331, 10000/144/606.
⁵⁷Washburne, internal minute no. 7, 30 Oct 1945 and memo, George Filatov, USSR Rep, Allied Commission, Italy, to Ed Sub, 26 Oct 1945, NARA, RG 331, 10000/144/606 and 564.
⁵⁸Bowman, *Zones of Strain*, p. 97.
⁵⁹*Ibid.*, pp. 134-135; Novak, *Trieste, 1941-1954*, pp. 410-411.
⁶⁰Novak, *Trieste, 1941-1954*, pp. 298, 410-411.

[61]Carleton Washburne, *Il bene del mondo* (Florence: La Nuova Italia, 1965), p. 110.   The English language original is *The World's Good* (New York: John Day, 1954).   On the morrow of liberation Guido De Ruggiero had predicted an irrepressible upwelling of Italian nationalism in his "Il pensiero politico europeo," *Idea* I, 6 (June 1945), 22.   1954 and 1955 in particular saw a heightened emphasis on patriotism at all levels of schooling throughout the Italian peninsula.   See Giorgio Canestri, "Scuola e politica in Italia dalla resistenza al sessantotto," in Quazza, ed., *Scuola e politica dall'unità ad oggi* (Turin: Stampatori, 1970), p. 117, and Circular, 21 May 1955, prot. n. 56/E/16040 (Gabinetto), AD, Min PI.

[62]Carleton Washburne, "Cultural Relations and the Education Subcommission," n.d., NARA, RG 331, 10000/144/Box 7.

[63]See also Thomas Fisher, "Allied Military Government in Italy," *Annals of the American Academy of Political and Social Sciences*, 267 (1950), pp. 116-119.

[64]Carleton Washburne, "Education in the Post-War World," p. 4, n.d., NARA, RG 331, 10000/144/605.   Washburne visited the Soviet Union during the 1920s, where he was impressed with the progressive and even "democratic" aspects of the new nation's school system before it had been recast under Stalin.   See further Carleton Washburne, *New Schools in the Old World* (New York: John Day, 1926).

[65]Washburne, *Che cos'è l'educazione progressista?*, p. ix.   This candid statement has attracted considerable comment among Italian historians.   See Fornaca, "Politica scolastica degli Alleati," 277; Tomasi, *Scuola italiana dalla dittatura alla repubblica*, p. 81; Francesco Susi, *La scuola italiana dopo la seconda guerra mondiale* (Rome: Societa Editrice Libreria, 1981), p. 23.

CHAPTER 7

COUNTER-REFORMATION

For all their great achievements, the Italians
have failed to make and to declare and to
attempt to live by the greatest discovery of
which man is capable, and which is the true
measure of his civilization; that every man is
sacred even in a secular sense, that no one by
accident of birth is better than his fellows.

--Angelo Pellegrini
Immigrant's Return (1951)

Limits to Reform

The drawn-out Italian campaign had been a frustrating one for
the American reformers. Washburne and his colleagues were
handicapped by their small numbers (in comparison with the
educational teams subsequently posted to occupied Germany and
Japan)[1], and by the conservative policies of their military
government superiors. For the first year of Anglo-American
occupation, the Allied Control Commission had its hands full simply
propping up King Victor Emmanuel's make-shift government in
Brindisi and in Salerno. From the outset in Sicily, top Allied
leaders respected the political and social sensitivities of the
Vatican, which they valued as an additional guarantor of stability
and order. Following the liberation of Rome, a vigorous purge of
the civil service was soon cut short lest it paralyze the
"co-belligerent" Italian state and saddle the ACC with unwanted
administrative responsibilities. In the north, the Allies and
central Italian authorities throttled political and educational
innovations by the Resistance for fear of an uncontrollable
revolution.

A large portion of the Education Subcommission's time and
attention was necessarily devoted to physical reconstruction and
relief operations. As the attacking party, the Allies were
responsible for most of the damage caused to schools. Aerial
bombardments in particular destroyed many buildings in
German-controlled territory. Fascist propagandists made much of
the October 20, 1944 bombing of a primary school outside of Milan
in which 174 children and 15 teachers perished. In liberated
areas, too, there is no question but that the larger Allied
military presence interfered with popular education. In rural
areas adjacent to the front, transport-clogged roadways were
impassible to pupils and teachers alike. In the larger towns and
cities, the numbers of child "street vendors, toots and bootblacks"

increased markedly following the arrival of Allied armies. In some cases American offers of food and supplies for needy children only compounded short-term hardship. In Rome the promise of American school supplies encouraged local shopkeepers to charge exorbitant prices for pencils, ink, pens, blotters and paper, since the rich could afford even high prices and the poor would "eventually benefit from American generosity."[2]

Despite a myriad of such frustrating incidents, reformist educators hoped that far-reaching positive reforms could be instituted soon after the cessation of hostilities. Like their colleagues in Germany and Japan, they seem to have underestimated the lasting obstacle posed by the war's legacy of physical and material deprivation. Rural schools remained without doors and windows for years after the end of the war. A teacher in one Umbrian village recorded that local inhabitants had ransacked his classroom of doors, desks, an electric lamp and notebooks at the close of the 1945-46 school year. Communal authorities then refused to make good these losses.[3] In Rome many primary schools still had no heat in the fall of 1948; subsequently an influenza epidemic swept the city and forced schools to close early for Christmas vacation.[4] As late as 1951, 38% of Neapolitan children were anemic and 75% showed signs of rickets. In the Abruzzese town of Marsica--setting of Ignazio Silone's novel *Bread and Wine*--a 1951 survey conducted by a Communist women's group revealed that 40% of local children were effected by tuberculosis, typhus, rheumatism or infectious diseases.[5]

All efforts to reorient the pedagogical and political attitudes of Italian schoolteachers were deeply conditioned by the latters' severe economic difficulties. As a group teachers had always been underpaid; during the war, their salaries lost any sensible relationship with the spiraling cost of living. By the end of 1945, prices had increased some twenty-five fold over their 1938 level, while the average teacher's pay grew only about five-fold.[6]

Here again, Allied military forces bore significant responsibility for this difficult state of affairs. Throughout the campaign, American authorities in particular refused to withhold any of their men's pay, despite the fact the fact that a private disposed of as much money as an Italian prefect.[7] Allied soldiers' willingness to pay inflated black market prices was catastrophic for native Italians. In 1940 a dozen eggs had cost 8.4 lire; in 1944, a single egg commanded 20 lire on the black market-- one quarter of many unskilled workers' daily wage.[8] AMG authorities made belated efforts to establish and enforce official prices only after serious public disturbances broke out in Naples in late 1943 and in Florence in late 1944.[9]

In the south, the Italian government increased schoolteachers' basic stipend and their wartime bonuses in July and November of 1943 and in the summer and fall of 1944. Although the increases were modest and slighted rural and small town instructors, they temporarily quelled some teacher discontent.[10]   Teachers assigned to remote rural schools faced another, more intractable fdifficulty: living accomodations were often unavailable or economically unfeasable.   Southern REO Joseph Murphy reported in November of 1944 cases of "rural teachers earning 1000 lire a month finding rooms available at the same price."[11]   Their only alternative was to commute for one or more hours each way by unreliable public transport over war-damaged roads.   Not surprisingly many of these individuals despaired of reaching their posts and took up work elsewhere.

In northern Italy the Fascist republican regime in October, 1943 implemented an across-the-board 30% increase in salaries and wartime bonuses for teachers in its territory.[12]   Ironically Allied liberation resulted in the abrogation of this decree along with all RSI legislation.   The income of northern teachers was thus cut back for a period of several months while the Roman government considered how to incorporate them into its own pay and bonus schedule.   In response to intense teacher discontent, AMG granted state teachers an emergency raise in July of 1945.   Nonetheless, schoolteachers participated in a dramatic strike by northern civil servants on August 10, protesting the central government's failure to normalize their juridical status or to alleviate their economic distress.[13]

Following the conclusion of military hostilities, Arthur Vessolo expressed the concern that the material hardships of *maestri* and *professori* might leave them vulnerable to "all sorts of political extremism."   In the case of teachers, like other civil teachers, the greatest danger appeared to be not a swing to the left, but a return to Fascism.   Vessolo observed that, as in Italy following the First World War, even manual workers' wages had kept pace with the cost of living better than the pay of civil servants.[14]   By the fall of 1945, teachers throughout the peninsula despaired of maintaining even a minimal level of bourgeois respectability.   By this point, a pair of shoes cost the average schoolteacher nearly one month's salary.[15]   It is not hard to imagine the social resentments of Roman *maestri* at seeing their income dip beneath that of a streetsweeper.[16]   One wonders what percentage of teachers wound up casting their votes for the neo-Fascist *Uomo Qualunque* movement, with its renunciation of inept coalition governments and of the party system itself, during the early post-war years.[17]

Teacher unemployment, with all of its concomitant and insidious pressures towards docility and conformism, re-emerged with a vengeance at the end of the war.   Of Italy's 200,000 trained *maestri*, perhaps 120,000 were employed in state educational institutions in late 1945.   A far smaller number taught in private and parochial schools.   This left an army in excess of 50,000 jobless schoolteachers to congregate in the towns and cities of the peninsula, where their numbers were further swollen by instructors still unable or unwilling to take up posts in remote rural areas.[18]

Following the war, the *istituti magistrali* resumed the familiar pattern of graduating classes far in excess of the number of vacant teaching slots. The backlog of unemployed teachers from the late 1930s and early 1940s, coupled with the wartime destruction of thousands of classrooms, compounded the problem. As a result, the educational ministry delayed scheduling its first postwar general *concorsi* until 1948.[19] When *concorsi* for some 20,000 positions were finally announced, the government reserved a certain number of posts for war veterans and for victims of Fascist political or racial discrimination. This only lengthened the odds confronting the majority of the 75,000 to 80,000 candidates,[20] and may have temporarily bolstered their support for far right-wing political currents, particularly in the Mezzogiorno.

The lengthy and destructive military campaign which finally restored political liberty to Italy had another problematic ideological consequence. The dual occupation of the penninsula by the Germans from the north and by the Anglo-Americans from the south had gravely exacerbated the chronic problem of Italian unity. Even after the Allied victory, the territorial integrity of the Italian state remained in jeopardy. A persistent Sicilian separatist movement was only contained in 1947. Italy's peace treaties with the Allied powers, signed on February 10, 1947, awarded the Dodecanese islands to Greece, the Adriatic islands and most of Venezia Guilia to Yugoslavia, and several small frontier areas to France. To many Italians, this was bitter recompense for their declaration of war on Germany in October of 1943 and the ensuing sacrifices of the Italian resistance. Once the treaty had been signed, Italy had expected to join the United Nations; instead, this was denied due to Russian veto.[21]

These centrifugal pressures produced a powerful countervailing demand for disciplined, highly centralized government. Political support for decentralization had been strong during the liberation period; now, it waned. Italy's elementary schoolteachers numbered among the staunchest defenders of a strong central government. It had taken Italy's *maestri* decades to gain entry into the national civil service; they were not about to sanction any tampering with their newly won status. Sicilian and Aostan proposals for the regional administration of elementary schooling and elementary school personnel elicited vigorous protests from *maestri*. In January, 1948 the Catholic elementary schoolteachers' association denounced any "regional constitutional dispositions which might violate the national unity of the *categoria* of schoolteachers."[22] The National Schoolteachers' Union (SINASCEL), by then dominated by its Catholic faction, adopted a similar resolution. Ultimately advocates of regional autonomy were forced to settle for didactic rather than administrative decentralization. Thus the modified

Sicilian regional primary school *programmi* of 1951 permitted "themes related to Sicilian autonomy" to be incorporated into history, geography and *educazione morale e civile*. The syllabus also encouraged the study of "dialectic poetry of particular grace" in Italian language classes.[23]

Related to the post-war reaffirmation of strong centralized government was an unmistakable revival of nationalism. The crisis in Trieste catalyzed much of this sentiment. In 1954, the year Venezia Giulia was partitioned, the Minister of Public Instruction Gaetano Martino issued a strongly-worded call for increased emphasis on patriotism at all levels of popular schooling as a means of inculcating greater respect for civil order among Italian young people.[24] In May of the following year Martino's successor, Giuseppe Ermini, issued his own circular entitled "Civic and Patriotic Education in the Schools." The minister's circular made perfunctory mention of the value of international collaboration and brotherhood, before dwelling at length on the need to extol Italy's glorious civilization and culture.[25] Ironically, 1955 also saw Italy accepted at last as an equal member of the family of nations when she was invited to join the United Nations.

The Age of Gonella

The greatest single obstacle to American political and cultural influence in post-liberation Italy was Catholic integralism. Key leaders within the Christian Democratic party, supported by the Vatican hierarchy, aimed to supplant the legacies of both Liberal and Fascist Italy and to establish "integral" Catholic hegemony in the peninsula through a direct effort of social persuasion and mobilization.[26] In the realm of popular education, post-war Italy's most powerful integralists were Guido Gonella, Minister of Public Instruction from 1946 to 1951, and Maria Badaloni, founder and first president of the Catholic Elementary Schoolteachers' Association (*Associazione italiana maestri italiani*, or AIMC, established in 1945). Like many integralists, Gonella and Badaloni had attained their first political experience as militants within Catholic Action, and drew continuing inspiration from that highly motivated and disciplined organization. Following World War II Catholic Action's "civic committees" represented one avenue of the integralist crusade. Catholic professional and trade associations, among them AIMC, constituted another avenue. Under Gonella's resourceful command, the Ministry of Public Instruction became a third impartant avenue for a Catholic Counter-Reformation in Italy.[27]

As a university student, Gonella had taken an active part in Catholic Action's struggle with the Fascist Party between 1929 and 1931.[28] Later in the 1930s he was a frequent contributor to the Vatican newspaper, *L'Osservatore romano*. His forthright criticisms of Mussolini's domestic and foreign policy, issued under the pseudonym of *Acta diurna*, impressed a host of readers in Italy and abroad--among them Alcide De Gasperi. Gonella's personal integrity and considerable rhetorical talent prompted De Gasperi to invite Gonella to assist in founding the Christian Democratic Party in 1943. Between 1944 and 1946, Gonella edited the Christian Democrats' Roman daily newspaper, *Il Popolo*, and played a prominent role in drafting the party's fundamental program for its national congress, held in April, 1946.[29]

His earlier training served him well during the debates of the Constitutent Assembly, where he resolutely rejected non-Catholic calls for the separation of Church and State. On the balance, the Constitution which went into effect on January 1, 1948 favored the Catholics' position. Article 7 safeguarded the societal and educational privileges granted the Vatican by the 1929 Concordat. On the other hand, articles 33 and 34 sanctioned private and parochial schools, but stipulated that they receive no assistance from public funds.[30]

In July of 1946 Gonella succeeded the Labor Democrat Enrico Mole as Minister of Public Instruction. With the exception of the Popular Party's Antonino Anile, who served briefly in 1922, he was Italy's first confessional minister at *La Minerva*. Still, it did not take him long to make himself at home in the sprawling baroque palace in Trastevere. Despite the Christian Democrats' clear plurality within the Constituent Assembly and the first Italian parliament, he distrusted the unfamiliar and unpredictable parliamentary process. As much as possible, he preferred to direct the rehabilitation of post-war Italian schooling from within the corridors of the ministry itself. As a result, much of the school-related legislation adopted during the initial post-war decade concerned minor administrative questions.[31] Gonella quickly installed a trustworthy team of top administrators within *La Minerva*. In some cases repentant holdovers from the *ventennio*, such as Nazareno Padellaro, survived his purge, while non-conformist anti-Fascists like Giovanni Ferretti lost their posts. As minister Gonella expanded the central bureaucracy at every level, from top posts such as *ispettore generale* and *capo divisione* down to the most humble *comandi*.

Gonella's presence at *La Minerva* gave the Catholics formidable leverage in bidding for the allegiance of Italian teachers. Catholic professional associations enjoyed growing prestige and influence during the five years of Gonella's tenure. Under the leadership of Maria Badaloni, AIMC, the Catholic Elementary Schoolteachers' Association, made especially impressive strides. Founded in 1945, by 1950 AIMC had organized one-third of the *classe magistrale* under its banner.

As founder and first president of the association, Maria Badaloni shared the "non-political" orientation of most *maestri*. Like Gonella, she had been reared within Catholic Action; during the war, she had risen to the position of Assistant Director for Young Women of AC's Youth Section. Still in her twenties at the war's end, Badaloni's intense commitment to Catholic reformism was not matched by any particular sympathy for parliamentary politics. In 1946 and again in 1948, she refused Alcide De Gasperi's invitations to stand for the Constituent Assembly and the Chamber of Deputies (for the republic's first parliamentary session, 1948-1953) from the city of Rome. Badaloni preferred to devote her full energies to strengthening AIMC.[33]

During the latter 1940s, Badaloni and Gonella engineered an impressive series of reforms which redressed many of the *classe magistrale*'s long-standing economic and juridical complaints. In 1947, the ministry launched a nationwide campaign against teenage and adult illiteracy. Special classes taught by elementary school teachers were organized throughout the peninsula. Many of these courses were administered directly by AIMC. All told, more than ten thousand unemployed *maestri* found work in these classes.[34] This campaign was more effective as a form of political patronage than it was as a suppressor of popular illiteracy. The adult education classes were generally organized in provincial capitals, where jobless teachers congregated, but did little to touch those remote areas beset by the highest illiteracy rates. According to the 1931 census, 21.9 percent of all Italians above the age of six were illiterate; by 1951, the percentage had dipped to 12.9, and in 1961 to 8.4.[35]

Other ministerial initiatives addressed the concerns of currently employed and retired schoolteachers. Decree Law No. 499 of 2 May 1947 realized Guido De Ruggiero's earlier aspiration and removed the highly restrictive quotas (the *ruoli chiusi*) which had limited the number of schoolteachers who could be promoted beyond the lowest civil service grade of XII. In addition, this decree fully equalized the professional status of rural and urban *maestri*. The May decree narrowed but did not entirely close the juridical gap separating schoolteachers from other civil servants. Instructors received inferior benefits from the traditional schoolteachers' pension board, the *Monte Pensione*. They received no extra compensation for "overload" teaching or administrative responsibilities. Nor were they reimbursed for academic study or other forms of professional improvement. Decree Laws No. 1066 and 1128, dated 7 May, 1948, remedied each of these problems.[36] Gonella took particular pride in rehabilitating the *Consiglio Superiore della Pubblica Istruzione* which had ceased to function during the Fascist period. The new Superior Council was convened in 1949 and divided into primary, secondary and higher educational divisions. All of its members were educators selected by their peers.[37] Lay and Catholic teachers ran competing slates of candidates for each of the sections. In 1948, 1951 and again in 1954, the Catholic slate of candidates headed by Maria Badaloni captured six seats on the council's elementary section (the Third Section), while the lay slate obtained two. In the secondary section (the Second Section), however, clerical and anti-clerical forces remained evenly matched. Because of this ideological pluralism, Gonella subtracted a measure of responsibility from the council's jurisdiction in 1950, granting it instead to new National Didactic Centers staffed almost exclusively by orthodox Catholics.[38]

Despite his studied neglect of formal representative institutions, Gonella was not insensitive to the need for broadly based public participation in educational policy making. In 1947 he launched an elaborate nationwide inquest (the *Commissione Nazionale D'Inchiesta per la Riforma della Scuola*) to sound public opinion and then to draft a comprehensive proposal for the structural and didactic reform of the Italian school system. At long last the post-war "Constitent Assembly of the School" advocated earlier by Guido De Ruggiero got underway. As if to underlie the inquest's continuity with wartime reformist aspirations, Gonella included his six predecessors at La Minerva on the *Inchiesta*'s presiding commission.[39]

The Christian Democratic minister was determined to make his "constituent assembly" ad democratic and inclusive as possible, in deliberate contrast to Giovanni Gentile's "autocratic imposition" of 1923. Five subcommissions, composed of a cross-section of the nation's leading intellectuals and educators, drafted detailed questionnaires for primary, secondary and university schooling, adult education and artistic and musical instruction. An elaborate machinery of some 1500 local commissions compiled and tabulated the results, which were publilshed in periodical form in 1948 and 1949. Over 210,000 educators, as well as some 85,000 civil servants, journalists, union members and other concerned citizens completed the questionnaires.[40]

The task of tabulating this enormous volume of information and reporting the results to the wider Italian public fell to the Inquest's eleven-man Central Office, headed by the Trentine educator Giovanni Gozzer. Hampered by his staff's limited manpower and statistical inexperience, Gozzer availed himself of several administrative expedients. Individual educational institutions were directed to prepare collective responses to their questionaires. In addition to simplifying the eventual burden placed on his office, Gozzer hoped that educators would benefit from the "pedagogical experience" of hammering out schoolwide consensuses.[41] Individuals dissatisfied with collegial outcomes retained the option of submitting their own responses to the central office.

The final issue of *La Riforma della Scuola* offered a lengthy yet curiously impressionistic portrait of the nation's educational preferences. In place of a comprehensive, quantitative breakdown of responses to each questionaire item, the report described how "slight" or "great" majorities of responsdents favored particular policy options.[42]

According to the *Riforma della Scuola* report, most Italians were dissatisfied with the "overly encyclopedic" 1945 elementary *programmi*. Interestingly enough, American-backed provisions for self-government within the classroom enjoyed broad support. So too did the incorporation of some form of student teaching in the training of aspiring *maestri*.

Most Italians were unprepared to emulate the American experience with comprehensive secondary schooling, however. The *Inchiesta* itself revealed that three quarters of those surveyed still wished to segregate those pupils preparing for advanced secondary study from those who would attend a terminal middle school and then enter the workforce. Within that three quarters majority, opinion was nearly evenly split between proponents and opponents of consolidation of the traditional classical and technical forms of secondary schooling.[43]

In 1949 the educational minister proceeded to select a predominantly Catholic commission (the *Commissione ministeriale per il progetto di legge di riforma della scuola*) to undertake the task of incorporating the *Inchiesta* results into a single, comprehensive reform package. The ministerial commission's recommendations in turn provided the foundation for Gonella's draft Legislative Proposal No. 2100 of July 13, 1951.

The improvement of intermediate level schooling (for pre-adolescents aged 11-14) provoked deep dissention within the reform commission. The "primary school faction" within the *commissione ministeriale*, led by Maria Badaloni, Giorgio Gabrielli and the Venetian central inspector Francesco Bettini, promoted "post-elementary schools" covering grades 6 to 8 but taught by elementary schoolmasters.[44] Such *scuole post-elementari* had operated successfully in the former Austrian possessions of Lombardy, Venetia and the South Tyrol; nationwide, they might become a practical means of providing schooling for the two out of three Italian young people who failed to complete their academic careers through age 14.[45] Among other arguments, Badaloni and her allies emphasized the "missionary" traditions of Italy's *maestri*. Compared with secondary school *professori*, they were far more willing to venture into the Italian hinterland and accept low-status, low-paying jobs.

The commission's "secondary school faction," led by Catholic Action's Gesualdo Nosengo and the Brescian pedagogue Aldo Agazzi, countered that all of the nation's young people required some form of unmistakably secondary schooling--particularly in light of the technological and political complexities of the twentieth century. Like most moderate and conservative Italian educators, Nosengo and Agazzi preferred that the new, inclusive middle school retain distinctive humanistic and technical tracks, while sharing a common core of subject matter (including civics) and permitting students to transfer from one track to the other. Neither camp won a clear-cut victory as the law finally submitted to parliament in 1951 provided for a tripartite division of intermediate education among classical, technical and post-elementary (termed *scuole secondarie normali* in the 1951 legislation) schools.[47]

This "compromise" sorely disappointed those educators who favored a single, comprehensive middle school for all Italians aged 11 to 14. The Marxist Dina Bertoni Jovine and the secular-progressive Lamberto Borghi charged that any segregation of educational tracks (and especially the terminal post-elementary school) would only freeze the children of the popular classes into an inferior socio-economic position.[48] Among the Catholics, Agostino Gemelli and Giovanni Gozzer also advocated a single school for Italian pre-adolescents.[49]

Gozzer and Borghi each praised the unitary form of secondary schooling prevalent in the United States.[50] As early as 1943, Carleton Washburne had spoken out against any Italian institutional arrangement which would prematurely segregate pre-adolescents into dissimilar educational tracks. As a USIS official after the war, Washburne was no longer in a position to shape the outcome of the *Inchiesta* or the ensuing draft law, although he was invited to testify on contemporary American educational practice before at least one of the *Inchiesta*'s subcommissions. At a 1948 news conference, the usually diplomatic Washburne amplified on that testimony, charging that Italians "still lacked a democratic conception of education" since they retained separate and unequal categories of lower secondary schools.[51]

Despite its auspicious beginning, Gonella's reform was scuttled by the Christian Democrat-dominated Chamber of Deputies in September of 1951. Indeed, the minister's school reform package was never even presented to the entire Chamber for a vote. A number of factors explain this anticlimactic denoument. Gonella's earlier determination to minimize parliamentary interference in educational matters caused resentment even among ideologically sympathetic deputies. Other conservative and moderate legislators appear to have been alarmed at the great expense which an organic reform of the nation's school system would entail.[52] Highly-placed ministerial functionaries did not hesitate to advertise their opposition to any alternation of the status quo. Leftists, on the other hand, ridiculed the minister for his failure to specify just how his reform would be financed.[53] His ministerial effectiveness ebbing away, the veteran integralist stepped down from *La Minerva* in July of 1951.

Catholic Apogee

The collapse of Gonella's legislative blueprint did not prevent his fellow Catholics from pursuing pedagogical change in other fora. Between 1950 and 1954, Gonella and his successor Antonio Segni created a network of "National Pedagogical Centers" charged with the tasks of promoting educational research, improving instructional methods and conducting in-service training programs for elementary and secondary school teachers.   Staffed almost exclusively by Catholics and a number of reformed idealists, these centers helped to reintroduce Italian educators to international developments in educational psychology and instructional practice.[54]

Complementing such official initiatives was the spontaneous renewal of Catholic pedagogy which had been underway since the late war years.   Particularly attractive was Gesualdo Nosengo's "Pedagogy of the Gospel," which focused on Jesus himself as a model teacher.   Jesus' unflagging sense of servanthood along his own *via dolorosa* could help Italian teachers make sense of their sufferings and sacrifice during and following the war.[55]   The Catholic emphasis on compassion, charity and the redemption of Italy's war-hardened youth appealed to many in a way that American progressive formulae of encouraging "learning by doing" or converting the school into a model society could not.   The majority of Italian parents and teachers wished to insulate the young from the traumas of the adult world, and not to immerse the young in that world.[56]

In   December,   1950,   a   new   ministerial   Didactic   Council (*Consulta Didattica*) headed by Giovanni Gozzer began to draft new *programmi* to update the Allied-sponsored elementary curriculum of 1945.   From the outset, the Deweyian elements within the 1945 elementary *programmi* had provoked reservations among conservative and particularly Catholic pedagogues.   These educators agreed that children ought to study "self-government" as a societal objective. But the pupils' immaturity prevented them from employing that process resposibly.   Thus exercises in *autogoverno* were no substitute for the authority of the *maestro* in the elementary grades.   More broadly, Catholics and others expressed fears that the curriculum's emphasis on social and civic education eclipsed the inner life of the student.   The 1945 curriculum's "vague" and "generic" religion component only compounded this weakness.[57]

All the discussion and debate of the previous several years bore fruit in June of 1955, when Minister Giuseppe Ermini promulgated new *programmi didattici* for Italy's primary schools. All mention of *autogoverno* was dropped from the new national curriculum's   introduction   and   from   the   section   specifically concerned with *educazione morale, civile e fisica*.   In an equally sharp break from the preceding, Allied-sponosored syllabus, the new *programmi* made orthodox Catholic religious instruction the "cornerstone and coronation" ("*fondamento e coronamento*") of the nation's elementary schooling. In reaction to the non-ideological, experimental methodologies recommended to teachers in the 1945 *programmi* the new syllabus directed *maestri* to ground their teaching   in   Italy's   "humanistic   and   Christian   educational tradition."[58]

Ermini's most audacious step was his attempt to extend this rigorously orthodox pedagogy into the realm of secondary education.

He centralized didactic control over the heretofore autonomous *scuole post-elementari* through an unusual "appendix" tacked onto the new primary school *programmi*. Meanwhile, he refused to authorize the construction of any additional *scuole medie* or *scuole di avviamento professionale*. Ermini relinquished his post with the fall of the Scelba government in July. However his immediate subordinates faithfully carried forth his program into the fall of 1955.[59] In a circular dated September 10, 1955, the Director General of Elementary Education mandated the creation of three-year post-elementary schools throughout the peninsula. This represented perhaps the most flagrant of a decade of attempts by Christian Democratic educational officials to bypass parliament and to implement fundamental educational reform via ministerial directive rather than legislative action.[60]

These initiatives on behalf of the *scuola post-elementare* unleashed a firestorm of criticism. The Second Section (for secondary education) of the *Consiglio Superiore della Pubblica Istruzione* quickly invalidated the September 10 circular.[61] More broadly, the controversy aroused by the new primary school curriculum, and especially by proposals for a nationwide system of *scuole post-elementari*, compromised the neo-Guelf design for dominion over Italian civil society. The deep differences among Catholics over middle school education which had wracked Gonella's ministerial commission deepened. During the latter 1950's, the Catholic Secondary Schoolteachers' Association, UCIIM, publicly broke with its junior sister AIMC over the need for post-elementary schools.[62]

Cultural Pluralism and Democratic Dialogue

In the mid-1950s, conservative Catholic stewardship of the Ministry of Public Instruction was also challenged. The Liberal Martino ministry of February to September, 1954 interrupted nearly a decade of continuous Christian Democratic possession of the post of educational minister. This brief ministry had not been in a position to alter the pro-clerical policies of its predecessors.[63] These policies were tested more stiffly by the Social Democratic Rossi ministry between July of 1955 and May of 1957. Rossi appointments broke the clerical monoply within the *Centri Didattici*. The Social Democratic minister also spoke out in defense of individual teachers who might wish to be exempted from teaching religion for reasons of personal conscience.[64] Not all of Rossi's policies were inimical to the Church, however. In 1957 Lamberto Borghi and other militant anti-clerics lashed out at a legislation which expended the participation of private school instructors in the examining boards for the secondary school *esame di stato*: such a change, they charged, could only "further the subjugation of civil to ecclesiastical society."[65] In fact, though, the spell had been broken. None of Rossi's Christian Democratic successors--even the die-hard integralist Giuseppe Medici--ruled *La Minerva* the way Guido Gonella once had.

A new spirit of cooperation between Catholic and lay educators also took root outside the halls of government. In February of 1956 the weekly journal "Amici del Mondo" sponsored an independent conference on the origins and nature of the problems which continued to plague Italian popular education. Participants ranged from the Communist Mario Alicata to the Catholics Luigi Pedrazzi and Giovanni Gozzer. Gozzer was later to describe the conference as a watershed in the history of Italy's post-war dialogue on educational reform. For the first time, a genuinely representative spectrum of the nation's Catholic and lay cultural traditions concurred that they had been working at cross-purposes. Rather than defending state or parochial institutions in their present forms against the "threat" posed by the other, Italy's educators neede to harness their energies to the task of creating a more genuinely tolerant and democratic public school system.[66]

The new spirit of dialogue encouraged Catholic and Marxist educators to reexamine the Deweyan pedagogical legacy, which now ceased to be monopolized by lay moderates. Although the new *programmi* declared the aim of assuring the "integral formation" of the child "according to Italy's humanistic and Christian educational tradition" they held back from imposing any particular methodology in the nation's *maestri*. This solicitude for the professional discretion of the individual teacher was accompanied by a strong emphasis on the unique personal worth of each pupil. Except in the area of religion, pupils were encouraged to acquire knowledge independently and experimentally as much as possible.[67] In place of uniform year-by-year instructional plans, the new curriculum revolved around instructional "cycles." The first cycle (grades one and two) dispensed with discrete subject matter altogether, in recognition of the "globality" of young children's interests. The second cycle (grades three, four and five) incorporated the conventional subjects, while reminding the instructor that the inculcation of skills should not be allowed to stymie the cultivation of the child's imagination. Henceforth in elementary schools the promotion of pupils was made almost automatic within each cycle.[68]

Even sympathetic Catholic commentators conceded that the new curriculum was based on a rather generic and imprecise understanding of child psychology. The mid-1950s saw a group of researchers at the Salesian University at Rome undertake important initiatives in developing psychological tests and devising other applications of modern experimental psychology for primary and secondary education.[69] Other Catholic pedagogues brought back ideas for novel institutional arrangements from visits to the United States. As early as 1949 Luigi Palma and Agostino Gemelli were introducing their countrymen to the role of psychological and vocational counseling in contemporary American schools. Gino Corallo, pre-eminent Italian Catholic authority on John Dewey, praised the American use of home rooms, which he described as "substitutes for the family within the very bosom of the school."[70]

During the first post-war decade the Italian Communist party had allocated educational reform a low priority. During the Constituent Assembly party leaders had compromised with the Christian Democrats, agreeing to retain clerical educational and social privileges sanctioned in the 1929 Concordat in order to gain support for economic planks such as the right of all citizens to work. Prominent Communist intellectuals ridiculed the lay progressives' faith in purely educational reform as a means of securing greater social and economic justice; effective social reform could only follow a fundamental shift in political power. During the late 1940s and early 1950s, Mario Casagrande, Lucio Lombardo Radice (son of the famous idealist pedagogue) and others dismissed Deweyian progressivism as the pernicious "therapy of a new liberalism" which only obscured the revolutionary importance of the class struggle.[71]

In the mid-1950s, however, a number of developments sparked the beginning of a new openness and a concern for educational questions. The diffusion of Gramsci's prison writings within the Italian Communist Party encourages leftist intellectuals to focus greater attention on schools as key components of the "ideological apparatus of the state."[72] Dina Bertoni Jovine's history of popular schooling in the 19th and early 20th centuries, published in 1954, dramatized to other party activists the pivotal role of traditional forms of elementary and secondary education in defining and perpetuating class divisions in Italy. In November of 1955 Bertoni Jovine and Lucio Lombardo Radice launched *La riforma della scuola*, the PCI's first nationwide journal addressed specifically to the problems of popular schooling. Like its lay progressive and Catholic competitors *I diritti della scuola* and *Scuola Italiana moderna*, *La riforma della scuola* included not only critical and historical articles, but also a didactic insert in each issue containing suggested lesson plans for *maestri*. The most important contributor to these didactic inserts was the Florentine teacher and party activist Bruno Ciari. Introduced to Dewey's thought by Ernesto Codignola, Ciari insisted that the progressive legacy of innovative classroom techniques for promoting social awareness complimented the larger Gramscian program of cultural revolution. Early issues emphasized the French communist educator Celestine Freinet's new method for permitting a group of students to operate their own press and print their own newspaper and even simple textbooks. Practical exposure to techiques such as Freinet's enabled first Ciari and then other Communist educators to view Dewey in a positive light.[73]

The new intellectual toleration and political flexibility of Italy's Catholic, lay progressive and Marxist cultures permitted their ministerial and parliamentary representatives to remove the last serious obstacles to effective and popular schooling through age 14. The persistent elementary school building program initiated by Antonio Segni finally corrected the traditional imbalance of ministerial budgets in favor of secondary and superior education. In 1960 the educational ministry abolished the middle school entrance exam; henceforth satisfactory completion of the fifth (final) elementary grade was considered sufficent preparation for secondary study. Then in July of 1962 new legislation mandated the free supply of textbooks for all state elementary school pupils.[73]

The culmination of the new multipartisan drive for egalitarian and inclusive popular schooling was the establishment of a single, comprehensive form of middle school. In January, 1959 the Communist senators Ambrogio Donini and Cesare Luporini introduced legislation which would create a truly inclusive *scuola media unica*. The proposed law would eliminate Latin from the curriculum--the key distinguishing feature of Bottai's old *scuola media* in comparison with the less prestigious *scuole d'avviamento professionali*. In its place the Communist projected a "new humanism" rooted in historical and scientific studies to serve as the central axis of the new comprhensive middle school. The Donini-Luporini bill was immediatly waylayed by conservative defenders of Latin, who extolled the *lingua madre* as both the cornerstone of Italian culture and an unrivaled predictor of the academic performance of the pupil.

Finally in 1962 a historical compromise was hammered out under the leadership of the Socialist deputy Tristano Codignola. The new *scuola media* created by Law No. 1859 of Dcember 31, 1962 was the first completely comprehensive lower secondary school in any of the member nations of the Council of Europe. Latin remained as a required subject of study in the first two years of the new middle school curriculum, while it became optional in the third year. History, civics, science, Latin and a new subject called "technical applications" (*applicazioni tecniche*) all found places in the new school's curriculum. But Latin, which was optional in the third year, was omitted from the subjects covered in the *scuola media* graduation examination (*l'esame di licenza*). It remained a necessary prerequisite for entry into the *liceo classico*, which in turn offered the widest access to university faculties.[75]

The compromise legislation formed one of the cornerstones of Prime Minister Amintore Fanfani's historical "Opening to the Left," which included the PSI within the governing coalition for the first time since 1947. Socialist and Christian Democratic votes as well as the support of the smaller lay progressive parties assured passage of the bill despite the opposition of the PCI on the one hand and the neo-Fascist *Movimento Sociale Italiano* on the other. Communist intellectuals criticized the compromise for its equivocation over Latin and thus its failure to provide a "rigorous and consistent cultural model" for Italy. But in the pluralistic Italy of the early 1960s, the contours for such a consensus were only beginning to emerge.[76]

Still, a profound transformation had occured in the nature of Italian popular schooling. For the first time in the peninsula's history, all young people through age 14 were offered a common form of primary and middle school education, regardless of their socio-economic status or geographical origin. Italy's economic miracle had stimulated an unprecedented demand for schooling. The nation's political and educational elite had been forced to respond by extending Italy's network of five-year primary schools to even the most remote rural areas, and by creating western Europe's first completely unitary system of middle schools. At last, the pernicious doctrine of the the "two peoples," segregating "those who think" from "those who merely feel," was being overcome.

The events of latter 1960s exposed a related, though subtler, form of eltism within Italian education. Unlike primary and middle schooling, upper secondary and university education remained virtually unchanged in structure or content for a quarter of a century following the defeat of Fascism. The contradiction between a modernizing, rapidly expanding popular sector and a rigid upper tier of educational institutions exploded in 1969. Outmoded syllabi, inadequate facilities and--especially--escalating unemployment among university graduates all played a role in the marches, stikes, and occupations which rocked Italian schools for the next decade. Belatedly, some restructuring of the Italian university system followed in the 1980s. Despite the massive challenge posed by the student movement, a less polemical, more individualistic, consumeristic ethos also reasserted itself within Italian youth culture.[77]

The intensely partisan scrutiny of popular education by Italy's political leaders has continued unabated. The 1955 elementary curriculum remained in force for thirty years--longer than any other in the history of modern Italy. During this period the Christian Democratic Party retained its near monopoly of *La Minerva* and firmly resisted calls for further curricular revision. Meanwhile, however, Italian society became markedly more secular in its customs and values. In 1984 the Republic of Italy and the Vatican concluded a new Concordat, thereby superceding the 1929 Lateran Accords. Among other changes, the Church was forced to renegotiate its privileged position within Italian public education.

The question of religious instruction proved particularly delicate for the 60-member commission convened in 1983 by the Ministry of Public Instruction to revise the national elementary curriculum. After two years of intense ideological and pedagogical debate, the new curriculum was promulgated in 1985. The Church's concessions were more limited than one might have anticipated.

True, the new elementary curriculum abandons the proposition that the Catholic faith serve as the "root and flower" (*fondamento e coronamento*) of all popular education. Religious instruction is provided only for families which request it.[78] Yet in the Concordat of 1984, the Italian state reaffirmed the values of Catholicism as a course of study, in view of its historical contributions and ongoing cultural presence in the life of the nation. Consequently, the state pledges to offer Catholic religious instruction as an optional course of study at all levels of pre-university public instruction. Pupils chosing to study Catholic religion must suffer no "discrimination": the alternative to catechism class should be another academic subject, and not merely free study time. To date, this last cumbersome directive has proved impracticable to implement. Such rulings are suggestive of the Church's continuing success in defending its "special place" within the Italian classroom.[79]

In other respects, the new curriculum does carry forward the progressive mission first spelled out in 1945. It invokes a scientific approach to the task of *educazione alla convivenza democratica*--education for a common democratic life. The democratic ethos is to be acquired actively and experimentally. Through a continuous series of projects and experiments, pupils should develop athe confidence, curiousity and open-mindedness necessary for good citizenship. Openness to the wider world is also nurtured by foreign language study, now extended down into the primary grades.[80]

The dynamics of American-Italian cultural relations have changed profoundly since the Second World War. During the *secondo dopoguerra*--the late 1940s and the early 1950s--Italy was not ready for wide-scale progressive education. The integralist impulse of Pius XII's Church was incompatible with Washburne's goal of sweeping yet somehow "non-partisan" educational reform. Nor could American initiatives, no matter how well-intentioned, escape the stigma of having originated under military rule. Only in the ensuing decades have many Italians chosen to look abroad for pedagogical inspiration. The Deweyian tradition in particular has served as a common point of reference in a lively dialogue between secular-progressive, Catholic and Marxist educators over the aims and means of democratic schooling. The key players in this ongoing debate are not disinterested outsiders, but committed intellectuals deeply engaged in Italian political life.

ENDNOTES

[1]See Epilogue, p. 179.

[2]Cremaschi, *Cinquant'anni*, p. 197.   Monthly Reports, REO, Lazio Umbria Region, Jan and Feb 1945, NARA, RG 331, 10000/144/279.

[3]Registro for grade V, 1945-46, Archvio, Otricoli elementary school.

[4]Registro, Classe V maschile, sezione D, January 1949, Scuola elementare E. Pistelli, Rome.

[5]*L'Unità*, May 17, 1951, p. 8.

[6]Cremaschi, *Cinquant'anni*, p. 212; Vessolo, "Italy Under Allied Military Government," 582.

[7]Benson and Neufeld, "American Military Government in Italy," 138-140.

[8]Hill, *In the Wake of War*, p. 56; on wartime prices and salaries under the Fascist regime and the RSI see "Relazione della commissione di studio," Prima assemblea di insegnanti elementari di Milano, ACS, Seq Part del Duce, Carteqgio Riservato--RSI, Busta 76, Fasc. 646, sootofasc. 13.

[9]Harris, *Allied Military Administration*, p. 377.

[10]*I diritti della scuola* XLV, 3 (Nov 1944), vii and XLV, 5 (Jan 1945), xxi-xxii.

[11]Educational Report, REO, Southern Region, Naples Zone, 8 Nov 1944, NARA, RG 331.

[12]These increases are summarized in *I diritti della scuola*, XLV, 4 (Dec 1944), 43.

[13]Memo, Vessolo to Education Subcommission, Allied Commission HQ, 25 June 1945, NARA, RG 331, 10000/144/364; *I diritti della scuola* XLV, 13 (Sept 1945), 129.

[14]Vessolo, "Italy under Allied Military Government," 582; Benson and Neufeld, "American Military Government in Italy," 141.

[15]Letter, Washburne to W. H. Kilpatrick, 15 Nov 1945, NARA, RG 331, 10000/144/583.

[16]*I diritti della scuola* XLV, 13 (Sept 1945), 129.

[17]Kogan. *Political History of Post-War Italy*, pp. 33, 47.

[18]De Ruggiero, "Esperienze," p. 99.

[19]*Ibid.*; Genovese, "I professori," in Tomasi, ed. *Scuola di base*, p. 71; Inteview, Dante Grossi, March 10, 1982.

[20]*Il maestro*, III, 12 (1947), 4.

[21]Grindrod, *The Reconstruction of Italy*, pp. 29-30; Annibale Tona, "Redenzione," *I diritti della scuola* XLV, 10 (June, 1945), 89-90.

[22]"Autonomie regionali" and "Scuola e Regione," *Il maestro* IV, 2 (February, 1948), 3, 6.

[23]*Modifica ai programmi delle scuole elementari della Regione Siciliana* (S. Maria Capua Vetere: Ernesto Schiano, 1951).

[24]Guido Quazza, *Scuola e politica dall'unita ad oggi* (Turin: Stampatori, 1977), p. 117.

[25]Ministerial Circular 21 May 1955, Prot. 56/E/16040, Gabinetto, Min Pl, AD.

[26]Tomasi, *Scuola italiana dalla dittatura alla repubblica*, pp. 113-114.

[27]Di Lalla, *Storia della democrazia cristiana*, pp. 222-224.

[28]R. J. Ciruzzi-Wolfe, "The Federazione universitaria cattolica italiana. Catholic students in Fascist Italy," *Risorgimento* III, 1-2 (1982), 67.

[29]Di Lalla, *Storia della democrazia cristiana*, 152, 165-166; Canestri and Ricuperati, *Scuola in Italia dalla legge Casati*, pp. 227-228.

[30]Tomasi, *Scuola italiana dalla dittatura alla repubblica*, pp. 285-301; Fornaca, *Problemi della scuola italiana*, pp. 175-227.

[31]Susi, *Scuola italiana dopo la seconda guerra mondiale*, p. 46; Mario Alicata, *Intelletuali e azione politica* (Rome: Riuniti, 1976), p. 227.

[32]Giovanni Ferretti, "Guerra all'intelligenza" in his *Scuola e democrazia*, pp. 17-19.

[33]Interview, Maria Badaloni, 4 May 1982.

[34]"Scuola popolare," *Il maestro* IV, 1 (1948), 1.

[35]*Annuario statistico dell'istruzione italiana*, 1956, p. 397 and 1963/1964, p. 670.

[36]The transferral of retired *maestri* from the *Monte Pensione* to the general *Opera di Previdenza* per gli impiegati dello Stato increased the retirement benefits of a teacher after 35 years of service from 61,000 to 161,000 lire. L. Andronico, "la portata del nuovo provvedimento," *Il maestro* IV, 4 (1948), 4. An excellent synopsis of all of these reforms is contained in *Il maestro* XI, 21 (Nov 1955), 5.

[37]Guido Gonella, "Inaugurazione del Consiglio Superiore delle Antichita e Belle Arti," 4 Dec 1948 and "Inaugurazione del Consiglio Superiore della Pubblica Istruzione a sezioni riuniti, " 29 July 1949, reproduced in Guido Gonella, *Cinque anni al Ministero della Pubblica Istruzione*, vol. 2 (Rome: Giuffre, 1983), pp. 26-60; Enzo Robaud, *Disegno storico della scuola italiana* (Florence: Le Monnier, 1961), p. 115.

[38]*Il maestro* VII, 6 (June 1951), 1; X, 11 (June 1, 1954), I and XI, 21 (Nov 1, 1955), 6.

[39]Of the six, Adolfo Omodeo had already passed away in 1946 and Giovanni Cuomo and Guido De Ruggiero died prior to the completion of the commission's labors.

[40]Santoni-Rugiu, *Il professore*, p. 150; Giovanni Ferretti, "La Riforma di Natale," reproduced in his *Scuola e democrazia*, pp. 25-28.

[41]As provincial superintendent in Trento, Gozzer had collaborated with Washburne's USIS office on a number of educational projects in the immediate post-war years. Interview,

Giovanni Gozzer, 1 June 1982; *La Riforma della Scuola*, Nr. 11 (Jan 1949), 80.
[42]The full text of the Inchiesta questionnaire on elementary education is reproduced in *Il maestro* IV, 5 (1948), 7. For the questionnaire's questions on middle school education see Canestri and Ricuperati, *Scuola italiana dalla legge Casati*, pp. 237-239.
[43]*La Riforma della Scuola*, supplement to Nr. 16, 54, 57, 67. See also the detailed region-by-region responses on pp. 74-122.
[44]Interview, Aldo Agazzi, 13 May 1982.
[45]Borghi, "Riforme e spese," in *Dibattito sulla scuola*, pp. 211-213; Justman, *The Italian People and Their Schools*, 7; Giorgio Galli and Alessandra Nannei, *Italia, Occidente mancato* (Milan: Mondadori, 1980), p. 123.
[46]See for example Salvatore Sarchioto, "I Docenti," *Il maestro* VI, 1 (1950), 5 and "L'adolescenza e i suoi educatori," *Il maestro* VI, 4 (1950), 7.
[47]*Ibid.*; Interview, Aldo Agazzi, 13 May 1982.
[48]Bertoni Jovine, *Scuola italiana dal 1870*, pp. 443-462.
[49]*Ibid.*, p. 455; G. Nosengo, "Discussione sulla 4 lezione (Gemelli), Settimana Sociale dei Cattolici d'Italia, XXVIII, Sept. 25-Oct. 1, 1955. Trento, Italy. *Società e scuola* (Rome: ICAS, 1956), p. 315; Giovanni Gozzer, *La scuola ponte* (Trento: Arti grafiche "Saturnia," 1948), pp. 9-11.
[50]Gozzer, *La scuola ponte*, pp. 9-11; Tomasi, *Scuola e pedagogia in Italia, 1948-1960* (Rome: Riuniti, 1977), pp. 165-166.
[51]Maria Letizia Balzani, "La scuola negli Stati Uniti," *La scuola e l'uomo* V, 6 (June, 1948), 5.
[52]Rafaele Ciasca, "Scuola e cultura," in *Aspetti di vita italiana contemporania* (Rocca San Casciano: Cappelli, 1957), p. 226.
[53]Susi, *Scuola italiana dopo la seconda guerra mondiale*, p. 46.
[54]Tomasi, *Scuola italiana dalla dittatura alla repubblica*, p. 116; Canestrii, "Scuola e politica in Italia dalla Resistenza al sessantotto," in Quazza, ed., *Scuola e politica*, p. 116; Bertoni Jovine, *Scuola italiana dal 1870*, pp. 450-455.
[55]G. Nosengo, "Un titolo e un programma," *La scuola e l'uomo* (supplemento per gli insegnanti al *Bolletino di Studium*), 29 July 1944, 1, 4; G. Righetti, "Apostolato," *Il maestro* (supplemento alla rivista "Il maestro," edito dalla Sezione Maestri di Azione Cattolica), 1944/45, 2, 4.
[56]"Controluce: Il dramma dell'apolitico," *I diritti della scuola* XLV, 1/2 (Sept-Oct 1944), 32; Angelo Magni, "Apoliticita," *I diritti della scuola* XLV, 3 (Nov 1944), 36; Michele Mastropaolo, "Partiti e Comuni," *I diritti della scuola* XLV, 8 (April, 1945), 73.
[57]Giuseppe Catalfamo, "Per la ricostruzione dei programmi," *Scuola di base* I, 4 (Oct-Dec 1954), 5; Giovanni Gozzer, "Originalita dei nuovi programmi," *Scuola di base* II, 3-4 (July-

Dec 1955), 10-11; Questionnaire response, Michele Riverso (5/15/82).

[58]Ministero della Pubblica Istruzione, *The Programs of Italian Primary School. Text and Comments* (Rome: Centro Didattico Nazionale per la Scuola Elementare e di Completamento dell'obbligo scolastico, 1958), pp. 14-18, 27, 28.

[59]Tomasi, *Scuola e pedagogia in Italia, 1948-1960*, pp. 159-160.

[60]Susi, *Scuola italiana dopo la seconda querra mondiale*, p. 58.

[61]Bertoni Jovine, *Scuola italiana dal 1870*, pp. 462-466.

[62]Susi, *Scuola italiana dopo la seconda querra mondiale*, pp. 60-61.

[63]Pasquale D'Abbiero, "Alcune cause dell'invadenza clericale," in Gorresio, ed., *Stato e Chiesa*, p. 233.

[64]Falconi, *La Chiesa e le organnizzazioni cattoliche*, pp. 129, 130.

[65]Borghi, "Scuola e Chiesa in Italia," in Gorresio, ed., *Stato e Chiesa*, pp. 153-154.

[66]Susi, *Scuola italiana dopo la seconda querra mondiale*, pp. 11-54.

[67]Incatasciato, "La didattica nella scuola elementare," in Tomasi, ed., *L'istruzione di base*, p. 126.

[68]Interview, Attilio Frajese, 3 February 1982.

[69]The Salesian University's journal *Orientamenti pedagogici*, established in 1954, became an important forum for such scientific pedagogical research.

[70]Luigi Palma, "La psicologia dell'orientamento e la selezione nella scuola primaria," *Il maestro* V, 9-10 (1949), 8-9.

[71]Dario Ragazzini, "Tra americanismo e pedagogia," *La riforma della scuola* 22, 8/9 (1976), 15-23; Tomasi, *Scuola e pedagogia in Italia, 1948-1960*, pp. 74-83.

[72]Tomasi, *Scuola e pedagogia in Italia, 1948-1960*, p. 122. On Gramsci, see also V. Gerratana, "L'opera di Gramsci nella cultura italiana," *Rinascita* (1954), 749.

[73]Ragazzini, "Tra americanismo e pedagogia," 15-23.

[74]Interview, Marco Cecere, 11 February 1982. On the traditional imbalance in ministerial budgets, see G. Gabrielli, *Commento ai programmi didattici per le scuole elementari*, p. 73.

[75]Susi, *Scuola italiana dopo la seconda querra mondiale*, p. 64.

[76]Canestri and Ricuperati, *Scuola in Italia dalla legge Casati*, p. 197.

[77]Clark, *Modern Italy 1871-1982*, pp. 364-366, 374-375; Ginsborg, *History of Contemporary Italy*, pp. 298-309, 424-425.

[78]Giuseppe Acone, "La religione nei nuove Programmi della scuola elementare" in Giovanni Gozzer, *I programmi della scuola elementare*, (Rome: Armando, 1986), p. 26.

[79]White, "Carleton Washburne--l'influenza deweyana sulla scuola italiana," *Scuola e Città*, XL, 2 (28 Feb 1989), p. 55.

[80]Fabrizio Ravaglioli attributes the underlying "rationalistic" pedagogy of the new programs to Harvard psychlogist Jerome Bruner. Despite his influence, however, Bruner cannot be cast in the kind of guiding role played by Washburne four decades ago. See Fabrizio Ravaglioli, "La 'Premessa' dei nuovi Programmi della scuola elementare" in Gozzer, *I programmi della scuola elementare*, p. 26.

EPILOGUE :

THE AMERICAN INTERVENTION IN COMPARATIVE PERSPECTIVE

The traumatic history of the early twentieth century has severely tested the millenial Western equation of self-knowledge and self-rule. Since Plato's time pedagogues and philosophers have advocated improved education as the surest foundation for just and rational government. In the late eighteenth century Rousseau and Jefferson highlighted the role of popular schooling in the establishment of enlightened self-governance. By the dawn of the twentieth century liberal statesmen on both sides of the Atlantic had gone far toward realizing this democratic creed by legislating compulsory, universal elementary education. In the United States and in Germany, these initiatives were carried out by state governments; elsewhere, they were promoted by national authorities.[1] Meanwhile Old and New World experimentalists proclaimed a "Copernican revolution" in the school, and placed the attitudes and behavior of the pupil rather than the teacher at the center of their theories and methods. In Maria Montessori and the Agazzi sisters Italy produced several of Europe's most creative pedagogical innovators, although her statesmen lagged behind their transalpine peers in implementing an effective system of national education.[2] In the United States, a broad pedagogical movement associated most closely with the name of John Dewey promised to harmonize the conflicts of a rapidly industrializing, multi-ethnic society within the walls of scientifically based, child-centered and socially responsive "progressive schools." Progressive local public school systems were established in a number of midwestern communities, foreshadowing the movement's conquest of America's pedagogical mainstream in the 1920s and 1930s.[3]

The First World War and the ensuing rise of totalitarianism took democratic reformers and educators by surprise. Individually and collectively, Western man demonstrated nightmarish capacities for violence, intolerance and willful abnegation before charismatic leaders. In Mussolini's Italy, Stalin's Russia and Hitler's Germany, schools became enormous straightjackets of political regimentation. With its celebration of audacity and physical prowess and its scorn of sedentary deliberation, Fascism in particular proclaimed itself the quintessential doctrine of the young. In the surviving democracies between the wars, intellectuals questioned the axiom that expanded formal schooling and increased literacy could only strengthen self-government. Psychologists, political scientists and other observers were struck by the *de facto* domination exercised by elites even in the surviving democracies. Some categorically denied the ability of contemporary mass men to fulfull the traditional duties of citizenship.[4] Pedagogical progressives countered by portraying their movement as the New World's best answer to Old World totalitarianism. Yet even as American pedagogical progressivism achieved its widest level of public acceptance, it also encountered a swelling tide of searching, highbrow social and political criticism.[5]

Ironically, it required a second world war to restore many skeptics' faith in their countrymen and in democracy. The campaign against the Axis powers also opened up new vistas and enhanced political influence to progressive American educators. In their eyes, the most challenging terrain for educational reconstruction lay overseas--particularly in the enemy nations of Italy, Germany and Japan. Twenty five years earlier, Woodrow Wilson had tried and failed to "make the world safe for democracy" by means of diplomacy and treaty-making. Now a new breed of internationally-minded reformers within and outside of government looked beyond legal and political measures, focusing on the social, cultural and economic foundations of democracy. As John Dewey argued in his *Freedom and Culture*, written in 1939, cultural attitudes and habits lay at the basis of all successful governments: "political institutions," he insisted, "are an effect, not a cause."[6]

Scholarly studies of wartime and immediate post-war American foreign relations have only begun to focus on America's post-war experiments with international cultural reconstruction. As Pier Paolo D'Attorre has noted, American scholars have concentrated their attention on the United States' post-war impact on Germany and Japan. For their part, Italian scholars have been slow to branch out from traditional preoccupations with Italian politics and Cold War diplomacy. In fact, the growing American influence on other Western societies since World War II lends itself to a comparative approach.[7]

Italy was the first of the former Axis nations to be invaded, and the American reconstruction effort there presaged the better-known reeducation campaigns waged in Germany and Japan. Marlene Mayo's recent research has documented how wartime preparations for German reeducation encouraged planners for the Japanese campaign to formulate similar, far-reaching objectives in the latter theater.[8] The illustrative and comparative significance of the Italian reconstruction effort, however, has not yet been studied in systematic fashion.

The Anglo-American Education Subcommission in Italy, which numbered 18 officers at its peak in mid-1944, was dwarfed by the American educational presence in Germany and then in Japan. In American-occupied southern Germany, the Education and Religious Affairs staff expanded from 15 in May, 1945 to 40 in early 1947, and was still larger by the end of the decade. In Japan the Education Division employed some 63 American and native specialists in December, 1947.[9]

Among the veterans of the Italian campaign, George Geyer and T. V. Smith played the most significant roles in the German and

Japanese theaters.   Geyer spent two years in Germany as an educational officer after serving as REO in Naples in 1943-44. Following his return to the United States he helped to recruit additional American educators for service in Germany.[10]
T. V. Smith contributed in a variety of ways to both the German and Japanese reeducation programs. He had helped briefly with pre-invasion planning for Germany while in London in January of 1944.   Following his return to the United States at the end of 1944, he taught German prisoners of war at several U.S. military installations.   He also served on the staff of the University of Chicago's training program for military governors in Japan.   Then in the spring and summer of 1946, he participated in the U.S. Education Missions to Japan and Germany, which played key roles in defining positive reconstruction objectives for those two nations.[11]
In Germany and Japan, as in Italy, a phase of physical reconstruction and ideological purification necessarily preceeded the period of substantive positive reform.   Because of the rapid consolidation of Allied military control in Germany and Japan, the first phase was shorter in these nations (lasting from the fall of 1944 in Germany and from mid-1945 in Japan through mid-1946) than in Italy.   Because the Germans and the Japanese had proved themselves by far the most threatening of the Axis nations, the second phase (mid-1946 through 1951) lasted far longer than in Italy.[12]
In each theater, Allied military commanders immediately closed down all educational institutions pending the thorough purging of both teachers and materials.   George Geyer came away from the Italian theater convinced that the goal of "defascistization" had been seriously compromised by AMG's policy of rapid and staggered school reopenings.   With Geyer's encouragement, the first U.S. Education Advisor in Germany, John Taylor, resisted his superiors' impatience to "get the children off the street," insisting that schools reopen on a uniform basis only after preliminary vetting was completed and an adequate number of acceptable non-Nazi textbooks had been stockpiled.[13]
Vetting in all three theaters was plagued by inequities and inconsistencies. Despite official Allied promises to apply uniform criteria to all civil servants, teachers suffered more severely than many other, often more highly paid government officials.   In Italy and Japan--and to a lesser extent in Germany--Americans bequeathed this thankless task to trusted domestic agencies as soon as possible.[14]
Italian teachers received by far the most lenient treatment. The overall purge rate for educators there was approximately five percent.   By contrast a fourth of Japan's teachers were either purged or resigned in order to avoid the threat of a purge.[15]   In Germany, American authorities carried out an even more draconian house-cleaning.   Over one half of the native teacher corps in the American zone was removed for ideological reasons.   By way of

contrast, the British fired between 15 and 20 percent of the educators in their zone. As a result, northern German schools avoided some of the practical difficulties experienced in areas such as Wurttemberg-Baden, where the pupil:teacher ratio soon exceeded 100:1, and the average age of "acceptable" elementary schoolteachers was over 50. Such situations led T. V. Smith to comment that in Germany the British had struck a better balance between the motives of "political purity" and "pedagogical efficiency."[16] Smith also claimed that in Italy, unlike Germany, Allied officials had been able to make their vetting judgments stick. In fact, in all three countries large numbers of teachers who had lost their posts under Allied or American occupation retrieved them in subsequent years.[17]

The screening and replacement of authoritarian and militaristic textbooks proved more tractable in Japan and particularly in Germany than it had been in Italy. For the first year of the American occupation in Germany, educational specialists rounded up and reproduced millions of copies of textbooks dating from the Weimar republic. Prior to the outbreak of the war, Taylor and his mentor (and successor in Germany) Richard Alexander had stockpiled Weimar period titles on sensitive subjects, such as history and biology, at Columbia Teachers' College. Consequently the Americans did not have to revise or reissue any official state series, as they had in Italy. Instead, all Nazi books were simply impounded. Perhaps because of their more relaxed approach to vetting, the British chose to apply tougher standards to instructional materials in their zone. They discovered defects even in many Weimar texts, thus confirming their suspicion that the Nazis had "thrived on ideas already present" in Germany. By late 1946 this particular question became passe, as local scholars across Germany were busily engaged in turning out politically acceptable, more up to date texts.[18]

In Japan, American specialists reluctantly took over the central ministry's elaborate machinery for the censorship and control of textbooks in order to eliminate militaristic and ultra-nationalistic teachings from all school materials. As in Italy, they initially retained standardized state series of elementary and secondary textbooks and teachers' manuals, instructing teachers and students to delete all objectionable passages. By the end of 1945, however, they felt compelled to take more vigorous action. They categorically suspended the teaching of history and geography on the grounds that these had been based on "myth" rather than "fact." The traditional ethics and morals course (*shushin*), with its "emphasis on submissiveness" was also banned. These subjects were eventually replaced by new, integrated texts and courses in social studies.[19]

By early 1946 American educators were forced to decide how extensive the positive reform of German and Japanese schools would have to be in order to put them on a firm democratic footing. T.

V. Smith consistently urged his fellow educators to practice self-restraint. Beyond the elimination of explicitly authoritarian and nationalistic content from the schools, the occupiers would do well to allow local populations maximum self-determination. "To purify the best of what a culture already practices," he asserted, "is to come as close as presently possible to perfection."[20]

Neither of the 1946 educational missions heeded these words of caution. Both groups issued reports more reminiscent of Washburne's "maximalist" approach than Smith's "minimalism" in Italy. In order to "eliminate social attitudes conducive to authoritarianism" Americans in both Germany and Japan urged the creation of comprehensive, unified primary and secondary school systems open to all students. Six years of elementary instruction would be followed by three years of obligatory secondary schooling in which all students would study a common core of subject matter. Those pupils able to continue their studies could then choose among a variety of more specialized upper secondary institutions.[21]

Pedagogically as well as structurally, the reformed schools were to encourage independence on the part of teachers and students. Teachers gained the right to select their own textbooks, and were encouraged to tailor lesson plans to the particular needs of local students. New courses in civics and contemporary history and classroom experiences with self-government would build initiative and social conscience among students. The new Japanese Fundamental Law of Education, enacted under close American tutelage in March, 1947, officially committed Japanese popular schooling to "the full development of the personality of the individual," whereas the old law had aimed at providing "good and faithful subjects of the emperor."[22] As Edward Beauchamp has put it, the American Mission to Japan's final report—which formed the basis for all subsequent reeducation policy in Japan—was "tantamount to a wholesale adoption of the American educational system and its philosophy."[23]

While some liberal British observers applauded the Americans' ambitious initiatives, the majority expressed strong reservations over the "Americanization" of schools in the former Axis nations. With the exception of Robert Gayre, British officials in Italy had displayed a strong concern over the dangers of introducing sweeping educational reforms in the midst of administrative and social chaos.[24] In their zone in Germany, the British carried out a thorough denazification of didactic materials, but deliberately kept structural tinkering at a minimum.[25] In Japan, one British diplomat asserted that the Americans were falling into the same "snags and pitfalls of imperialism" which his nation had encountered in India, the site of MacCauley's attempt to introduce a "fantastically unsuitable educational system" during the previous century. So pronounced was the Foreign Office's disapproval that it declined to send even a single British representative to participate in the Americans' reeducation program in Japan.[26]

The far-reaching reconstruction of popular schooling in each of the ex-Axis nations deeply concerned the Vatican. Among interested outsiders at the time, the Roman hierarchy may well have been most disturbed about the precedent which Italian reeducation might set in Germany and Japan. Cardinal Spellman and other high-ranking Catholics on both sides of the Atlantic vigorously defended the rights of parochial schools in Berlin when these appeared to be threatened by local authorities in 1947 and 1948. American Education Advisor Richard Alexander's "Kulturkampf" in Bavaria prompted a chorus of protests, led by Pope Pius XII himself.[27] When the United States government decided to send a team of specialists to evaluate the early progress of Japanese reeducation, Monsignor John Carroll pointed out that America's educational missions to Italy and Germany had been "completely dominated by secularistic educators." As a result American diplomats saw to it that the Catholic presidents of Georgetown and Notre Dame Universities were included on the 27-member mission to Japan.[28]

Efforts to decentralize and streamline German and Japanese education along American lines met with only partial success. American authorities had little difficulty in convincing the particularistic Germans to scrap the federal educational authority created by the Nazis in 1934 and return policy making to the individual *Lander*.[29] In Japan, the decentralization of the indigenous school system was more difficult. The occupiers conceeded the highly centralized Meiji regime's efficiency in introducing six years of compulsory primary education during the 19th century: by 1920, Japan had joined Germany among the world's most literate nations. But American observers also maintained that Japan's hierarchical educational system had resulted in ultranationalistic and "monolithic thought and action" prior to and during the Second World War. Only an American-style patchwork of local, non-partisan citizen school boards could eliminate the threat of such behavior in the future. Between 1945 and 1948 concerned Japanese educators countered by noting that decentralization was not a universal prerequisite for democracy, citing the highly centralized French, Belgian and Australian school systems. Nevertheless Education Director Mark Orr and his American colleagues were adamant: the jurisdiction of the Japanese Ministry of Education was curtailed and a system of local elective school boards established, with authority to determine curricula and hire and fire personnel. After eight tumultuous years, the Japanese parliament modified this arrangement in 1956, granting local government heads the right to appoint all school board members.[30]

On the other hand, the streamlined 6-3-3 elementary and secondary structure introduced during the occupation was enthusiastically received by the Japanese.[31] Southern and Western Germans living under American occupation took to structural reform much more reticently. Proposals to extend common elementary much more reticently.   Proposals to extend common elementary schooling from four to six years, and to create comprehensive secondary schools were either rejected or pigeonholed by each *Landtag* in the American zone.   As in Italy, many teachers and parents resisted the proposition that "the terms 'elementary' and 'secondary' should not mean two types or qualities of education, but rather two [equal and] consecutive levels, as was the case in America."[32]   Only in Berlin were American educators successful in collaborating with representatives of the other occupying powers and with local German officials in integrating all pupils at both the primary and secondary levels into unitary educational institutions.   In this instance, interestingly enough, American and Soviet representatives championed as "egalitarian" a consolidated school system which British and French specialists accepted only begrudgingly.[33]

The progressive drive for pedagogical modernization encountered the greatest resistance in Catholic South Germany, particularly in Bavaria.   American specialists were unsuccessful in their efforts to consolidate into new multidenominational institutions the many small confessional primary schools located in rural areas, despite the alleged "inferior educational standards" prevalent in the latter.[34]   Even the relatively tame proposal to equalize the professional preparation of elementary, secondary and vocational school teachers by requiring some university training for all was rejected on the grounds that this would undermine the predominantly parochial secondary pedagogical institutes.   Bavarian church leaders were anxious to shelter nuns teaching in kindergartens from any such requirement.   Ultimately, the only American-sponsored reform adopted in Bavaria was the introduction of free tuition and textbooks for elementary and lower secondary school students.[35]   This modest denouement created considerable frustration among interested onlookers in the United States.   Idealistic and impatient as ever, Robert Koopman concluded in 1953 that the American intervention had "failed," by not implementing a common school system capable of dissolving Germany's "caste system."[36]

In the long run, however, American proposals did serve as useful reference points for indigenous reform across West Germany. By the early 1960s, student councils had taken root and social studies and contemporary history had made their way into curricula in each *Land*.   Primary and secondary school teachers alike studied modern pedagogical techniques with West Germany's expanded university system.   By 1962 most West German educators agreed on the need for a uniform primary school through grade six, although they continued to disagree over the desirability of a common curriculum in the middle school years.[37]   These strictly pedagogical changes do not by themselves explain the striking evolution of a democratic political culture and a more egalitarian society in West Germany since the Second World War.   But by the early 1960s, West German popular education had certainly begun to reflect and reinforce those trends.[38]

In Japan a new, American-sponsored system of popular schooling facilitated a similar transformation. After World War II Japanese political authoritarianism and a pattern of almost feudal rural social relations rapidly gave way to a fundamentally democratic and egalitarian social and political order.[39] A combination of external and internal factors would seem to explain the immediate impact of "progressive" pedagogical reform in Japan. The American educational team there combined a clear mandate for basic reconstruction equivalent to that sanctioned in Germany with a level of sympathy and even trust for the occupied population more like that demonstrated in Italy. The weight of public opinion and the lobbying of the Japanese Teachers' Union played key roles in establishing the new streamlined and decentralized school system. More longstanding historical traditions are also very important. Japan's cultural, political and financial commitment to national education since the establishment of the Meiji regime has far-outstripped Italy's, and may well exceed those of Germany and the United States. Over the past century, the Japanese state has also demonstrated a receptivity to external institutional forms unmatched in the histories of unified Germany or Italy.[40]

In each of the defeated Axis nations, the American progressive tradition played a noteworthy role in overturning authoritarian legacies and stimulating the growth of democratic alternatives. Briefly in 1943 and 1944, Italy dominated the attention of reconstructionist policy-makers and of the American public; thereafter, the occupations of Germany and Japan became more inportant. Particularly in Japan, the American intervention paid immediate dividends in the form of sweeping social and educational reform. Yet in the ensuing decades, Japan has begun moving away from the liberal democratic ethos undergirding American-style progressivism in favor of a more conservative, nationalistic outlook.[41] Meanwhile, a newly reunited Germany has entered a period of intensive social, cultural and economic introspection. Italy, however, has remained remarkably open to foreign cultural influences.[42] Having weathered the successive tempests of Fascism, military occupation and post-war Catholic triumphalism, Italians emerged in the 1960s determined both to broaden their horizons and enhance their standard of living. This climate of expectations has made contemporary Italy, even during the turbulent decade of 1968 to 1978, a hospitable setting for the transplantation and elaboration of the progressive ideal.

ENDNOTES

[1]William Boyd, *The History of Western Education* (London: Black, 1950), pp. 408-410.

[2]*Ibid.*, pp. 412-417.

[3]Lawrence Cremin, *The Transformation of the School. Progressivism in American Education, 1876-1957* (New York: Random House, 1964), pp. 128-160, 179-186.

[4]Edward A. Purcell, Jr., *The Crisis of Democratic Theory. Scientific Naturalism and the Problem of Value* (Lexington: University of Kentucky Press, 1973), pp. 11, 95-114.

[5]Cremin, *The Transformation of the School*, pp. 324-327.

[6]Purcell, *The Crisis of Democratic Theory*, p. 212.

[7]Pier Paolo D'Attore, "Guerra fredda e trasformazioni delle societa occidentali nella storiografia americana," *Italia contemporanea*, 140 (Sept, 1980), 97-102.

[8]Marlene J. Mayo, "Psychological Disarmament: American Wartime Planning for the Education and Re-education of Defeated Japan,1943-1945." in *The Occupation of Japan, Educational and Social Reform: the proceedings of a symposium sponsored by the MacArthur Memorial Old Dominion University. The MacArthur Memorial Foundation, October 16-18, 1980* (Norfolk: Gatling, 1982), pp. 33-35, 57-61.

[9]*Ibid.*, p. 200; Tent, *Mission on the Rhine*, pp. 47-49, 304; *The Occupation of Japan*, p. 200.

[10]Tent, *Mission on the Rhine*, pp. 28, 108, 173.

[11]*Ibid.*, pp. 113-123; Robert K. Hall, *Education for a New Japan* (New Haven: Yale University Press, 1949), p. 77; Smith, *A Non-Existent Man*, p. 173.

[12]For the overall periodization of American occupations, see Robert Wolfe, ed., *Americans as Pro-consuls. United States Military Government in Germany and Japan, 1944-1952* (Champaign-Urbana: University of Illinois Press, 1983).

[13]Tent, *Mission on the Rhine*, pp. 28, 42-43.

[14]*Ibid.*, p. 45; Hall, *Education for a New Japan*, pp. 429-440; T. V. Smith, "Personal Impressions of Current Education in Italy, Germany and Japan," *The Educational Record* XXVIII, 1 (January, 1947), 27.

[15]William K. Cummings, *Education and Equality in Japan* (Princeton, Princeton University Press, 1980), p. 30.

[16]Smith, "Current Education," 25-27; Tent, *Mission on the Rhine*, pp. 50-57, 107, 222.

[17]Smith, *A Non-Existent Man*, p. 197.

[18]Tent, *Mission on the Rhine*, pp. 8, 26, 27, 166; Robert F. Lawson, *Reform of the West German School System, 1945-1962* (Ann Arbor: University of Michigan, School of Education, 1965), p. 58; Smith, "Current Education," 29.

[19]Hall, *Education for a New Japan*, pp. 414-478; Norman Graebner, "Occupation Policy and the Schools of Yokohama," and Toshiyuki Nishikawa, "The Postwar Educational Reform in Japan--Thirty Years After the Allied Occupation," in *The Occupation of Japan*, pp. 221, 264.

[20]Smith, *A Non-Existent Man*, pp. 193.

[21]Lawson, *Reform of the West German School System*, pp. 39-40; United States High Commission for Germany. Division of Cultural Affairs. Educational Advisory Staff. *Prewar German Education and the Objectives of the U. S. Education Program in Germany* (Frankfurt: Office of the U.S. High Commissioner for Germany, 1952), pp. 2-5.

[22]Tent, *Mission on the Rhine*, p. 117.

[23]Frank Sackton, "Education and Social Reforms in Japan" and Edward Beauchamp, "Education and Social Reform in Japan: The First United States Educational Mission to Japan, 1946," in *The Occupation of Japan*, pp. 7, 187.

[24]See for instance Arthur Vessolo's characteristic remarks in "Italy: Education," 580.

[25]Lawson, *Reform of the West German School System*, p. 57.

[26]Gordon Daniels, "Social Reform in Post-War Japan: British Perspectives on Education and Land Reform" in *The Occupation of Japan*, pp. 460-461.

[27]Tent, *Mission on the Rhine*, pp. 154-155, 243-244.

[28]Roy DeFarrari, *Memoirs of the Catholic University of America 1918-1960* (Boston: St. Paul Editors, 1962), pp. 381-382; Beauchamp, "Education and Social Reform in Japan," p. 182.

[29]Tent, *Mission on the Rhine*, pp. 164, 251; Sackton, "Education and Social Reforms in Japan," and Harry J. Wray, "Decentralization of Education in the Allied Occupation of Japan, 1945-1952" in *The Occupation of Japan*, pp. 4-5, 148.

[30]Nishikawa, "The Postwar Educational Reform, " p. 273.

[31]*The Occupation of Japan*, pp. 236-238.

[32]Tent, *Mission on the Rhine*, p. 117.

[33]*Ibid.*, pp. 238-250.

[34]United States High Commission for Germany. *Prewar German Education*, pp. 8-10, 23-24.

[35]*Ibid.*, pp. 47-49; Tent, *Mission on the Rhine*, pp. 154, 158, 166.

[36]*New York Times*, February 17, 1953, as cited in Lawson, *Reform of the West German School System*, pp. 49-50.

[37]*Ibid.*, pp. 145-155; Tent, *Mission on the Rhine*, p. 251.

[38]Lawson, *Reform of the West German School System*, p. 204.

[39]Cummings, *Education and Equality in Japan*, pp. 3-6; King, *Education for a New Japan*, pp. 405-429; Makoto Aso and Ikuo Amano, *Education and Japan's Modernization* (Tokyo Ministry of Foreign Affairs, 1972), pp. 55-67.

[40]Toshio Nishi, "Education During the Meiji-Taisho Showa Periods" and Sato Hideo, "The Present Status of Studies and Resources on Educational Reform in Japan After World War Two" in *The Occupation of Japan*, pp. 16-17, 300-301.

[41]Andrew Barshay, "Imagining Democracy in Postwar Japan: Reflections on Maruyama Masao and Modernism." Paper delivered at American Historical Association Annual Meeting. New York, December 30, 1990.

[42]In the spring of 1988 I taught a seminar on "The American Progressive Tradition" as a visiting Fulbright lecturer at the University of Perugia.   My Italian students were far more curious and better informed about the United States than my stateside Western Civilization students tend to be about Europe.

APPENDIX I

Ministers of Public Instruction

July, 1943 – June, 1968

Minister	Party Affiliation	Tenure in Office
Leonardo Severi	-------	7/43-2/44
Giovanni Cuomo	-------	2/44-4/44
Adolfo Omodeo	Action Party	4/44-6/44
Guido de Ruggiero	Action Party	6/44-12/44
Vincenzo Arangio Ruiz	Liberal	12/44-12/45
Enrico Mole	Democracy of Labor	12/45-6/46
Guido Gonella	Christian Democrat	6/46-7/51
Antonio Segni	Christian Democrat	7/51-7/53
Giuseppe Bettiol	Christian Democrat	7/53-8/53
Antonio Segni	Christian Democrat	8/53-1/54
Egidio Tosato	Christian Democrat	1/54-2/54
Gaetano Martino	Liberal	2/54-9/54
Giuseppe Ermini	Christian Democrat	9/54-7/55
Paolo Rossi	Social Democrat	7/55-5/57
Aldo Moro	Christian Democrat	5/57-2/59
Giuseppe Medici	Christian Democrat	2/59-7/60
Giacinto Bosco	Christian Democrat	7/60-2/62
Luigi Gui	Christian Democrat	2/62-6/68

Apostolic Delegation   3329 Massachusetts Ave.
U.S.A.   Washington, D.C.

                                         Feb. 14, 1944

My dear Mr. Stull,

With further reference to my recent letter regarding the teaching of religion and the general educational policies to be followed in the schools of Italy under the military government of the Allies, I have the honor to present for your esteemed consideration the accompanying memorandum which has been presented to me by the V. Rev. Monsignior Walter Carroll, of the Vatican Secreatariate of State.

M. Carroll is presently in the United States, whither he returned at the earnest request of their Eminences Cardinal Ascalesi of Naples and Cardinal Lavitrano of Palermo who have viewed with consternation the first steps being taken for the reorganization of the Italian schools. It was the wish of their Eminences that M. Carroll should come to present in person a view of the actual situation in order that proper steps might be taken to forestall possible lamentable abuses or to remedy those that may already been caused.

It is superfluous for me to observe that the teaching of religion occupies an important and even essential place in any satisfactory program of education for Italy, in view of its predominantly and traditionally Catholic background.

With sentiments of esteem and with every best wish I remain

                         Sincerely yours,

                         A. G. Cicognani
                         Archbishop of Laodicea
                         Apostolic Delegate

Memorandum

The Allied educational programme for Italy is at present under the direction of Lt. Col. Gayre of the British Army, an Oxford scholar, member of the Church of England and scientist of repute.

The principle members of his staff are Major T. V. Smith, Major
Carleton Washburne and Major Koopman, of the American army.

These latter are said to be bent on encouraging leftist
elements in Italian education, and imposing, under the guise of
"freedom of thought," educational programs not only devoid of
traditional Christian influence of any kind, but designed to
deprive children, parents and the Church of the elementary rights
recognized by every society in which the principles of justice and
freedom prevail.

Colonel Gayre, because of powerful backing in England, up to
now has succeeded, not without great difficulty, in preventing the
American members of his staff from putting into practice policies
which he and the mass of the Italian people rightly regard as
arbitrary, unjust and perilous to the true welfare of the people
and the stability of the nation. There are indications that these
American officials have in mind the deChristianization of
education. They are already regarded in Italy as extreme
doctrinaires and superficial educational experimentalists. The
inevitable result of their program, if permitted to be put into
effect, will be the preparation for, if not the establishment of,
an anti-religious educational regime with no provision for the
freedom which prevails in the educational systems of England and
the U.S.

Now it is learned that Colonel Gayre, the only obstacle in the
way of those who would carry out such a program, is about to be
recalled to London and that he will be suceeded in the normal
course of events by any one of the above-mentioned American
officials, with the other two remaining as his assistants. This
news has created consternation among those interested in promoting
genuine education in the country. Shocking as they find the
present condition of affairs, they feel that the situation that
would follow the departure of Colonel Gayre would be nothing short
of disastrous. It might be noted that the Italian people have been
utterly dismayed to find themselves victim of policies and programs
alien not only to their concept of freedom but to traditions and
practices recognized as inviolable under the Constititution of the
United States.

Thus, these American officials, it may be truly said, have not
only failed to win the confidence of the majority of the Italians
of goodwill, but have done immeasurable harm. As Allied troops
move forward, the gravity of the situation will be greatly
accentuated. So critical is the situation already that it is felt
to be of the gravest importance that it be brought to the attention
of the highest authorities of the United States Government, so that
immediate steps may be taken 1) that Colonel Gayre be retained in

his present post and 2) that an immediate change in the American personnel of his staff in Italy and Sicily be effected by the American authorities.

Washington, D.C.
14 February, 1944

C O N F I D E N T I A L

ALLIED CONTROL COMMISSION
SICILY REGION HEADQUARTERS
APO 394

3 March 1944

SUBJECT: Conference with Bishop Carroll and Mr. Mohler.

TO   :   Regional Commissioner.

1. In reviewing church-state relations shortly before he left, Lt.
Col. Charles Poletti, then RCAO, asked me to put in written form
for our files a report on my conference with Bishop Carroll and Mr.
Mohler. I am complying with this request with apologies for my
tardiness.

2.   The Bishop was introduced to me as a representative of the
Vatican. Mr. Mohler was introduced as secretary of the American
Bishop's Welfare Conference.   The latter took no part in the
conference apart from the usual friendly interchanges at the
beginning.
      Sinse these two functionaries called on me at the behest of
the RCAO and at the time when the Head of the Subcommission was
visiting the Region, I arranged to show them every courtesy and to
have Lt. Col. Gayre in the conference.   After the usual
pleasantries Bishop Carroll opened the discussion of church affairs
by stating that he believed that AMG was "attempting to set up an
anti-fascist government." This puzzled us both but he elucidated
by objecting to the appointment of Omodeo as Rettore at Napoli
(which appointment was not made by Lt. Col. Gayre) and other
liberal sounding activities.   The Bishop stated that (a) no
non-catholic should be appointed to a public office such as the
Napoli post and (b) that there were no educational affairs in which
the Church should not be consulted.
      Later the matter of replacements of faculty members at the
University of Palermo was discussed. The Lt. Col. stated that he
had removed 12 professors of permanent status.   At this point the
Bishop interjected "and replaced them with communists." He also
mentioned several names of supposed communists which included two
of the best-known socialists in Palermo.   One of these persons,
Ferretti, had not been appointed by AMG.
      The Bishop also discussed the matter of programs of study

prepared by AMG.   He objected to anticlerical influences.   We explained our policy of neutrality as evidenced by the fact that we withdrew Part II of the program of the elementary school, because it was susceptible to an anticlerical interpretation.   The Bishop then indicated that we should recognize that for all of us, the next enemy would be Communism.

Personally, I took no part in the first half of the discussion.   I interposed an objection at the point when he stated that a non-catholic should not hold public office by pointing out that the preservation of freedom of religion was a mandate to AMG.

The blatant statement about Communism prompted me to state to the Bishop that he was proposing a policy contrary to the achievement of our main objective--a lasting peace.   I also pointed out that his accusation to the effect that Lt. Col. Gayre had replaced fascists with communists was entirely contrary to the facts in the case.

My interpretation of the conference is as follows: to the extent that Bishop Carroll was representing his higher authority (a matter open to question) we can conclude that the Church is seeking political power utterly regardless of its effect on world peace.   The position taken was the most dangerous threat to our policies that I have encountered in military government since it was entirely contrary in every respect to the principles of democracy.

G. R. KOOPMAN
Major, A.U.S.

APPENDIX IV

National Curriculum for the Elementary Schools

Foreword

(From the Ministerial Decree of Feb. 9, 1945)

The curriculum which follows reflects a keenly felt desire to equip Italy's elementary schools to contribute as effectively as possible to a rebirth of national life.

An essential precondition for that rebirth is a new form of learning which fruitfully associates the world of "culture" with that of "labor." Only in this way will culture cease to be the sterile accumulation of disembodied notions, and labor the unreflective expression of brute force. This aspiration hails back to our first Risorgimento, in which thought and action conjoined became both symbol and vehicle of national education.

While combatting instrumental illiteracy, the elementary school must not neglect a far more pernicious spiritual illiteracy, which takes the form of civic immaturity, lack of preparation for political life, sheer expediency in the workplace and insensitivity toward social problems in general.

The new Italian elementary school must encourage a lively sense of human fraternity which superceeds the petty limits of nationalism and promotes instead a calm willingness to work and serve one's country with honest intentions. To this end a clear understanding of ethical problems is developed through each subject within the curriculum--in particular religion; moral, civic and physical education; labor; and history and geography.

Instruction in moral, civic and physical education will depend not on dictation in the old manner, but on. . . the experience of liberty through carefully-planned practice in self-government. .

Individual guidelines for each subject area are designed to overcome the fragmentary and disjointed instruction provided by the old curriculum. In this spirit moral and civic education--now joined by physical education--have again been included in the curriculum. Instruction in labor has an important social value. . . while the program of history and geography instruction reflects a more concrete understanding of the inter-relationships between man and his environment. The sciences reclaim in a single subject-area topics formerly treated in a helter-skelter fashion under the rubric of *nozioni vari*. These subject areas must not be regarded in isolation from one another; rather, they constitute a harmonic whole mirroring the organic consciousness of the student.

The realization of this educational program, devoted above all to the preparation of the pupil for civic life, will require more than the traditional "humanistic" training of instructors. The teacher will need a lofty sense of social responsibility which will make of him a true "*maestro* of life," both within the classroom and outside of it. . . In addition--let it be clearly said--he will need technical competence. He should continually perfect his didactic methods through reflection on the results achieved in the classroom, and through active participation in the modern Italian and international pedagogical movement.

The instructor should note. . . the recurring empasis on spontaneous collaboration between pupil and instructor. . .

This curriculum does not prescribe specific instructional methods for each subject area. . .

BIBLIOGRAPHY

Archival Collections

Charlottesville, Virginia. University of Virginia. Alderman Library. Manuscripts Department. Frank Bane and William Alexander Papers.

Florence, Italy. Centro-Studi Ernesto Codignola. Ernesto Codignola Papers.

New York, New York. Columbia University. Lehrman Library. Manuscripts Department. Charles Poletti Papers.

Otricoli (Province of Terni), Italy. Otricoli Elementary School. Archivio Deposito.

Rome, Italy. Archivio Centrale dello Stato.

Rome, Italy. Ministry of Public Instruction. Archivio Deposito.

Rome, Italy. Pistelli Elementary School. Archivio Deposito.

Suitland, Maryland. National Archives and Records Administration. Records of the Allied Control Commission in Italy.

Official Documents

Allied Commission. *A Review of Allied Military Government and of the Allied Commission in Italy, July 10, 1943, D-Day, Sicily to May 2, 1945, German Surrender in Italy.* Rome: Public Relations Branch, Allied Commission, U. S. Army, 1945.

Allied Commission. Education Subcommission. *La politica e la legislazione scolastica in Italia dal 1922 al 1943.* Rome: Garzanti, 1946.

Allied Commission. Education Subcommission. *Swan Song from the Ex-Director of the Education Subcommission, Allied Control Commission.* n. p., 1944 (?).

Coles, Harry L. and Albert K. Weinberg, eds., *Civil Affairs: Soldiers Become Governors.* Washington D. C.: Dept. of the Army, 1964.

Italy (Repubblica Italiana). Commissione Nazionale di Inchiesta sulla Riforma della Scuola. *La Riforma della Scuola.* Rome: Commissione Nazionale di Inchiesta sulla Riforma della Scuola, 1948.

Italy (Repubblica Italiana).   Instituto Centrale di Statistica. *Annuario statistico dell'istruzione italiana*. Rome: Istituto Centrale di Statistica, 1950.

Italy (Repubblica Italiana).   Ministero della Pubblica Istruzione, *La scuola italiana dal 1946 al 1953*. Rome: Ministero della Pubblica Istruzione, 1953.

_____. *La ricostruzione della scuola italiana dalla fine della guerra*. Rome: Centro didattico nazionale, 1950.

Moro, Renato.   *Legislazione della scuola elementare*.   2nd ed. Milan: Garzanti, 1950.

United States Information Service and Missione Americana per l'European Reconstruction Program in Italia, Ufficio Informazioni.   *Breve Storia degli Stati Uniti*.   Rome: Missione Americana per l'ERP, 1951.

United States. Office of Education. *Education Under Dictatorships and in Democracies*.   Washington, D. C.:   United States Printing Office, 1941.

United States Office of the High Commissioner for Germany. Education Advisory Staff, Division of Cultural Affairs. *Prewar German Education and the Objectives of the U. S. Education Program in Germany*.   United States Office of the High Commissioner for Germany, Frankfurt, 1952.

United States. State Department. *Foreign Relations of the United States*. 1943, Vol. 1., Washington D. C.

Zanobini, Luciano, ed., *Codice delle leggi sulla pubblica istruzione*. 2nd ed. Milan: Guiffre, 1960.

_____, ed., *Raccolta delle circolari sulla pubblica istruzione*. Vol. 1.: *Istruzione primaria*. 2nd ed. Milan: Giuffre, 1966.

National Curricula

Allied Military Government.   Education Division.   *Programmi di studio ed indicazioni didattiche per le scuole elementari per l'anno scolastico 1943-1944. Parte seconda. Consigli per la modernizzazione della scuola elementare*. Palermo: Tipografia IRES, 1943.

Cottone, Carmelo and Francesco Bettini. *I programmi di studio della scuola elementare.* Rome: Organizzazione editoriale tipografica, 1946.

Italy (Repubblica Italiana). Ministero della Pubblica Istruzione. *Programmi e orari d'insegnamento per gli Istituti Magistrali.* Rome: Libreria dello stato, 1945.

Italy (Repubblica Italiana). Ministero della Pubblica Istruzione. *Programmi per i vari gradi e tipi di scuola proposti dalla Consulta Didattica. Riforma della Scuola progetto di legge n. 2100.* Florence: Vallecchi, 1953.

Italy (Repubblica Italiana). Ministero della Pubblica Istruzione. *The Programs of Italian Primary School. Text and Comments.* Rome: Centro didattico nazionale per la scuola elementare e di completamento dell'obbligo scolastico, 1958.

Italy (Repubblica Italiana). Ministero della Pubblica Istruzione. Direzione generale dell'istruzione secondaria di primo grado. *Orari e programmi d'insegnamento per la scuola media statale.* Rome: Istituto poligrafico dello stato, 1963.

Elementary Textbooks

1945

Bargellini, Piero. *Letture per la IV classe urbana e rurale.* Naples: Dante Alighieri, 1945.

Campagnoni, Riccardo. *Umanità. Letture per la IV classe.* Rome: Edizioni Rome, 1945.

Mastropaolo, Michele. *Libertà e lavoro. Letture per la III classe.* Naples: Conte, 1945.

Piccola miniera. Sussidiari riuniti per la V classe. Various authors. Milan: Fratelli Fabbri, 1945.

Il seme d'oro series (grades 1-5). Various authors Milan: La Fiamma, 1945.

1946

Bartoli, Bianca and Alberto Albertoni. *Voci serene (a scuola bimbi!)* series (grades 1-5). Florence: Le Monnier, 1946.

Bertoni Jovine, Dina and Franceso Bertoni. *Sole sul cammino* series (grades 1-5). Milan: Mondadori, 1946. Jolizio, G. and L. Piccini. *Il sole ride al fanciullo*. Florence: Bemporad, 1946.

Novelli, Fortunato and Silvano Pezzetta. *Piccola vela* series (grades 1-5). Trieste: Editoriale Libreria, 1946.

Sichirollo, Augusto. *Piccole storie. Letture per la V classe.* Milan: Mondadori, 1946.

1947

La buona raccolta series (grades 1-5). Various authors. Milan: Signorelli, 1947.

Piccola sorgente. Sussidiario completo per la V classe. Various authors. Turin: SEI, 1947.

1949

Cerri, Giovanni, Maria Felicori Sarti and Antonietta Manzotti. *Fraternità* series (grades 1-5). Milan: Signorelli, 1949.

1950

Gaiba, Vera Cottarelli and Oreste Gasperini. *Spigolando* series (grades 1-5). Turin: Paravia, 1950.

Puccini, Mario and Vittorio Masselli. *Fiordimaggio* series. Turin: SEI, 1950.

1955

Bargellini, Piero. *Fratelli. Letture per il secondo ciclo, parte terza (V classe).* Florence: Vallecchi, 1955.

1957

Tempi nuovi. Sussidiario per la V classe elementare. Various authors. Bergamo: Minerva Italica, 1957.

1958

Scoprire. Albo sussidiario per la classi del secondo ciclo, parte terza (V classe). Various authors. Brescia: La Scuola, 1958.

Schoolteachers' Journals

I Diritti della Scuola. 1944-1949.

Il Maestro. 1945-1955.

La Riforma della Scuola. 1954-1955.

La Scuola di Base. 1954-1955.

Scuola e Città. 1950-1955.

La Scuola e l'Uomo. 1944-1945.

Scuola Italiana Moderna. 1945-1948.

Primary Articles

De Ruggiero, Guido. "Esperienze di un ministro." *Idea* I, 2 (January, 1945), 15-20 and *Idea* I, 2 (February, 1945), 6-14.

_____. "Problemi della scuola. La scuola elementare." *Realtà politica* 5 Jan 1945, 5-6.

Ferretti, Giovanni. "I servizi dello stato per gli scambi culturali con l'estero." *Il Ponte* V, 2 (February 1949), 135-146.

Fisher, Thomas R. "American Military Government in Italy." *The Annals of the American Academy of Political and Social Science* 167 (1950), 114-122.

Gabrielli, Giorgio. "Se e perchè necessaria una riforma dei programmi." *Scuola di Base* I, 4 (1954), 5-19.

Gozzer, Giovanni. "Missione a Ginevra." *Scuola e Professionalità.* (May, 1970), 7-11.

Graziussi, Graziano. "America ed Europa." *Scuola e Città* IV, 11 (November 1953), 379-380.

Mason, John Brown.   "Lessons of Wartime Military Government
   Training." *The Annals of the American Academy of Political
   and Social Science* 267 (1950), 183-192.

Neufeld, Maurice.   "The Failure of AMG in Italy."   *Public
   Administration Review* VI (Spring, 1946), 137-148.

Pesce, Domenico.   "La scuola media 'progressiva' in
   America." *Scuola e Città* IV, 7-8 (August, 1953), 276-283.

Smith, Thomas Vernor. "Personal Impressions of Current Education
   in Italy, Germany, and Japan." *The Educational Record* XXVIII,
   1 (January, 1947), 21-32.

Vessolo, Arthur.   "Italy: Education Under Allied Military
   Government." *Yearbook of Education*, 1948, 578-591.

Washburne, Carleton W. "Education Under Allied Military Government
   in Italy." *The Educational Record* XXVI, 10 (October, 1945),
   261-272.

_____. "La riorganizzazione dell'istruzione in Italia." *Scuola
   e Città* XXI (1970) 273-277.

Primary Books

Amici del Mondo. *Dibattito sulla scuola*. Bari: Laterza, 1956.

Codignola, Ernesto. *Le scuole nuove e i loro problemi*. 4th ed.
   Florence: La Nuova Italia, 1962.

Cremaschi, Luigi. *Cinquant'anni di battaglie magistrali*. Rome:
   I diritti della scuola, 1952.

De Ruggiero, Guido. *Il ritorno alla ragione*. Bari: Laterza,
   1946.

De Young, Chris. *Educazione pubblica americana*. Florence: Le
   Monnier, 1946.

Dewey, John. *Democracy and Education*. New York: Macmillan, 1916.
   (Italian translation, tr. E. Enriques Agnoletti. *Democrazia
   e educazione*. Florence: La Nuova Italia, 1949.)

_____. *The School and Society*. Chicago: University of Chicago
   Press, 1899. (Italian translation, tr. E. Codignola and L.
   Borghi. *Scuola e società*. Florence: La Nuova Italia, 1949.)

Durante, Antonio. *Memorie di un maestro*. Rome: Riuniti, 1974.

Friedrich, Carl J., ed. *American Experiences in Military Government in World War II*. New York: Rinehart, 1948.

Gabrielli, Giorgio. *Commento ai programmi didattica per la scuola elementare*. Turin: Paravia, 1946.

Gayre, George Robert. *Italy in Transition; Extracts from the Private Journal of G. R. Gayre*. London: Faber and Faber, 1946.

Gonella, Guido. *Cinque anni al Ministero della Pubblica Istruzione.*, Vol. 1: *La rinascita della scuola dopo la seconda guerra mondiale*. Milan: Giuffre, 1983.

_____. *Cinque anni al Ministero della Pubblica Istruzione*. Vol. 2: *Libertà della scuola e nuovi orientamenti scolastici*. Vol. 2: Milan: Giuffre, 1983.

Gozzer, Giovanni. *La scuola per tutti. Idee e programmi per la scuola dagli 11 ai 14 anni*. Rome: U.C.I.I.M., 1956.

_____. *La scuola ponte (osservazioni--esperienze--problemi della scuola media)*. Trento: Arti Grafiche Saturnia, 1948.

Hill, Robert M. *In the Wake of War: Memoirs of an Alabama Military Government Officer in World War II Italy*. University, Ala.: University of Alabama Press, 1982.

Holborn, Hajo. *American Military Government. Its Organization and Practice*. Washington, D. C.: Infantry Journal Press, 1947.

Justman, Joseph. *The Italian People and Their Schools*. Tiffin, Ohio: Kappa Delta Pi, 1958.

Koopman, George Robert. *Democracy in School Administration*. New York: Appleton-Century-Crofts, 1951.

Matthews, Herbert. *Education of a Correspondent*. New York: Harcourt, Brace, 1941.

_____. *The Fruits of Fascism*. New York: Harcourt, Brace, 1943.

Omodeo, Adolfo. *L'età del risorgimento italiano*. 5th ed. Naples: Edizioni scientifiche italiane, 1946.

_____. *Lettere. 1910-1946*. Turin: Einaudi, 1963.

Omodeo, Adolfo. *Libertà e storia.   Scritti e discorsi politici.*
     Turin: Einaudi, 1960.

Pellegrini, Angelo M. *Immigrant's Return.* New York: Macmillan,
     1951.

Settimana Sociale dei Cattolici d'Italia, XXVII. Pisa, Sept. 18-25,
     1954. Atti. Published under the title *Famiglie di oggi e mondo
     sociale in trasformazione.* Rome: Edizioni I.C.A.S., 1954.

Settimana Sociale dei Cattolici d'Italia, XXVIII. Trento, Sept.
     25-Oct. 1, 1955. Atti. Published under the title *Società e
     scuola.* Rome: Edizioni I.C.A.S., 1956.

Smith, Thomas Vernor. *Democracy Versus Dictatorship: Teaching
     American Youth to Analyze and Understand Their Own and the
     Enemy's Way of Life.* Washington D. C.: National Educational
     Association, 1942.

_____. *The Democratic Tradition in America.* New York: Farrar
     and Rinehart, 1941.

_____. *The Democratic Way of Life.* Chicago: University of
     Chicago Press, 1926.

_____. *A Non-Existent Man, an Autobiography.* Austin: University
     of Texas Press, 1962.

Washburne, Carleton W. *La formazione dell'insegnante negli Stati
     Uniti.* Florence: La Nuova Italia, 1958.

_____. *A Living Philosophy of Education.* New York: John Day,
     1940. (Condensed Italian translation by M. Goretti, G. Rombo.
     Filosofia vivente dell'educazione. Florence: Le Monnier,
     1957.)

_____. *Le scuola di Winnetka.* Florence: La Nuova Italia, 1953.

_____. *What is Progressive Education?* New York: John Day, 1952.
     (Italian translation, *Che cos'è l'educazione progressiva?*
     Florence: La Nuova Italia, 1953.)

Widmar, Bruno. *La tragedia della scuola italiana.*   Florence:
     Poligrafico fiorentino, 1951.

Dissertations and Theses

Colombo, Daniela. "Gli insegnanti tra impegno antifascista e sindacalizzazione della categoria. Le vicende dell' AIDI attraverso la revista `La Voce della Scuola.'" Tesi di Laurea. University of Rome. Facolta di Magistero, 1980.

Day, Douglas Charles. "The Shaping of Postwar Italian Politics: Italy 1945-1948." Ph.D. Dissertation, University of Chicago, 1982.

Domenico, Roy. "Sanctions Against Fascism: The Politics of Purges in Italy, 1943-1948." Ph.D. Dissertation, Rutgers University, 1986, (publication forthcoming by University of North Carolina Press).

Hearst, Joseph Robert. "The Evolution of Allied Military Government Policy in Italy." Ph.D. Dissertation, Columbia University, 1959.

Koon, Tracy Hutchins. "Believe, Obey, Fight: Political Socialization of Youth in Fascist Italy, 1922-1943." Unpublished Revised Phd. Dissertation, 1982, (subsequently published under same title by University of North Carolina Press).

White, Steven F. "Italian Popular Education Between Fascism and Democracy 1943-1955." Ph.D. Dissertation, University of Virginia, 1985.

Zamperini, Nara. "Biblioteche scolastiche e lettteratura per l'infanzia in Umbria in periodo fascista." Tesi di Laurea. Universita di Perugia. Facolta di Magistero, 1977.

Secondary Articles

Aga-Rossi, Elena. "La politica del Vaticano durante la seconda guerra mondiale." *Storia contemporanea*, 6 (1975), 881-99.

Argento, Elmiro. "Continuity and change in Italian Education, 1859-1923." Canadian Historical Association. *Historical Papers/Communications Historiques*. 1978, 94-105.

Borrowman, Merle. "Social Forces Influencing American Education." *Yearbook of the National Society for the Study of Education* 60, 2 (1961), 144-153.

Cavazzoli, Luigi. "Vita quotidiana e seconda guerra mondiale."
    Italia contemporanea, 174 (March, 1989), 101-106.

D'Attore, Pier Paolo.   "Guerra fredda e trasformazioni delle
    societa occidentali nella storiografia americana."   *Italia
    contemporanea*, 140 (September, 1980), 83-103.

De Grazia, Victoria. "Mass Culture and Sovereignty: The American
    Challenge to European Cinemas, 1920-1960," *Journal of Modern
    History*, 61:1 (March 1989).

Fisher, Thomas P. "American Military Government in Italy." *Annals
    of the American Academy of Political and Social Sciences*, vol.
    267 (1950), 114-122.

Fornaca, Remo. "La politica scolastica degli Alleati in Italia ed
    in Piemonte dopo la liberazione." *I problemi della pedagogia*,
    2 (1975), 256-280.

Gallerano, Nicola.   "L'influenza dell'amministrazione militare
    alleata sulla riorganizzazione dello stato italiano (1943-
    1945)." *Italia contemporanea* 115 (1974), 4-22.

Garosci, Aldo. "Adolfo Omodeo III, Guida morale e guida politica."
    Rivista Storica Italiana LXXVIII, 1 (March, 1966), 140-183.

Mazzatosta, Teresa Maria.   "Educazione e scuola nella Repubbulica
    Sociale Italiana."   *Storia contemporanea* IX,1 (February,
    1978), 63-101.

Miller, James E.   "Epurazione Mancata: The Failure of
    Defascistization in Italy."   Paper delivered to American
    Historical Association Convention, December 28, 1981.

Ostenc, Michel. "L'ecole pendant le fascisme." *Revue d'histoire
    moderne et contemporaine*, XXX (July-September, 1983), 401-407.

Pavone, Claudio, "Sulla continuita dello stato nell'Italia 1943-
    45." *Rivista di storia contemporanea* 2 (1974), 172-205.

Ragazzini, Dario.   "Tra americanismo e pedagogia (la fortuna di
    Dewey)." *Reforma della scuola* 22, 8-9 (1976), 15-23.

Roberts, David D.   "Benedetto Croce and the Dilemmas of Liberal
    Restoration." *The Review of Politics*, 44, 2 (April, 1982),
    214-241.

Schapp, Jeffrey. "Cultural Integration and Disintegration in the
    Europe of 1992." *Italian Journal*, IV, 5 (1990), 3-6.

Varese, Claudio. "Appunti sul programma dell'istituto magistrale." *Società*, (April-June, 1946), 404-414.

White, Steven F. "Carleton Washburne: l'influenza deweyana nella scuola italiana." *Scuola e Città*, XL, 2 (28 Feb 1989), 49-57.

_____. "An Experiment in Regional Government: Piedmont Under Partisan and Allied Rule, 1945." Paper delivered at the American Historical Association Annual Meeting, Washington, D.C., December 28, 1987.

_____. "The Politics of Psychology in Post-Fascist Italy." Paper delivered at the American Historical Association Annual Meeting, New York, December 29, 1990.

Woolf, Richard J. "Catholicism, Fascism and Italian Education from the Riforma Gentile to the Carta della Scuola 1922-1939." *History of Education Quarterly*. 20, 2 (Spring, 1980), 18-23.

Secondary Books

Agazzi, Aldo. *Panorama della pedagogia d'oggi*. Brescia: La Scuola, 1950.

Alicata, Mario. *Intellettuali e azione politica*. Rome: Riuniti, 1976.

Allum, P. A. *Politics and Society in Post-War Naples*. Cambridge: Cambridge University, 1973.

Ambrosoli, Luigi. *Libertà e religione nella riforma Gentile*. Florence: Vallecchi, 1980.

_____. *La scuola in Italia dal dopoguerra ad oggi*. Bologna: Il Mulino, 1982.

Amici del Mondo. *Dibattito sulla scuola*. Bari: Laterza, 1956.

Aquarone, Alberto. *L'organizzazione dello stato totalitario*. Turin: Einaudi, 1965.

Aso, Makoto and Ikuo Amano. *Education and Japan's Modernization*. Tokyo: Ministry of Foreign Affairs, 1972.

Barbagli, Marzio. *Disoccupazione intellettuale e sistema scolastico in Italia*. Bologna: Il Mulino, 1974.

Bellucci, Maria and Michele Ciliberto. *La scuola e la pedagogia del fascismo*. Turin: Loescher, 1978.

Bertoni Jovine, Dina. *La scuola italiana dal 1870 ai giorni nostri*. Rome: Riuniti, 1958.

_____. *Storia della didattica dalla legge Casati ad oggi*. Rome: Riuniti, 1976.

_____. *Storia della scuola populare in Italia*. Turin: Einaudi, 1954.

Binchy, Daniel A. *Church and State in Fascist Italy*. London: Oxford University Press, 1941.

Borghi, Lamberto. *Educazione e autorità nell'Italia moderna*. Florence: La Nuova Italia, 1951.

Boyd, William. *The History of Western Education*. London: Black, 1950.

Brenna, Ernestina. *Il primo passo sulla via del magistero. Guida practica per tirocinanti e neo-maestri*. Bergamo: Istituto italiano d'arti grafiche, 1947.

Broccoli, A. *Educazione e politica nel Mezzogiorno d'Italia*. Florence: La Nuova Italia, 1968.

Cambi, Franco. *La scuola di Firenze (Da Codignola a Laporta 1950-1975)*. Naples: Liguori, 1982.

Canestri, Giorgio and Giuseppe Ricuperati. *La scuola in Italia dalla legge Casati a oggi*. Turin: Loescher, 1976.

Carlyle, Margaret. *Modern Italy*. London: Hutchinson, 1957.

Casadio, Quinto. *Gli ideali pedagogici della Resistenza*. Bologna: Edizioni Alfa, 1967.

Castronovo, Valerio, et. al., *L'Italia contemporanea, 1945-1975*. Turin: Einaudi, 1976.

Chapman, Charlotte Gower. *Milocca: A Sicilian Village*. Cambridge Mass.: Schenkman, 1971.

Clark, Martin. *Modern Italy, 1871-1982*. London: Longman, 1984.

Counts, George S. *School and Society in Chicago*. New York: Harcourt, Brace, 1928.

Covello, Leonard. *The Social Background of the Italo-American School Child*. Leiden, Netherlands: E. J. Brill, 1967.

Cummings, William K. *Education and Equality in Japan*. Princeton: Princeton University Press, 1980.

De Conde, Alexander. *Half Bitter, Half Sweet. An Excursion into Italian-American History*. New York: Scribners, 1971.

De Ferrari, Roy. *Memoirs of the Catholic University of America 1918-1960*. Boston: St. Paul Editors, 1962.

De Fort, Ester. *Storia della scuola elementare in Italia*. Vol. I Milan: Feltrinelli, 1979.

Delzell, Charles F. *Mussolini's Enemies: The Italian Anti-Fascist Resistance*. Princeton: Princeton University Press, 1961.

Di Lalla, Manlio. *Storia della democrazia cristiana*. Vol. 1. Turin: Manetti, 1979.

Di Nolfo, Ennio. *Le paure e le speranze degli italiani (1943-1953)*. Milan: Mondadori, 1986.

Ellwood, David W. *L'alleato nemico. La politica dell'occupazione anglo-americana in Italia 1943-1946*. Milan: Feltrinelli, 1977. (Revised English edition *Italy 1943-1945*. New York: Holmes & Meier, 1985)

Fadiga Zanatta, Anna Laura. *Il sistema scolastico italiano*. Bologna: Il Mulino, 1976.

Falconi, Carlo. *La Chiesa e le organizzazioni cattoliche in Italia (1945-1955)*. Turin: Einaudi, 1956.

_____. *Popes in the Twentieth Century*. Boston: Little Brown, 1968.

Federaziono Nazionale Insegnanti Scuole Medi. Sezione Firenze. *Problemi attuali della nostra scuola (programmi e metodi)*. Florence, FNISM, 1954.

Filippi, Tommaso. *Un anno di scuola*. Rome: I diritti della scuola, 1946.

Fiorentino, Fiorenza. *La Roma di Charles Poletti (giugno 1944-aprile 1945)*. Rome: Bonacci, 1986.

Flynn, George Q. *Roosevelt and Romanism. Catholics and American Diplomacy, 1937-1945.* Westport, Conn.:   Greenwood Press, 1976.

Fornaca, Remo, ed. *La libertà nell'educazione.* Turin: Paravia, 1975.

_____. *I problemi della scuola italiana dal 1943 alla Costituente.* Rome: Armando, 1972.

Forti, Marco and Sergio Pantasso, eds. *Il Politecnico. Antologia Critica.* Milan: Lerici, 1960.

Galli, Giorgio. *Storia della Democrazia Cristiana.*   Bari: Laterza, 1978.

Galli, Giorgio and Alessandra Nannei. *Italia, Occidente mancato.* Milan: Mondadori, 1980.

Garin, Eugenio. *Cronache di filosofia italiana.*   vol. 2.   Bari: Laterza, 1966.

_____. *La cultura e la scuola nella società italiana.*   Torino, Einaudi, 1960.

_____. *Gli intellettuali italiani del XX secolo.*   Rome: Riuniti, 1974.

Ginsborg, Paul. *A History of Contemporary Italy: Society and Politics, 1943-1988.* London: Penguin, 1990.

Gorresio, Vittorio, ed. *Stato e Chiesa.* Bari: Laterza, 1957.

Gozzer, Giovanni, ed. *I programmi della scuola elementare. Dalla teoria alla pratica.* Rome: Armando, 1986.

Gozzer, Giovanni et. al. *Programmi della scuola media. Strutture e valutazioni.* Rome: Armando, 1981.

Grindrod, Muriel. *The Rebuilding of Italy.   Politics and Economics, 1945-1955.*   London: Royal Institute of International Affairs, 1955.

Grossi, Dante. *Giorgio Gabrielli e il metodo globale naturale.* Rome: Selemia, 1979.

Guzzetti, G. B. *Il movimento cattolico italiano dall'unità ad oggi.* Naples: Edizioni Dehoniane, 1980.

Hall, Robert King. *Education for a New Japan.* New Haven: Yale, 1949.

Halperin, S. William. *Italy and the Vatican at War. A Study of Their Relations From the Outbreak of the Franco-Prussian War to the Death of Pius IX.* Chicago: University of Chicago Press, 1939.

Harper, John. *America and the Reconstruction of Italy, 1943-1948.* London: Cambridge University Press, 1987.

Harris, Charles R. S. *Allied Millitary Administration of Italy, 1943-1945.* London: H. M. Stationery Office, 1957.

Heiney, Donald. *America in Modern Italian Literature.* New Brunswick: Rutgers University Press, 1964.

Jemolo, Carlo Arturo. *Chiesa e Stato in Italia.* Turin: Einaudi, 1971.

Jucker, Ninetta. *Italy.* New York: Walker, 1970.

Kogan, Norman. *Italy and the Allies.* Cambridge, Mass.: Harvard University Press, 1956.

_____. *A Political History of Post-War Italy.* New York: Praeger, 1966.

_____. *A Political History of Post-War Italy. From the Old to the New Center-Left.* New York: Praeger, 1981.

Kolko, Gabriel. *The Politics of War.* New York: Random House, 1968.

Lawson, Robert F. *Reform of the West German School System 1945-1962.* Ann Arbor: University of Michigan School of Education, 1965.

Levi, Fabio, Umberto Levra and Nicola Tranfaglia eds. *Storia D'Italia.* Florence: La Nuova Italia, 1978

Levine, Irving R. *Mainstreet Italy.* Garden City: Doubleday, 1963.

Lombardi, France V. *I Programmi per la scuola elementare dal 1860 al 1955.* Brescia: La Scuola, 1975.

Macciocchi, Maria Antonietta. *La donna "nera:" "consenso" feminile e fascismo.* Milan: Feltrinelli, 1976.

212   *Progressive Renaissance*

Mack Smith, Denis. *Italy: A Modern History*. 2nd ed. Ann Arbor: University of Michigan Press, 1969.

Mafai, Miriam. *Pane nero. Donne e vita quotidiana nella seconda guerra mondiale*. Milan: Mondadori, 1987.

Mangoni, L. *L'interventismo della cultura. Intellettuali e riviste del fascismo*. Bari: Laterza, 1974.

Marraro, Howard R. *The New Education in Italy*. New York: S. F. Vanni, 1936.

Masselli, Vittorio. *I programmi della scuola primaria*. Naples: Morano, 1955.

_____. *La scuola di tutti*. Sesto S. Giovanni: Bietti, 1965.

May, Arthur J. *Europe Since 1939*. New York: Holt, Rinehart and Winston, 1966.

Mercuri, Lamberto. *L'epurazione in Italia 1943-1948*. Cuneo: L'Arciere, 1988.

_____. *La guerra psicologica. La propaganda anglo-americana in Italia 1942-1946*. Rome: Archivio Trimestrale, 1983.

_____. *1943-1945: Gli Alleati e L'Italia*. Naples: Edizioni Scientifiche Italiane, 1975.

Miller, James. *The United States and Italy, 1943-1950: The Politics and Diplomacy of Stabilization*. Chapel Hill: University of North Carolina Press, 1986.

Minio-Paluello L. *Education in Fascist Italy*. London: Oxford University Press, 1954.

Mitchell, B. R. *European Historical Statistics, 1750-1970*. London: Macmillan, 1975.

Myers, Francis M. *The Warfare of Democratic Ideals*. Yellow Springs, Ohio: Antioch College Press, 1956.

The Occupation of Japan, Educational and Social Reform. The proceedings of a symposium sponsored by the MacArthur Memorial, Old Dominion University, the MacArthur Memorial Foundation, October 16-18, 1980. Norfolk: The MacArthur Memorial; published by Gatling Printing and Publishing Co., 1982.

Orlando, Diega. *C. W. Washburne e l'esperimento di Winnetka.* Brescia: La Scuola, 1971.

Pecorini, Giorgio. *Dizionario della scuola democratica. Guida pedagogica, storica e giuridica alla gestione sociale della scuola.* Milan: Emme Edizioni, 1977.

Purcell, Edward A., Jr. *Crisis of Democratic Theory. Scientific Naturalism and the Problem of Value.* Lexington, Kentucky: University of Kentucky Press, 1973.

Quazza, Guido, ed. *Scuola e politica dall'unità ad oggi.* Turin: Stampatori, 1977.

Ragazzini, Dario. *Repertorio bibliografico di storia dell'educazione.* Florence: Sansoni, 1986.

Ricuperati, Giuseppe. *La scuola italiana e il fascismo.* Bologna: Consorzio Provinciale Pubblica Lettura, 1977.

Robaud, Enzo. *Disegno storico della scuola italiana. Riferimenti cronologici legislativi e bibliografici.* Florence: Le Monnier, 1961.

Santoni-Rugiu, Antonio. *Ideologia e programmi nelle scuole elementari e magistrali dal 1859 al 1955.* Florence: Luciano Manzuoli, 1980.

_____. *Il professore nella scuola italiana.* 2nd ed. Florence: La Nuova Italia, 1968.

Sassoon, Donald. *Contemporary Italy: Politics, Economy and Society since 1945.* London: Longman, 1986.

Schmitt, Hans A. ed. *Historians of Modern Europe.* Baton Rouge: Louisiana State University Press, 1971.

Sciacca, Federico Michele, A. Ciribini Spruzzola and G. Castiglioni. *Commento ai programmi di Filosofia-Pedagogia-Psicologia.* Milan: Marzorati, 1947.

Semeraro, Angelo. *Dina Bertoni Jovine e la storiografia pedagogica del dopoguerra.* Manduria: Lacaita, 1979.

Serant, Paul. *I vinti della liberazone. L'epurazione nell'Europa occidentale alla fine della seconda guerra mondiale.* Milan: Borghese, 1966.

Sinistrero, Vincenzo. *La politica scolastica 1945-1965 e la scuola cattolica.* Rome: Fidae, 1967.

Sisinni, Francesco. *La scuola media dalla legge Casati ad oggi.* Rome: Armando, 1969.

Spadolini, Giovanni. *L'Italia dei laici. Lotta politica e cultura dal 1925 al 1980.* Florence: Le Monnier, 1980.

Sprigge, Cecil. *Benedetto Croce: Man and Thinker.*   New Haven: Yale University Press, 1952.

Susi, Francesco. *La scuola italiana dopo la seconda guerra mondiale.* Rome: Societa Editrice Libraria, 1981.

Tannenbaum, Edward. *The Fascist Experience. Italian Society and Culture 1922-1945.* New York: Basic Books, 1972.

Tent, James F. *Mission on the Rhine.   Re-Education and De-nazification in American-occupied Germany.*   Chicago: University of Chicago Press, 1982.

Tomasi, Tina.   *Idealismo e fascismo nella scuola italiana.* Florence: La Nuova Italia, 1969.

_____. *Massoneria e scuola dall'unità ai nostri giorni.* Florence: Vallecchi, 1980.

_____. *Scuola e pedagogia in Italia, 1948-1960.* Rome: Riuniti, 1977.

_____. *La scuola italiana della dittatura alla repubblica, 1943-1948.* Rome: Riuniti, 1976.

Tomasi, Tina, ed. *L'istruzione di base in Italia (1859-1977).* Florence: Vallecchi, 1978.

Tyack, David. *The One Best System: A History of American Urban Education.* Cambridge, Massachusetts: Harvard University Press, 1979.

Volpicelli, Luigi. *Storia della scuola elementare a Roma.* Rome: Armando, 1963.

Webster, Richard A. *The Cross and the Fasces. Christian Democracy and Fascism in Italy.* Stanford: Stanford University Press, 1960.

Wolfe, Robert, ed.   *Americans as Proconsuls.   United States Military   Government   in   Germany   and   Japan   1944-1952.* Champaign-Urbana: University of Illinois Press, 1983.

Zambaldi, Ida.   *Storia della scuola elementare in Italia.*   Rome: Libreria Ateneo Salesiano, 1976.